Lala Lajpat Rai

Lala Lajpat Rai

Edited by
Shiv Gajrani
S. Ram

Commonwealth

Lala Lajpat Rai

Edition : 2027

ISBN 978-81-311-0184-1

Published by :

COMMONWEALTH PUBLISHERS (P) LTD.

4831/24, Govind Lane,
Ansari Road, Darya Ganj,
New Delhi - 110002
Ph. : 23272541, 23242541
e-mail : commonwealthpublishers2016@gmail.com

Distributed by :

ARJUN PUBLISHING HOUSE

4831/24, Govind Lane,
Ansari Road, Darya Ganj,
New Delhi - 110002
Ph. : 23272541, 23242541
e-mail : arjunbooks2001@gmail.com

Laser Typesetting by :

Dimple Computers

Delhi

Printed at :

Milan Enterprises

Delhi

Contents

Preface

Lalaji was a strong man and a great nationalist. He was truly a great son of the soil. He was a prolific writer among his contemporary nationalist leaders and a fighter. How this lion of Punjab lived and died in the process of achieving the goal of freedom of his country has been explained, through the life and works of Lala Lajpat Rai.

Authorities on this subject are many. His life story and his contribution to freedom struggle is a real saga of Indian history. Many scholars have written extensivaly on the subject. We record our acknowledgements to them.

Labrarians and their staff members have been kind and co-operative. We thank them all.

A word of appreciation for my publisher who has made available this biography, in its present form, for wider intellectual persuits.

Authors

1

Birth, Parentage and Environment

Lala Lajpat Rai's Life Reads Like An Epic

Atleast this country there are very few Boswells and there are still fewer Morleys. A Boswell can present his hero as he lived from day to day and can vivify his personality with the help of revealing anecdotes. A Morley can write an extensive and detailed biography which is at once cool and fervid. It can give a picture of the man but more clearly it can sum up his achievements. Lajpat Rai could have been a fit subject for all these different types of biographers, but the fates have not been kind to him.

Yet there is no need to despair. The best biographer of Lajpat Rai will be Lajpat Rai himself for all time to come. Any one who is interested in him will have to go through his innumerable works in order to have a complete picture of the man. One should read his books on Education.

Politics and History, his biographies of some of the heroes of India and the world, and his innumerable articles, all these reveal the man with all his enthusiasm and limitations, for everything that he wrote was vibrant with his personality. In this respect he is like Gandhiji. Both of them have what has been so aptly described the didactic impulse, the desire to communicate their impressions, their views and their experiences. This urge has a two-fold purpose—on the one hand, it means self-expression and on the other hand it is a desire to influence other people.

In spite of the fact that the essential man can be seen in his writings, it is not possible to ignore the external facts of his life, for they relate both to his heredity and environment, and these, as we know, shape mainly the trend of one's life.

'Lajpat Rai was born in 1865 in Jagraon, in the district of Ludhiana—a district which is known mainly as the home of militant Sikhs, Lajpat Rai came, however, of an Aggarwal family, which though not blessed plentifully with the goods of this world was rich in self-esteem and independence of spirit. His father, L. Radha Kishan, was a teacher of Urdu in a Government school, but it seems this service had not shackled his spirit. On the one hand, he admired Swami Dayanand Saraswati to the point of adoration, and on the other he had no end of regard for Sir Syed Ahmed. If Swami Dayanand Saraswati embodied in his person the renascent Hinduism, Sir Syed represented reformed Islam and united nationhood. For a long time Sir Syed exemplified all that was the best in Indian nationalism, but when he broke away from the Indian National Congress, his admirer received a rude shock and expressed a sense of disillusionment in an article which was published in the Press. Lajpat Rai's mother was one of those noble women who are destined to build up a home by their piety, thrift, wifely devotion and strong motherly affection. It is no wonder that Lajpat Rai once said "All that I am I owe to my father and mother."

If one looks at all this critically, one finds a rich heritage for Lajpat Rai. The heroic way of life or the military attitude of the soul, as Emerson puts it, came to him from the soul where he was born. His interest in the reform of Hinduism and his enthusiasm for united Indian nationhood came to him from his father. In addition to these he got from him that burning desire for self-expression which was such a mighty weapon in his hands. All his genius for constructiveness and the basic spiritual quality of his nature were the gifts which he inherited from his mother. It is true, his parents did not give him much in the way of worldly possessions, but surely from them he got much by way of intellectual; emotional and spiritual endowment.

Lajpat Rai went to school, as other children. It is, however, sad to relate that no school-fellow or teacher of his has given us any interesting reminiscences of his school days. But a few things are clear. He was a promising student and one on whom this so called education did not have a deadening effect. In his school days he acquired a passion for reading, writing and speaking, which stood him in good stead throughout his life. But he was not merely a bookish lad. He felt interested in life around him. Then he came to Lahore and joined the Government College. After passing his Intermediate Examination, he sat for the examination in Law. In 1895 he was a full-fledged Vakil.

We must remember that his student days at Lahore were the blossoming time of his genius. Youth is a remarkable period in one's life. It is the time when one makes friends and imbibes enthusiasm, and all these determine a man's future. Lajpat Rai was lucky in both because the times were so propitious. He came to make friends with Mahatma Hans Raj and Pt. Guru Datt, and all these three played a vital part not only in each other's lives but also in the life of the province. At the same time the Punjab was in those days electrified by the gospel that the Arya Samaj preached. To ardent spirits it brought a message of national regeneration and spiritual uplift.

Lajpat Rai fell under its spell and it left abiding impression on his life. He threw himself heart and soul into this Movement, and became its champion in the Press as well as on the platform. He wrote frequently for an English Weekly, which the Lahore Arya Samaj published, and he lectured very often from its platform. He became in a short time one of the major hopes of this Movement. When Swami Dayanand, the founder of this Movement, died, he delivered an oration at a public meeting in Lahore which stamped him as one of the leaders of this Movement. His identification with this movement meant that he was to play a leading role in social reform, religious uplift and educational progress, for these are the three objects for which the Arya Samaj has always stood. One of these took concrete shape on the death of Swami

Dayanand Saraswati. To perpetuate his memory the Arya Samajists resolved to found the Dayanand Anglo-Vedic College, Lahore. For several years to come the energies of the Arya Samajists went into the building up of this institution. It became the focus of Lajpat Rai constructive endeavours also, and he did his very best to make it an instrument of national education.

Lajpat Rai set up his practice at Hissar, and made a name for himself as a lawyer. There, too, he found two kindred souls—L. Chura Mani and Pandit Lakhpat Rai. All three worked hard to further the mission of the Arya Samaj and to consolidate the position of the D.A.V. College, Lahore. Needless to say they gave both their time and money selflessly. For several years Lajpat Rai religiously donated a part of his income for this purpose.

Hissar was, however, too small a place for a person of Lajpat Rai's dynamic energies, so he shifted to Lahore. There he built for himself an enviable practice as a lawyer. But more than this, Mahatma Hans Raj and he built up a network of Arya Samaj and educational institutions. Both of them, along with a host of others, made the Arya Samaj a power for good in the Punjab.

1888 was a fateful year in the life of Lajpat Rai. So far the Arya Samaj with its programme of social reconstruction, educational expansion and spiritual revival had monopolised all his attention. But now he entered the political field. It may be asked why he did so. There are some who believe that Lajpat Rai found the field of the Arya Samaj too small for him and, therefore, entered the bigger field of politics. There are others who think that his association with the Arya Samaj had only been a preparation for his political work. I do not think this is true. He really believed in some aspects of the mission of the Arya Samaj and worked wholeheartedly for them. But when all is said and done, one cannot but feel that Lajpat Rai was a patriot first and last and his interest in the Arya Samaj was also due to the fact that in it he found the means of national reconstruction. But he found after some years that the movement of Indian freedom was the most pressing one, and so, as a soldier of freedom, he joined it. It was characteristic of him that he prefaced his entry into politics by writing and publishing a number of biographies. This, it should be remembered, was his intellectual and spiritual preparation for the task. He wrote biographies of Italian patriots, such as Mazzini and Garibaldi and heroes of India, such as Sivaji, Shri Kishna and Swami Dayanand Saraswati. At the same time he wrote a series of letters to Sir Syed Ahmed Khan, in which he criticised his secession from the Congress. In spite of it, it should be remembered that Sir Syed Ahmed had at one time a very potential influence on the thoughts of Lajpat Rai.

That very year he went to attend the session of the Indian National Congress at Allahabad. It is thought that this session was convened by Pandit Ayodhya Nath in spite of the opposition of the authorities. To Lajpat Rai this was a very intriguing situation, and could not but react to it in the way in which he did. All kinds of oppressions were abhorrent to his nature and he could not but take up arms against them. He rose to the full height of his stature and struck vigorously. He was, in fact, one of those who are at their best in dangerous situations, for these call forth for utmost courage. Like a Knight of old, he went joyfully into the fray. This was his first contact with the Congress, and he kept it up as long as he lived. The Congress dominated his life ever after, and politics came to occupy a major role in his life.

In a short time he came to be one of the leading politicians of India. His position as such was recognised not only by the people but also by the Government, but far more by the people than by the Government. His views were solicited on every public question, and his counsel was sought in every difficult situation. It should, however, be remembered that on all such occasions he acted like a true patriot. He did not seek any favour and did not yield to any fear. In 1901, the Government appointed the Famine Commission before which he was called as a witness. His evidence was so valuable and weighty that the Government had to change its policy with regard to the orphans and helpless children left in the wake of the famine. In 1905, Lajpat Rai had to give practical proof of his solicitude for the masses. This was the year when a devastating earthquake occurred in Kangra. This brought about untold loss of men and property. Lajpat Rai could not see this spectacle of misery and sit quietly. The Lahore Arya Samaj organised relief committee, of which he became the secretary. In this connection be toured all over the Punjab and collected donations. He rendered much useful assistance to the people and earned their life-long gratitude.

That very year the Indian National Congress passed a resolution that two representative Indians should be sent abroad to acquaint the public with the conditions in India.

Gopal Krishna Gokhale and Lajpat Rai were selected for this purpose. Lajpat Rai toured England and delivered several speeches, in which he explained clearly what the British Raj had done in India. But more valuable than this was the message that he brought for India from abroad. This was threefold : He was so struck with the educational systems that he saw abroad that on his return to India he felt it incumbent to make efforts to nationalise education. He also felt that the final test of a good Government was the general welfare of the masses. He came to realise it very vividly that for this purpose the Government should be in the hands of the people. At the same time he came to believe in the unlimited efficacy of the Swadeshi movement. He thought that this should be made the common religion of all Indians, and it should provide a meeting ground for Indians of various shades of thought and opinion. Some of these ideas he advocated vigorously at the Surat Session of the Indian National Congress in 1907.

1907 also marked another landmark in the life of Lajpat Rai, for he was deported to Mandalay that year. This is how it came about. Attempts were made in the Punjab to increase the water rate, and this caused a great deal of disaffection amongst the Zamindars. There was widespread agitation against this measure in which Lajpat Rai took a leading part. At a public meeting in Lyallpur he delivered a fiery speech, as a consequence of which he was deported. In Mandalay, he wrote the well-known book, *The Story of My Deportation*. After some months he was released. The first thing that he did on regaining liberty was to file a suit against an English newspaper, which had been defaming him by describing him as a seditionist. He won the case, and whatever money he got by way of damages he gave away in charity. Another thing that he did was seek election to the Lahore Municipality. He was able to create so much enthusiasm for his candidature that even the deaf, the dumb and the maimed went to vote for him. It is said that one mute person took Lajpat Rai's photo with him to show for whom he was voting. In the Municipality he showed a great deal of civic interest and did much for the citizens.

In 1914 Lajpat Rai went to England, and from there he left for America, where he stayed for about six years. He left India because he did not feel safe during the reign of Sir Michael O'Dwyer. In the United States he spent his time in lecturing on Indian affairs and in writing books. He founded the Indian Home 'Rule League, and wrote *Arya Samaj, England's Debt to India, Young India* and several other books. He made very helpful friends there, whom he succeeded in interesting in the cause of India. There he earned a reputation for himself as a publicist in whose integrity the Americans could trust. When he left America, all his friends felt very depressed. It should be remembered that life in America was not a bed of roses for him. He used to cook his own meals and used to live mainly on the earnings from his articles and books which were not very abundant.

In 1920 Lajpat Rai came back to India, and his fellow-countrymen were jubilant. In Bombay, at Delhi and Lahore he received addresses of welcome. Then in September 1920 he was elected President of the special session of the Indian National Congress in Calcutta. It was at that session that Mahatma Gandhi presented his programme of non-co-operation. Lajpat Rai at first opposed it. But that very year at the Nagpur Session of the Congress, he joined hands with

Mahatma Gandhi. He threw himself heart and soul into this Movement. Since one of the items of this new programme was the boycott of schools and colleges, he founded the National College at Lahore. He started also the Tilak School of Politics, which was something like the London School of Economics. In addition, he collected nine lakhs of rupees for the Tilak Swaraj Fund in about ten days. He made a whirlwind tour in the Punjab for this purpose, and so great was the regard of the people for him that wherever he went the people gave him their money ungrudgingly.

In December 1921, he was arrested, because public meetings had been forbidden and he had presided over a meeting of the Punjab Provincial Congress Committee. He was tried and was sentenced to one year's regorous imprisonment. The message that he gave to the people at that time was full of patriotic fervour and showed that the man was made of steel. After a few months, as a result of public agitation in the provincial council, he was released, but was again arrested. During this term of imprisonment he fell seriously ill. When it was found that his condition was critical, he was released and in order to recoup his health he went to Solan. He had hardly recovered fully from his illness when Pandit Moti Lal Nehru founded the Swaraj Party, Lajpat Rai joined it, and was elected to the Central Assembly. There once again he made himself famous by his fearless advocacy of the national cause. After sometime he found that the Congress was not doing its duty by the Hindus, so he inaugurated the Hindu Sangathan Movement and worked strenuously for the unification of the Hindus. Then he sought re-election to the Assembly and it was under his lead that the resolution advocating the boycott of the Simon Commission, which was coming to India to explore the possibilities of further constitutional development in India, was passed. In the meantime he paid a flying visit to Europe, and on his return from there he undertook a fiery campaign against the Simon Commission. Then the Nehru Report was published, in which Pandit Moti Lal Nehru and his colleagues, taking up the challenge of the Secretary of State for India, outlined a scheme of Swaraj for India. Lajpat Rai was so impressed with it that he undertook to tour over the whole of India so as to do propaganda work in its favour. He had hardly begun his work when the Simon Commission arrived at Lahore on the 20th of October, 1928. Lajpat Rai led a procession of citizens of Lahore to demonstrate their disaffection with the Simon Commission. This was declared illegal and in order to disperse the crowd, the police made a *lathi* charge. Lajpat Rai received grievous hurt on this occasion and as a result of it was taken ill. He never recovered from this illness and passed away on the morning of the 17th of November 1928, due to heart failure.

Thus passed away Lajpat Rai, and by his death was left a void in the public life of India, which could never be filled. But he left behind a glorious legacy—the legacy of high and selfless patriotic endeavour. One may judge him by any standard and one will come to the conclusion that he was great. Yet his greatness is not some kind of self-aggrandisement but that based on service to others. Three things stand out pre-eminently in his life, and these alone can be his title to immortality. First, he had a genius for making friends, and friends of the right type. At college he made friends with Mahatma Hans Raj and Pt. Guru Dutt. At Hissar he won the confidence of Pt. Lakhpat Rai and Lala Chura Mani and when he came to Lahore, he had a noble band of friends. His friends were not confined to one place but were spread over almost all the countries of the world. His friendships were, however, not based on superficial social relationships, but on a deep love of some common cause and on a willingness to suffer and make sacrifices for the cause. Even if a person met him casually, he was impressed with his flaming patriotic ardour. His patriotism was hot, however, merely of the sentimental type; it was militant on the one hand; it was a constructive force on the other. No one could be more aggressive than Lajpat Rai when a wrong had to be set right or some injustice had to be redressed.

He was also in his element when some solid work had to done for the Nation. It is needless to give a list of such things for they will fill several pages. It is enough to remember that there was hardly any sphere of national welfare to which he did not contribute something. If he had a patriot's fervour, he had also a patriot's lot. Imprisonment, deportation, self-imposed exile, all these were his and he bore them cheerfully. But in every situation he found friends, who shared his suffering or collaborated with him in his work. Another thing that distinguished him was his gift of self-expression. This he cultivated throughout his life. He was a bookman and a voracious reader. But all that he read, he shared with others through his writings and his speeches. The number of books that he wrote is very large, and he was one of those rare persons to whom public speaking came naturally. At the age of eighteen, he was the ornament of the platform of the Arya Samaj and to the last day of his life he retained this oratorical ability. Yet he was not merely an academic speaker. He had the highest kind of oratory—oratory which stimulates people into action. He was above all a born leader of men. He could lead Movements as very few men could. To enumerate the Movements to which he made a very vital contribution will be futile. One can say only this much that all progressive Movements, social, religious, educational, economic and political, found in him a great champion.

His patriotism he translated into several concrete things, most of which have already been enumerated. There is hardly any aspect of our national life which he did not enrich. In a way he covered the whole field of education. His contribution to the D.A.V. College, Lahore, is already well known. Besides, he founded the National College, the Tilak School of Politics and the Dwarkadass Library.

At one time he drew up a scheme of primary education which, it is a pity, he could not put into force. On journalism, too, he left his impress. He founded the "Bande-Matram," an Urdu Daily and the "People" an English Weekly. In the field of business also he left his mark. The Punjab National Bank Ltd., owes a great deal to him and it was be who sponsored the Lakshmi Insurance Co., Ltd. No one could be more keen on philanthropy than he was. The destitute children of the Nation found in him a father, and he built a home for the consumptives, known as "The, Gulabdevi Hospital." Almost every Movement in India found in him a friend. The Kisans, the workers, the youth of India, he befriended every one of them. In the last period of his life, be founded the Servants of People Society so that patriotic young men should be able to devote all their time and energy to national service without the dread of starvation. He stimulated the feeling for social reform and unification among Hindus, but more than anything else, he remained a life-long worker in the cause of national unity. For national service, he founded in the Indian National Congress the most befitting instrument, and he served it wholeheartedly. To speak the truth, he served his country at home as well as abroad, by his pen as well as with his tongue, through the legislature as well as outside. It is no small wonder then that his name will ever remain enshrined in the grateful hearts of his countrymen.

Parentage

Barely ten days to the opening event of the season of Chrismas festivity, and, of a sudden, Sir Hugh Gough, the British. Commander-in-Chief, cancels his grand ball fixed well in advance for the eleventh evening of December.

In the cold season of 1845 things looked pretty grim. The grand ball had to be sacrificed because the British at Ambala got the news that the Sikh army was on the march eastwards and had crossed the Sutlej—the waters that the British had ever insisted must separate Ranjit Singh's domain from theirs. West of Ambala and the Sutlej, Ranjit Singh's successors still ruled, though the British held isolated outposts at Ludhiana and Ferozepore.

Much was at stake for both parties. The Governor-General himself, Henry Hardinge, came down to share the work and worry of the Commander-in-Chief. In the campaign that followed, he would often be seen sitting down to his despatch-boxes under no other canopy than that of a tree, for urgent papers must be dealt with before his camp paraphernalia arrived.

Battle was joined on December 18 at Mudki. Henry Hardinge, himself a tried soldier, directed a part of the British forces, not from a remote and sheltered headquarters but by galloping into the field the moment heavy cannonade was heard.

Some remonstrated with him for his thus exposing himself, but to no effect. Could he be thinking of the great Macedonian who had once fought on the neighbouring soil and paid scant regard to like remonstrance? Hardinge was a tried soldier, and he was aware of how large the stakes were.

On the Sikh side, as a writer of history remarks, "hearts to dare and hands to execute were numerous, but there was no mind to guide and animate the whole". The unlettered but extremely shrewd Ranjit Singh, Lion of the Punjab, had already been dead more than six years. Ranjit Singh had left behind a splendid army, but no worthy successors to put it to good use and to steer the ship of State.

Not more than 48 km from the field of battle, at Jagraon, the same fateful day in December 1845 saw the birth of Radha Kishan, father of the child who grew up to revive the old title, Lion of the Punjab.

At Mudki the Sikhs lost. The war had begun well for the British. A few more battles on the neighbouring fields, and all was up. In a month's time at Jagraon itself, the Ferozepore force joined that from Ludhiana. In two months the war had ended. The British denounced the treaty they had so keenly pressed on Ranjit Singh. They had cleared the Upper Sutlej finally. In the next four years the beyond-Sutlej Punjab too was theirs.

When British raj came to the Punjab, the particular branch of Agarwals with which we are here concerned had for generations been living in Malerkotla and the neighbouring territory. Like all Agarwals elsewhere they were a trading and money-lending community, but here they gained additional prestige by filling important administrative offices. In particular they had supplied for generations the *khazanchis* or custodians of the exchequer to the Muslim rulers of Malerkotla, a small state in the south-eastern part of the Punjab.

Malerkotla town is by train some 45 km from Ludhiana, to the south, and has a population of more than 20,000 souls. Originally Maler and Kotla were two distinct townships. The beautiful Moti Bazar connecting the two is a 20th century addition. The Agarwals of our story were more in evidence at Maler, the bigger of the twins. History tells us of a local disturbance in the turbulent Sikh days which put the clan on the trek, though not for long. In fact, some of them sought shelter next door, not three furlongs away, in Kotla (literally, the "walled" township). The others were scattered in the Ludhiana and Ferozepore districts, but continued to be known as Malerys.

As part of this trek Lajpat Rai's ancestors arrived at Jagraon, a township in the Ludhiana district but not far from Ferozepore. The ancestral house is still there. So also is the school named after their father by Radha Kishan's sons, during his life-time, and since then elevated to college status.

Radha Kishan's father had been an employee of the new rulers, a Patwari—the time-honoured village official who keeps the land records—in a village not far from Jagraon. He was short of stature and, on his grandson's showing, "very painstaking and courageous... very intelligent and wise and sociable". He had all the virtues and failings of the shopkeeper, that is, of his ancestors through the centuries. In keeping with the code of that class, he was fond of making money in all possible ways. Traditionally a patwari being an ill-paid but indispensable village functionary—one might almost call him a dignitary—suffers from no inconvenient scruples, especially as the law connives at and custom insists on providing many simple ways to extra cash or amenities. His salary is recognised merely as a retainer or, say, as a supplement to his "extras". To this day when "anti-corruption" campaigns started by those in high authority are advertised so loudly, a patwari without these "extras" is nearly as common as a white crow. Truly speaking, a large part of the petty fees exacted by a patwari is what would properly be called appreciative "tips" rather than outright bribes. All Patwaris collect these tips; the banya Patwari may merely have asked for them with greater zest. With this hereditary love of money he combined the adaptability of his stock, A trading community could not be very long-lived when political upheavals were common, unless it displayed exceptional resourcefulness in adapting, itself to circumstances. The Muslim rule in Malerkotla. its clasnes with the Sikhs, the panicky trek to Jagraon, the petty tyranny in everyday life under the Muslim Rais of Raikot, a spell of Ranjit Singh's Ahluwalia proteges of Kapurthala, the arrival of the British after the Sikh defeat on the battle-field—all these bewildering buffets of history this adaptable clan seems to have thriven on.

The short-statured Malery banya patwari had had no schooling worth the name. He was acquainted with the ingenious "short-long hand" of the banya's ledgers, called the "Mahajani", but had no acquaintance with Persian and Urdu in which the land records were maintained. His was the advantage, however, of having come from a stock which accepted any situation in which it was placed, and adapted itself quickly to the altered circumstances. Possibly those who had the advantage of knowing Persian and Urdu were yet trying to get their own bearings in the quick and cataclysmic changes that history had staged. These practical people, however, wasted little time in idle gazing and futile introspection. They were adepts in trimming their economic sails to any political wind that blew. So they would supply a patwari, and one who would well manage his business in spite of his handicaps. They furnished a patwari, because in the tossing about by history they had found their feet earlier than those with the necessary training and qualifications. Their patwari ran true to type and like his *jat bhais* he was orthodox and strict in his religious observances. He performed his devotional rites twice a day regularly, and hospitably cultivated the company of the ascetic gurus—Shvetambara (white-robed) Jain sadhus.

His wife was a bit "different". Not in being illiterate, or in her incapacity to count beyond twenty—handicaps common to most women of her generation—but in not being money-minded.

"I have not seen another woman," says Lajpat Rai of his grandmother, "as righteous, as pure-hearted, as hospitable, as generous and as simple. She was incapable of keeping money and her husband never gave her much. All her life she never used a lock and never kept a key in her custody. She was not fond of jewellery or of dressing well. She was so generous that practically all she got from her husband was given away to her neighbours."

Could the invisible fingers that join chromosomes and prepare the packet of heredity combine this woman's generous indifference towards money with the money-shrewdness and practical sense of her husband?

This "different" woman, we are told, was also a study in abnormal psychology—a subject, if you like, for parapsychology, or for psychical research. Occasionally the spirit of her husband's deceased sister seemed to possess her. The family would gather round her and consult her as an oracle, whenever she was in this state of trance. She would foretell the future or make revelations about matters not known to anybody. Later events corroborated her prophecies: the family anyway had great faith in her. Her grandson had often seen her, as a boy, in such a trance, and wrote what we have just quoted, without offering any explanation of the phenomenon, adding only that "tricks or fraud or humbugging my grandmother knew not", and that "she kept excellent health and seldom fell ill".

Her husband showed indications of a *wanderlust,* though we are not aware if he ever undertook really long tramps in those pre-railway days. His last illness lasted but a day, and he died practically in harness.

Born of these parents, Radha Kishan exhibited an unusual interest in religion. Macaulay had already written his famous note on educational policy in India, when Radha Kishan went to school. The madarsah set up by Macaulay's countrymen in Radha Kishan's village was conducted by a Maulvi and imparted what was known as Persian education. Radha Kishan was a bright pupil, ever securing the top position in the class, and in the final Normal School examination he came out first in the Punjab, securing the full quota of marks in "exact learning", *i.e.,* in mathematics and physical science. He was more than merely intelligent, much more than a mere winner of prizes and positions in examinations. He had an intellectual sturdiness about him that gave to things of the mind a definite precedence over the mere running after cash. He had not his mother's complete apathy towards money, nor was he like his father prone to "making money by all possible means." He evinced great interest in religion; but to him this did not signify the routine ritual that had been accepted by his ancestors for centuries. He wanted to study, to ponder, to scrutinise and only then to accept. The one religion that he could study at his school was that of his teacher, a pious Sunni Mussalman, "very firm in his religion and honest and righteous". His lofty character, we learn, made his Islam contagious, for several of his non-Muslim pupils embraced Islam later in life. Some of those who fought shy of apostasy, in their heart of hearts renounced their own faith in favour of the pious teachers. So did Radha Kishan. He said his *namaz,* fasted during the *Ramzan,* and he sought friends amongst the ulema. For years he was on the verge of formal conversion but fought shy of it fearing the tremendous domestic difficulties it would for certain bring in its trail. He studied Islam with a sincere devotion to truth. Ever responsive to new stimuli, he combined the receptive quality with the critical. When Sir Syed Ahmad Khan started his liberal interpretation of Islam, which came to be dubbed popularly as "natural theology", Radha Kishan avidly drank in the new tenets. He read with zest all that Sir Syed wrote, and for years was in correspondence with him. Once in a letter he asked Sir Syed if to become a Musalman it would be necessary for him to cease to be Radha Kishan, and to be known by an Islamic name. Sir Syed's reply suited Radha Kishan admirably, for it said that change in name was not in the least fundamental, the essentials being a firm monotheistic faith in Allah, and in Muhammad as his prophet. This reply must have gone a long way in appeasing Radha Kishan's conscience.

Duni Chand, the lawyer, shared with his intimate friend, Radha Kishan, his peculiar faith, and his peculiar difficulties about apostasy. One day, however, it appears, the two friends resolved to embrace Islam openly. With this intention they set out for the masjid. Radha Kishan's wife somehow came to know of their plans and successfully thwarted them! She had felt bitterly, as any Hindu woman would, the heresy of her husband, but she had tolerated it with the tact and adaptability peculiar to Hindu wives. Her parents believed in the Sikh Gurus. She had been taught their *bani* in her childhood, and in Radha Kishan's house she kept up her regular recital of *Japji*, the Sikh mattins. Radha Kishan would bring his Muslim friends to his house to dine with him. In those days of orthodoxy (though not of political 'communalism') this was regarded as outrageous in a Hindu home. But Radha Kishan's wife created no scenes. She satisfied her husband by serving his friends in her own plates and afterwards satisfied orthodoxy by cleansing the plates (of metal, as usual in Hindu homes) in fire. A non-vegetarian Agarwal in those days was regarded by his people as little short of a monster. But Radha Kishan who in his thinking had ceased to be Jain or Hindu and Agarwal would at times carry home a meat dish cooked in the house of a Muslim friend. All these outrageous doings his wife put up with; but he knew she would draw a line somewhere—he knew exactly where. The day he became an avowed Muslim, he strongly suspected, she would leave his roof taking away the children and would seek either his father's roof or that of her own. "That my father did not become a convert to Islam... is nothing short of a miracle, and the credit of having wrought this miracle goes to my mother," so wrote Radha Kishan's son. But a friend of the family gave the credit for this *shuddhi* (or conversion back to Hinduism) miracle to the baby Lajpat in Gulab Devi's lap when she overtook her husband on the steps of the masjid and appealed to him in the name of their little one. While the father in Radha Kishan listened and hesitated, the babe bewildered by this unfamiliar scene started crying, and this coming at a tense moment supported the mother's beseeching so successfully that overcome by domestic emotion, the near-Muslim halted just as he was about to cross the barrier, and returned home unconverted.

Radha Kishan's wife must have been a wonderful woman in her own way. The handling of such an erratic husband made extraordinary demands on her tact. And again as a housewife she needed to be no less skilful in managing a house on his meagre income. As a teacher he was getting just twenty-five rupees a month. He was much too absorbed in his theological studies and in the pursuit of learning to bother about currying favour with the officials of his department, and so was never thought of in connection with any preferment, though superb as a teacher and so adored by his pupils. After years of keen interest in education Lajpat Rai wrote of Munshiji as a teacher : "In India I have never come across a better teacher," In his whole career he is said to have been granted an increment twice—each time a five-rupee one so that when he retired he had been getting the munificent salary of thirty-five rupees a month! His wife had to bring up a large family on this slender income. In all she bore him ten children; at the time of her death six of these, four sons and two daughters, were alive. How she managed to feed and clothe this large family and to observe in addition all the religious feasts and festivals and *samskaras*—for we are told she missed none of these—within this income seems little short of a miracle. Yet her bigger miracle was that of fortitude which her husband was for ever straining to a breaking-point by his sacrilegious enormities. She suffered deeply, but all in silence—a living monument of fortitude. No rows, no ugly scenes, and that made her suffering the more intense. Sorrow she kept strictly to herself. Lajpat, as a two-year-old, often watched her for hours shedding tears of grief at her husband's incorrigible ways. "For days together," wrote her son afterwards, "she would not taste her food, and would be sighing in grief with her children in her lap. But she would never think of deserting her husband. In fact she always lived with him and was never away from him for any appreciably long period of time"—we suppose to suffer, to serve, and thus to avert if possible the calamity of apostasy.

Good and remarkable in many ways, she was altogether unlettered. Her husband tried time and again to teach her, and later on her son tried too. But her frail health, the perpetual worry about her husband, the heavy household routine of a housewife on a meagre allowance for a large family, and the fact that most Hindu women of her generation even in families better favoured by fortune were uneducated, made her remain content with her unlettered lot.

Radha Kishan remained an "unofficial" Muslim till about his fortieth year. He not merely admired Islam zealously and sincerely, but cultivated in himself all the aggressiveness of a new convert in denouncing the religion and ritual of his forefathers. To have done so secretly or even privately would have been entirely unlike him. He wrote out his denunciations in newspaper articles which found ready publication in the Brahmo Press of those days. His attitude towards Hindu religion, philosophy and culture changed only when his son had become an ardent follower of the principles of a new Hinduism which the Arya Samaj had laid bare. He was able to show his father that beneath an exterior that had become ugly and even putrid, Hinduism at its core was pervaded by a beautiful aroma all its own. Radha Kishan was never wilfully blind but he knew no Sanskrit; and a keen seeker after truth as he was, the milieu of his school days had not favoured his seeing Hinduism in the true perspective. When he became aware of this lack he readily tried to correct himself. He studied all about Hinduism that was accessible to him. But he never joined the church for which his son so devotedly worked. His studies led him not to the Arya Samaj, but to *Vedanta.* The subtleties of the *Vedantic* philosophy held out a strong intellectual appeal and in his old age he found solace in the teaching of the 'Upanishads'.

All his life Radha Kishan remained a keen student of religion. He could not go to the Hindu source books as he had done in studying Islam. But whatever was available to him in Urdu (or even Hindi or Gurmukhi), he read with avidity and studied with industry and conscientious scrupulousness,

Besides newspaper articles he occasionally wrote small books and had some title to authorship. His religious studies resulted in a book in Urdu called *Tahqiqe Mazahib,* ("Inquiry into Religions"), a brief comparative study of the fundamental tenets of the principal religions, advertised as "the fruit of the author's study of different religions extending over a period of 22 years". We do not know whether Munshiji ever composed verse, but he is known to have sported the penname of 'Azad' as appropriately betokening his spirit and his outlook. His published tracts included one on metempsychosis called *Risalah-i-Tanasukh* in which he particularly compared the teachings of his erstwhile guru, Sir Syed Ahmad, with those of the Hindu philosophers, generally to the advantage of the latter. But he himself did not subscribe to the views of any one particular school. He joined issue with Swami Dayananda in his doctrine according to which even souls that had attained moksha (salvation) enjoyed such beatitude not eternally but for an essentially limited, though a very long period. This doctrine he found to be contrary both to the teachings of ancient Indian philosophers and to the dictates of his own reason. Radha Kishan throughout tried to be logical and terse and confined his attention only to the point at issue. He had his chapter and verse ready in support of his contentions and generally let the different philosophers he was discussing speak for themselves. His writing is dispassionate in the extreme, completely devoid of all attempts at decoration. In fact, it is ascetically bald, and definitely wanting in grace of presentation.

His studies in history resulted in an Urdu booklet of about

150 pages called *Bir Charitra* which was mainly a selection from Todd's *Annals and Antiquities of Rajasthan.* In a preface Munshi Radha Kishan speaks of the value, of historical study and shows his peculiar fondness for it. The book enjoyed a vogue for some time, and even a second edition was called for.

This fondness for reading he retained till his very end. I was privileged to be his neighbour, in the sense of occupying the room adjoining his at 2 Court Street, Lahore, when I joined the Servants of the People Society. Lala Lajpat Rai had given away the house to the Society and had built himself a smaller two-storeyed one in the same compound. His father did not shift to the new house, but continued to occupy in the old one a small low-ceilinged room in the south corner of the verandah. A cot and an office chair were about all the furniture one could notice in this room, besides the very conspicuously-unvarnished, crudely-planed thick strong plank of wood running continuously along three walls, at a convenient height. This shelving came handy for stowing away books, papers and odds and ends and underlined the ascetic aspect of the bed-cum-living room of Munshi Radha Kishan. This was perhaps the only room in the house the ascetic aspect of which never accepted a glass-pane in door, window or ventilator. In summer, of course, he slept on the verandah or in the open. In the morning he would get up and would be seen reading one of his favourite books, or last evening's paper—for, Lahore in those days boasted of no morning paper—till it was time for breakfast. After breakfast he would walk to the shop of his second son, Ranpat Rai (a paper merchant on Ganpat Road, Anarkali) and spend his day there, most of the time reading. His supper he used to have at Ranpat Rai's, after which he would return to his own small room at 2 Court Street, with the afternoon's *Bandemataram* in his hand. He never went to sleep without having first done his reading.

Among the books that he was particularly fond of was an Urdu translation of Draper's classic *Conflict between Religion and Science.* Often he would dip into this early in the morning or else pick it out in the evening for a read when going to bed. His other favourites were mostly books on religion or history.

When he died he was eighty-two. His death was keenly felt by Lajpat Rai—the more so because being in prison at the time he could not be by his death-bed for a filial fulfilment. He sent special instructions that all expenses for the obsequies must be met out of his (Lajpat Rai's) royalties as a writer which he regarded as a particularly pure portion of his fortune.

Birth

Munshi Radha Kishan taught for some eight years at the Government Middle School, Rupar, in Ambala district. During the Rupar days, early in 1865—January 28—he became a father. The first child, a son whom he named Lajpat Rai, arrived in a small mud house in his father-in-law's village, Dhudike. As is the custom largely even now, the expectant mother had moved to her father's home for her first child-birth. Dhudike is a small village in the Moga tehsil of the Ferozepore district, and about 8 km from Radha Kishan's own Jagraon, which is in the Ludhiana district.

The father happened to be away at Delhi for a short professional course. News reached him there that the new arrival was a puny thing. Tall and vigorous himself and devoted to physical exercise, this was not exactly what he had looked forward to.

Early childhood in malaria-infested Rupar did not go to make of Lajpat a model of health and vigour. When he grew up into a schoolboy he was more fond of books than of play. He became a constant victim to malaria, and early acquired an enlarged spleen.

The boy's schooling at first was largely carried on by Radha Kishan at home, where the lessons of the class-room were abundantly supplemented. The boy was intelligent and hardworking and as prize-winning as his father had been in his own day. The father taught him not merely the three R's, but soon began to interest him in that most interesting of all

R's— Religion. The boy read parts of the 'Quran' with his father and like him used to say his *namaz* and occasionally even observed the *Ramzan* fast.

Young Lajpat must have been puzzled about feelings about religion as he saw it practised in his home. His father's father was an orthodox Jain; his own father a firm, though an unofficial, Muslim; his mother in perpetual agony about her husband's Islam but scrupulously regular in her Sikh recitals. If ever he went to her parents' house he must have seen plenty of Sikhism in evidence. How could he help feeling perplexed whenever he took stock of his situation even in a boyish way? Anyhow Munshi Radha Kishan succeeded in imparting to his son the contagion of religious enquiry and curiosity which continued unblunted through mature years, even though the boy before very long gave up Islamic observances.

From his father he also inherited his fondness for the study of history which in fact meant a fondness for the 'epic' in the widest possible sense. Radha Kishan started the boy early on Firdausi's immortal *Shahnama,* which is regarded as the Persian counterpart of Homer's epic or of Vyasa's *Mahabharata*. Again and again he read parts of Firdausi with his father, and when he had grown up, he continued to read them all by himself. The studies at once satisfied a craving, and created an appetite for more. It is to the early schooling in *Shahnama* that Lajpat in later years traced his passion for books of history, and it might be it was the dramatic declamations of Firdausi's heroes that first kindled in the child's mind an interest in oratory. Perhaps to this schooling might even be traced his life-long fondness for the dynamic, the heroic and the epic in any work. Like Vyasa and Homer, Firdausi is not content with a mere chronicle of what happens on the battle-field. In that sense he was very unlike the official historians of yore. He is all-embracing and presents an exhaustive picture of the life and culture of the times his verse celebrates. The boy nurtured on this intellectual diet naturally sought ever after in books of history the same large sweep, the same encyclopaedic range.

Preoccupation with the Quran and the *Shahnama* and rather frequent interludes of malaria notwithstanding, he did not neglect his school-books. Almost always he occupied the top position. Being also the youngest boy in the school he was looked upon as a prodigy. He completed the Rupur school course consisting of six forms. Soon after the closing of that school, Munshi Radha Kishan was transferred to Simla. He could not take his wife and children there because his meagre salary would not suffice to meet the expenses of that place. Lajpat had been sent to Lahore for further schooling. The education department granted him a stipend of seven rupees a month and from Lahore he went to Delhi. He was there for about three months, but the climate of Delhi did not suit the sickly boy. By then the father had gone away to Simla, and Lajpat went with his mother to their home in Jagraon.

Before he was thirteen and while yet at the middle school, the boy had been married. Of course it was an arranged match, in the orthodox way, linking one Agarwal family with another. Radha Devi, the bride, came from a Hissar family and had seen there more affluence than was visible at the house of the ill-paid teacher. We shall have occasion to speak of her and of the married life of the couple later. For the moment we are concerned with the education of the bridegroom. After having left Delhi, and having spent a few months at home at Jagraon, he joined the Mission High School at Ludhiana, where also he was granted a stipend as a promising boy, and where again he fell ill and left the school after a few months. About this time Munshi Radha Kishan again received orders of transfer, this time to Ambala. There his wife and children joined him. At Rupar two more children were born to him—Mela Ram, who died young, and a daughter. In his Ambala days, three more sons were born—Ranpat Rai, Dhanpat Rai and Nand Lal, later named Dalpat Rai in better consonance with the names of his brothers. Also, incidentally, a Dalpat Rai at Lahore was a very successful lawyer in those days.

Sickly Lajpat had not been at Ambala quite two months when he fell dangerously ill, and for nearly four months had to be nursed in bed. This time it was an abscess which had to be operated on twice or thrice. Thinking of those days he later wrote :

> "I have been a source of trouble and anxiety to my parents all my life, but that year I put them to so much trouble that I can never possibly forget it."

All the same he matriculated that year. In fact, he did a double matriculation. The University of the Punjab was yet in its infancy, and Dr. Leitner was trying various experiments to pattern it differently from the other universities. The infant university did not enjoy much prestige even in its home province, whereas the diplomas and degrees granted by the Calcutta University were at a premium. Lajpat solved the problem by taking both the examinations, the Calcutta, and the Punjab ones. He was successful in both, and got a first class in his Calcutta examination, in spite of his long illness. For his Calcutta matric he took up Persian as second language, but in the Punjab he was examined in Arabic and Urdu and physical science, besides all the Calcutta subjects. His father had been keen that he should learn Arabic, and in early boyhood he devoted a good deal of time to Arabic accidence and syntax; but in reality he was not much interested in the study, and his success in the examination was a *tour de force*. Dr. Leitner's university turned out barely 106 matriculates that year; the educational factories were working slow and Lajpat Rai stood somewhere in the middle of the turnout.

STUDIES AND INFLUENCES

Studies

Lajpat's further education became a serious problem. The boy was no doubt gifted and keen on his studies. To his father so genuinely interested in education, it would have been painful indeed to wean such an eager and promising lad away from his books so soon, and yet where was the money to send him up to college? The difficulties were formidable, but eventually Radha Kishan made up his mind to give his son the benefit of a college education, whatever hardship that might entail on the family at home. A man of Munshiji's independent character could not go about begging support from friends. The only friend whose help he is said to have ever sought was a much respected Musalman of Jagraon, one Sajawal Biloch, who had been his schoolmate, probably his class-mate, and with whom Radha Kishan's relations were cordial and intimate. Sajawal would have willingly financed the high-school education of the boy at Lahore. But it does not seem he was ever called upon to make good his word for, as we have seen, Lajpat's stay at Lahore for school education was extremely brief. For his college education he depended on the stipends he could secure and a meagre allowance of eight to ten rupees a month from home, which sum, of course, was a considerable part of his father's earnings.

In February 1881, a little after he had turned sixteen, Lajpat joined the only college that Lahore (or the Punjab) then boased of, the University or Government College.

The struggle with poverty at college must have been grim indeed. He had not seen prosperity at home, but a frugal standard within their slender means was maintained there, and whenever he fell ill, his parents could look after him. At Lahore, with the utmost that could be squeezed out of the family budget, supplemented by sundry stipends, he was constantly being reminded of his penury.

"For the first two or three months", he himself tells us, "I had to face great embarrassment. My eyes gave me great trouble. Besides, I had at times to go without food. After a good deal of struggle I succeeded in getting a stipend of three rupees a month from the university. I had come to Lahore merely with the idea of studying for an arts degree, but on the advice of certain fellow-students in the hostel I joined the law school also. Out of my monthly stipends I was paying two rupees as tuition fee in the Government College, three rupees in the law school and perhaps one rupee as hostel fee. My father could, with difficulty, manage only eight to ten rupees a month, and I had to live within that amount, Law books were pretty expensive, but I got the more essential among them rather cheap, by buying them second-hand, or I depended on friends for their loan. I used the same economy in securing the arts books and got along by borrowing these. My parents were undergoing great hardship for my sake, and were even prepared to run into debt. But I did not want to put them to this trouble, and so lived very frugally."

The grim struggle soon persuaded him that the first thing was to complete the law course and get the diploma that would enable him to earn a living. Liberal education soon came to occupy a subsidiary place in his plans. For his law examination he worked hard enough to qualify at the end of the year for Mukhtarship—and also for jaundice. He continued on the college rolls for two years more, but without passing any more university examinations. Frequent illness, the law-school priority, preoccupation with certain live issues in public life, and absorption in education of a type very different from the university curriculum, all combined in 1883 to keep his name out of the list of successful candidates in the intermediate arts examination.

But his Government College days were otherwise very important in his life. Here his class-mates included names that later became famous—Mahatma Hans Raj, Pandit Guru Dutt Vidyarthi, Raja Narendranath and Professor Ruchi Ram Sahni. A college class in those days was a smaller affair. Although the number of students taking the corresponding examinations of the successor universities at Chandigarh and Lahore, nowadays, runs well beyond 50,000 yearly, it is doubtful if any other year in the Punjab's academic annals has seen a batch that will outshine this 1882-83 galaxy. Five men who have had half as much to do with the shaping of the modern Punjab, as Lajpat Rai, Hans Raj, Narendranath, Guru Dutt and Ruchi Ram, all of whom took their intermediate examination in 1883, could not easily be named out of students in any class. Some of his comrades were for Lajpat Rai much more than mere fellow-students; in fact, Guru Dutt, Hans Raj, Lajpat Rai, Chetan Anand and Rai Shiv Nath, who formed a coterie at college, had a great deal to do with one another's lives even after their college days. A puritanic way of living was a common bond. Rai Shiv Nath, later an engineer in the U.P., was perhaps the most ascetic of them all. He went about barefoot and was a zealous collector of ancient Indian MSS, curios and books : his Dehra Dun house was indeed a private museum with a unique feature displayed in its geometrical reproductions of the old Aryan *yajnashalas* worked out from ancient texts with devotion and industry!

Not many among Lajpat's teachers at the Government College could by later judgement be regarded as nearly so important as the brilliant galaxy of his class-mates we have already mentioned. The only memorable names from amongst the teachers seem those of Dr. Leitner and Muhammad Hussain Azad. Dr. Leitner's ambition was to be a shaper of educational policy, but his plan of creating a sort of oriental seminary under the aegis of the University of the Punjab met with little success. But he has a claim to be remembered as the scrupulous and painstaking author of an important report on Indigenous Education in the Punjab which brought to light facts showing that literacy, far from being such a scarce commodity in the pre-British days, was perhaps commoner then than after a century of British rule. As a teacher he was brilliant and versatile, and covered a wide and variegated range extending over the Arts, Oriental and Law Schools. He also had a number of linguistic, mainly Oriental, studies to his credit. But administration was a different affair, and the official history of the university seems to suggest that the brilliant Dr. Leitner had to go because under him there was too much laxity regarding the funds and accounts of the university.

Muhammad Hussain Azad was shaping history at the Government College in a different way. Steeped in Persian and Arabic erudition, he was keenly aware also that literature and learning must change with the times, and he had addressed himself to the task of enriching Urdu and of making of it a better vehicle for the new literary requirements arising mainly out of the western impact. His verse is of little significance, but indubitably he ranks among the makers of Urdu prose. He produced the first comprehensive and systematic history of Urdu literature and so powerful and vivid was his style of writing that even where his facts have been shown by later research to be utterly baseless, his *obiter dicta* cannot be obliterated from the popular mind; for he is a clever literary portraitist, and his minutiae, and the anecdotes ingratiate themselves into the readers' imagination and abide there tenaciously. Historians may repudiate Macaulay when he says that a convict was offered the choice of reading Guiccardiani's *History* or working at the galleys, and after a trial of both chose the galleys as the lesser torture, but the story has stuck to Guiccardiani. Muhammad Hussain Azad had the same dangerous gift. When he made up his mind to give a particular character to an Urdu poet, always the stories came pat to support him. Most of the anecdotes he circulated about the ill-temper of the pathetic genius, Meer, have been found by later scholarship to be fables, but for generations Meer seems doomed to go down much as Azad portrayed him.

Lajpat Rai attended Azad's Arabic classes for only a few days, but those few days remained indelibly impressed on his memory. Azad could indulge in a broad joke even in the classroom, as Lajpat Rai learnt to his cost, the very first day. However, it was not because of banter that he left the Arabic class. He left it for more ponderable reasons. The language controversy was just then starting. In the United Provinces (now named Uttar Pradesh) a movement was afoot that resulted a few years later in the recognition of Hindi as the language of the law courts. In the Punjab the Arya Samaj was laying great emphasis on the importance of Hindi and Sanskrit for Hindus. Lajpat Rai's Samajist friends at college, having definitely espoused the cause of Hindi and Sanskrit, beseeched him to discard Arabic in favour of Sanskrit—of which he knew not a word—as a sacrifice for the cause.

Professor Azad's own attitude helped Lajput Rai in yielding to the importunity. Azad used to boast that as a Shia and as a Persian scholar he considered Iran and not India as his home. This offended the patriotic awareness already fast developing in young Lajpat's bosom and made him suspect that there was a de-nationalising influence lurking in the study of Arabic and Persian. The enemy lay in ambush, and he must beware. He made up his mind to leave his Arabic class and to give a trial to Sanskrit. But if he had made poor progress in Arabic, he was not destined to fare any better in Sanskrit. Even during his staunch Arya Samajist days, he had access to Sanskrit wisdom only through translations.

Let no one run away with the impression that Azad was a sort of anti-Hindi bigot. He was, in fact, neither anti-Hindi nor a hater of India. He loved India in his own way. Perhaps in a different set of circumstances no one would have accused him of hostility to Hindi, even though his own contribution went only to Urdu. Azad found that Urdu literature was not only poor but was definitely suffering from stagnation. Prose had attracted little talent, and verse was wasting lavish amounts of it in outmoded channels. If it continued in the rut into which it had then fallen, there was no hope of its ever coming out to serve the many uses to which modern minds might put it. The modernising of Urdu literature had its birth in the Punjab. The initiative was taken by Muhammad Hussain. The great and almost unbelievable miracle of Urdu literature is that the modernising which is supposed to have come out of the impact of the West (made mostly through English) was achieved mainly by those who had little or no knowledge of English—by Azad and Hali, and next to them by Sir Syed Ahmad and Shibli. Amongst these four, the first place in the new movement must be given to Muhammad Hussain Azad. He set the movement going and under his influence it gathered momentum in the province. At his instance it was that Hali came down to Lahore and the combined efforts of the two resulted in something of a literary revolution. It was while Urdu was undergoing this invigorating metamorphosis that the Hindi movement made its appearance in the Punjab and the Hindi-Urdu question became one of the major controversies of the day.

Lajpat Rai threw in his lot with the Hindi enthusiasts. But he was not to shake off so easily the influence of Muhammad Hussain. He left his class, because he thought there was a danger of his falling under the spell of Azad's Iranian leanings. Yet his national pride was destined to derive nourishment from the writings of this very Muhammad Hussain; and, in his autobiography, he paid a handsome tribute to this influence on his life. His father had been his first great teacher, and he had formed the boy's mind mainly by teaching him Firdausi's *Shahnama*. Muhammad Hussain Azad was to be his second great teacher, for it was from his very well-written slender Urdu book, *Qasis-i-Hind,* that Lajpat first became aware of India's glorious past. These chapters of Indian history in the form of legend and story presented her past in language that made their author's pride in the Indian heritage highly infectious. Incidentally it proved to him that his father had not been altogether right in concluding that pre-Muslim India had nothing to boast of. Both the *Shahnama* and the *Qasis* he continued to read off and on long after his school and college days. Later on he became acquainted with Col. Todd's *Annals & Antiquities of Rajasthan;* these annals and Arya Samaj's revealing to him the manifold glories of India's ancient past changed for him the image of his motherland; but the beginning had surely been made by Azad's narratives in the *Qasis-i-Hind.*

His admiration for Muhammad Hussain Azad's dignified prose must also have started at this period of his life. At any rate it continued to the end of his days. Azad, Sir Syed, Shibli—these three were his perennial favourites.

Influences

The Hindi movement soon found in him an active missionary. This was in fact the beginning of Lajpat Rai's public life—a precocious beginning rather, for he was barely out of school. He and Guru Dutt and Hans Raj started their public careers with this movement, while (all three) still "freshers" at college. Guru Dutt and Lajpat Rai had a busy time collecting thousands of signatures to a pro-Hindi memorial.

The first public speech that young Lajput Rai made was in the cause of Hindi, at Ambala in 1882, when he was only eighteen. He had gone there especially for this propaganda. A subordinate magistrate happened to be among the audience and sent up a report to the Principal of the Government College who duly administered a warning to the young enthusiast pointing out that students were expected to keep at a safe distance from all such agitation.

Lajpat Rai's active participation in Hindi propaganda did not necessarily imply acceptance of the Arya Samaj. In fact for a time he wavered between the Brahmo and the Arya Samajas. The Punjab Brahmo Samaj was much under the influence of Nobin Chandra Roy, and unlike some other Bengali leaders of his day, Nobin Babu attached the utmost importance to the Hindi movement. He regarded Hindi as the foundation on which the entire edifice of Indian nationalism would one day rest. Agnihotri who later founded the Dev Samaj, the church without God, was in those days a pillar of the Punjab Brahmo Samaj. Lajpat had brought to Lahore an introduction to him from his father. Agnihotri was still a drawing master or Art teacher at the Government school, and was also editing an Urdu paper, called the *Biradar-i-Hind* (literally "Brother of India"). Munshi Radha Kishan used to attack the Arya Samaj and orthodox Hinduism in the hospitable columns of this paper. At Lahore Lajpat Rai was very much under the influence of Agnihotri Probably he went out occasionally with Agnihotri on lecturing tours. He read a paper on the life of Rammohun Roy at one of the Brahmo Samaj meetings. In 1882 he was formally initiated into the Brahmo Samaj by his father's friend. Agnihotri was a most eloquent public speaker and it is possible that the first realisation of what a mighty force a moving speech can be came to Lajpat through contact with him.

But Lajpat did not stay a Brahmo very long. At college, as we have already seen, his chief friends were Guru Dutt and Hans Raj and they frequently talked of the Arya Samaj to him. Guru Dutt was a prodigy; his towering intellect, his vast fund of knowledge in all branches of learning, his all-round dazzling brilliance made a profound impression on Lajpat Rai's mind. Yet it was not Guru Dutt who enlisted Lajpat Rai for the Arya Samaj but another who, though he had few intellectual pretensions, undoubtedly possessed a magnetic personality and a sound judgement regarding men. This was Sain Das, then President of the Lahore Arya Samaj. He often used to go to the college hostel, in search of converts for his church, and he knew how to attract a promising young man when he saw one.

Sain Das happened to be present at the Brahmo Samaj meeting at which Lajpat Rai received initiation at the hands of Agnihotri. As he came out of the meeting Sain Das accosted him, and in a pitying tone remarked that a worthwhile young man had been misguided and entrapped.

Inside the Punjab Brahmo Samaj, things seemed moving towards a crisis, with three factions striving for ascendancy. The bickerings bewildered the young lad from Rupar and Jagraon.

Towards the end of the year the Arya Samaj at Lahore was celebrating its anniversary. Lajpat Rai had heard a lot about this other Samaj from his friends, Guru Dutt and Hans Raj. At the time of the anniversary curiosity led his footsteps towards the Arya Samaj. He had never before witnessed an Arya Samajist gathering. Having watched the anniversary meeting the first day, he went there the next day too. The principal speaker that day was one who knew him well and had great affection for him. He took him aside to the top of the building to show him a draft of the speech he was about to deliver, and it must have flattered the young student thus to be invited to give his opinion.

Lala Sain Das urged him to join the Arya Samaj. Lajpat Rai agreed. "Indescribable joy illuminated Lala Sain Das's face."

Once in the Arya Samaj, he was soon in its inner counsels, and before long among its front rank leaders. Sain Das, President of the Arya Samaj at Lahore, soon after selected

Lajpat for a deputation to Rajputana and the United Provinces. He visited Meerut, Ajmer, Farrukhabad and other places, addressed public meetings, raised funds and everywhere met the Arya fraternity and exchanged notes with them. Growing intimacy with its working revealed the Samaj as a body extraordinarily fervent and dynamic, a well-knit determined lot that might work as the leaven for a vast quantity of inert dough. It provided just the environment that he had long yearned for : he had at last arrived where he felt at his ease.

It was not the theological or doctrinal superiority of the Arya Samajic teaching that had attracted him. It had rather been the patriotic zeal of its members, their ambition of restoring *Aryavarta* to its ancient glory, that inspired and permeated all activities sponsored by the Samaj and promoted by its members.

He had no doubt been influenced by the company of Guru Dutt and Hans Raj, his closest friends at college. How had these been drawn to the Samaj? Guru Dutt was precocious, and a much-talked-of prodigy of his day. As a very young lad he had displayed an interest in science and philosophy altogether beyond his years. He became a keen student of metaphysics. He had a facility for learning languages too. He studied Sanskrit while a schoolboy with the earnestness of an accomplished scholar of mature years. His studies in Western philosophy led him to the agnosticism so much in vogue among the European thinkers of the 'eighties and 'nineties. But his agnosticism was not without streaks of faith. Spiritualism with its promise of mystical experience fascinated him as much as agnosticism did with its intellectual challenge to belief. He became interested in yoga, and the subtleties of Sanskrit grammar and philosophy attracted him even more than Bentham and Mill and Herbert Spencer had done. Yet he was not merely a man of books. He took his books too seriously to be content merely with reading and academically pondering over them. He wanted life to tally rigidly with thought. He kept a journal which showed a perpetual struggle to secure this concord. Flesh was weak and would often fail. With this earnest man, however, every such failure called forth immediately an entry of self-reproach in his journal—and fresh endeavour. He had met a yogi in his early youth when he still vacillated between faith and agnosticism. This yogi made a profound impression on him and Guru Dutt wanted to accompany him as a disciple; but friends intervened, and the ties of home and friendship proved stronger than the love of yoga. It is said that the last shreds of his agnosticism vanished when he saw Dayananda on his death-bed. The dying founder of the Samaj won a convert who came to be regarded as the greatest intellectual among his followers. Guru Dutt was an eccentric. He would often put on winter clothes in summer and summer clothes in winter. By these austerities he sought to make his mind and body perfect and obedient tools. With some slight alteration somewhere in his methods he might perhaps have become a Gandhi long before Gandhi had been discovered even by himself. And perhaps out of this revised Guru Dutt you could have made not only a Gandhi but a couple of intellectuals too from what was left over. From out of the products of the University of the Punjab, for sheer intellect nobody attracted as much attention as Guru Dutt, with the possible exception of Har Dayal, another intellectual that Lajpat Rai was to have a good deal to do with in later years at Lahore and in Europe, and above all (through Har Dayal's followers and lieutenants) in the States.

These two, in fact, resembled each other much. Both were eccentric in personal habits as well as in their thinking. Both were too much weighed down by a heavy earnestness. Both possessed great gifts of mind and memory—curiosity, receptiveness, a strong will and a flair for languages and for expression, for logical thinking, for a contagious persuasiveness. Both pushed their thinking to the extreme, and could hop from one extreme to another—from the westernmost to the easternmost, or from a cosmopolitanism that left internationalism lagging far behind to the narrowest and most parochial nationalism, from agnosticism to perfect faith and spiritualism. Both had a remarkable knack of collecting around them friends and admirers who never tired of offering incense to them.

Both had a strong streak of asceticism. Har Dayal's remained unaffected alike in the midst of American materialism and the gaiety of Paris. If like Guru Dutt Har Dayal kept a journal and if it were unearthed one day it will be interesting to see if this too is full of self-reproach and of renewed resolutions for mortifying the flesh.

Those interested in yogic philosophy and exercises aim generally at personal salvation. But Guru Dutt did not lose his sense of social and collective values in this endeavour at individualistic perfection. Though he would not be reckoned amongst the 'politically-minded' he was by no means wanting in patriotism. As a student he had been as little examination-minded as his friend Lajpat Rai, but because of his greater precocity he could not help outshining all competitors in an examination. He was an equally keen student of Sanskrit and the Vedas, and of Western thought and modern science. He passed his M.A. in physical science in 1886 and because of his brilliant university career was offered an assistant professorship in physics at the Government College, Lahore. As his journal shows, he kept on wavering between continuing in this career and giving it up in favour of a yogic pursuit of perfection.

All the time, however, he continued to work hard for the Arya Samaj, by lecturing, by writing, by organising, by guiding and by exercising his personal magnetism on a large circle of friends and admirers. His intellectual gifts and attainments, and even more than these, his earnestness and sincerity and his readily sacrificing personal interest, profoundly impressed the youngest of the trio, Lajpat Rai. In shaping his own career Lajpat Rai at every step consulted him. Even apart from the service rules Guru Dutt's bias and temperament seemed removed from the sphere of politics. A directly political movement had not yet arrived—at least not in the Punjab. Even if it had, it is possible that "plunged in thought" Guru Dutt would have "let the thundering legions pass". But he was certainly patriotic in a broader sense, and the contagion that affected those coming within his orbit was not without an ingredient of patriotism. Lajpat was attracted by that part of Guru Dutt's idealism which demanded sacrifices in a cause, rather than by his high intellectual attainment or even yogic pursuit of personal perfection. This pursuit too he may have admired—somewhat from a distance, and with little inclination to emulate. In his pamphleteering fervour for the Samaj Guru Dutt was then editing a magazine in English, appropriately styled the *Regenerator of Aryavarta,* which rather suggested a patriotic mission. The patriotic side of Guru Dutt was to no small extent responsible for Lajpat Rai's being won over by the Arya Samaj. In choosing his own vocation he consulted Guru Dutt. At one stage he had to consider whether he should give up law and dedicate himself to the educational movement being set afoot by the Samaj. It was proposed that Hans Raj should work as headmaster (they had then started only the high school; the college was to come later) and Lajpat Rai should be his second in command. He himself felt diffident. Hans Raj had taken his B.A. degree—a rather rare bit of parchment then—while Lajpat Rai had no academic credentials. The trio pondered over the matter, and eventually it was decided that Lajpat Rai could be more useful to the college by continuing at the bar.

Guru Dutt himself had had a choice of careers before him—apart from the extreme alternative of discarding all worldly careers. He could have become an "extra assistant commissioner", a provincial civil service man, in other words. He had been offered this : he could go up the rungs of the ladder of administrative jobs, and with his rare gifts he might go as high as any Indian was in those days permitted. After some anxious thinking he decided that work at the Government College could suit him best. He continued there, though he was a member—and a very prominent one—of the D.A.V. College Society too.

Guru Dutt lived a life of voluntary poverty. His personal wants were very few and easily met. A large part of his salary always went to help others, and to buy books for which Guru Dutt had a passion. Hoarding money he regarded as a sin, and at his death it was found that he had saved nothing for his wife and children.

Before Guru Dutt died, two schools of thought had arisen in the Arya Samaj. One was dominated by men supposed to have a modern outlook, those who would think and talk in terms of what is practicable and expedient, rather than in terms of scriptural sanction of text and canon and of dogma. The other school denounced this worship of expediency and wanted to go by rigid principle and the letter of the text. It was generally believed that the first school was more political and patriotic in its outlook, while the horizon of the second school was dominated by dogma and theology. Guru Dutt was much respected by both. It was during his last illness that the cleavage became definitely pronounced. After his death the best tribute that was paid to him was that each party quoted him in its own support. Lajpat Rai's personal tribute to his dearly loved friend was paid in the form of a biographical sketch, published both in English and Urdu in the early 'nineties—Lajpat Rai's first claim to authorship, if we leave aside a few small tracts and pamphlets written for the Arya Samaj, and perhaps a minor professional production, dealing with criminal courts and litigation said to have been written during his Hissar days. This was by no means one of his important books; the author's craft had not yet been acquired by him, and the book bore marks throughout of an amateur hand and of haste. But one can perceive that even in the crudest of its pages breathes the feeling of tenderness that actuated the attempt. It is significant that Lajpat Rai began his career as an author with an essay on biography. Till the end he retained a fondness for biographies. As an author he was to attempt a number of biographies later on, some of which enjoyed considerable vogue; and, as we shall see, of all his books the one which helped most in bringing about a national awakening, especially in the Punjab, was his biography of Mazzini in Urdu.

Hans Raj, Lajpat Rai's other great friend at college, was

temperamentally a contrast to Guru Dutt. Without the dazzling brilliance of Guru Dutt, Hans Raj was endowed with gifts that made for greater stability. He too had joined the Arya Samaj before he came to college but he had not been directed thither by any Sanskrit erudition. He never acquired proficiency in Sanskrit, and could never have been much interested in yogic culture. He was actuated by a sincere passion to serve others, but he wanted to do so in the manner of a hard-headed practical man, and not that of an idealist pushing ideas to their logical extreme or seeking after perfection here and now. He could not draw round him a coterie of young enthusiasts, but be had a wonderful knack of managing things. He decided on a life of simplicity, even poverty and service. When the D.A.V. College was conceived, he identified himself with the institution, with almost a Jesuitical single-mindedness. His critics have averred that the institution had been intended to be just a means, not an end in itself, and that Hans Raj treated the means as an end. That, alas, is the common failing of those dedicated to institutions. Hans Raj's special talent was for organisation; he would build up an institution entrusted to his care, inch by inch with meticulous devotion to detail, a devotion bordering on an idolatry which in jealously guarding the idol at times checked rudely the onslaught of a great and dynamic movement embodying a national aspiration.

Hans Raj was not interested in the subtleties of metaphysics and of theology, Vedic grammar and exegesis. For him it was enough that the Arya Samaj as a progressive movement was destined to play a vital part in the reorganisation of Hindu society. In other words, he had been drawn to the Samaj more by its patriotic than its philosophical or dogmatic side.

Lajpat Rai stood midway between the extremes of perfectionist idealism and of expediency; but his approach to problems interesting the Arya Samaj was much nearer that of Hans Raj than that of Guru Dutt. For him as for Hans Raj the supreme merit of the Samaj lay in its social, educational and welfare work, and in its stimulating a patriotic awareness in Hindu society.

It was good for the friendship of this trio and, incidentally for the D.A.V. College, that their spheres of activity remained distinct. Lajpat Rai had intended to dedicate his life to the D.A.V. College, like Hans Raj, and not having a university degree, to be for ever his subordinate. It was likewise suggested that Guru Dutt should take over the D.A.-V. College as Principal. The results in either eventuality could have been disastrous. Temperamentally the three friends differed too widely from one another to make a good team. They were bound to differ at some stage, and then the consequences might have been ruinous as much for their friendship as for the institution equally dear to them all.

Early Training in Arya Samaj

Youthful and highly receptive, Lajpat Rai was drinking in through every pore of his being the ideas of the Arya Samaj—ideas that made up its real core rather than those that constituted its corpus of dogma. To understand the shaping of his outlook it is necessary to grasp the Samajic ideas of the 'eighties and the' nineties, and we need to know a little more here of the elderly men then guiding the destinies of the Samaj.

First of all there was Sain Das, at that time President of the Lahore Arya Samaj who, as we have seen, had been immediately responsible for winning over Lajpat Rai for the Arya Samaj. What was his conception of the mission of the Samaj? Was he interested keenly in theological and metaphysical subtleties, or in the yogic pursuit, or in the practice of austerities for the attainment of individual perfection and salvation of the soul? Or did all these things combined interest him less than serving his people through the Samaj in a more secular way, by promoting social, educational or relief and welfare work, and inculcating a spirit of patriotism and self-reliance among them? He himself held a clerical job in a Government office. He could not directly be connected with any political movement. We do not hear of any yogis whom he pursued for the deliverance of his soul. He carried no heavy load of Sanskrit grammar or theological erudition in his head. But he was one of the shrewdest men going in the Arya Samaj, with an uncanny judgment about men and affairs. A harder-headed man with greater abundance of common sense would be difficult to find. He had no pretensions to being an intellectual, but it is remarkable that he too had a claim to authorship. The only book that he wrote dealt not with Vedic exegesis or with Aryan philosophy, but curiously enough it was a translation of the essays of Francis Bacon. This may be some indication of the philosophy of life that guided this leader of the Arya Samaj.

Much controversy arose in later years as to whether the Samaj was a political or a religious movement. The truth is that the founder of the Samaj was a religious personage and not a politician; all the same his work had a conspicuous streak of patriotism running through it. And he attracted round him not a few who were drawn as much by his patriotism as by his learning and spiritual accomplishments, and to whom patriotism was a sort of religion and a religion void of patriotism meant nothing at all. Some of these men were bound by their inherent bias to play an active and important role later on in political movements, when these made their appearance. But it was absurd to look upon the Arya Samaj as a camouflaged school of political thought or as a semi-secret political movement which had put on a religious mask to deceive the authorities. We shall remember that though Dayananda is rightly regarded as the founder of the Arya Samaj, the Samaj as a movement and as an organisation was really the result of the joint deliberations of the Swami and several of his disciples and friends some of whom in their thinking attached the highest importance to social reform and to a patriotic renascence. The fundamental principles—the ten basic tenets—and the constitution of the Samaj were very largely drawn up by the Swamiji's Punjabi admirers and advisers, prominent among them being Rai Bahadur Mul Raj.

We may usefully indulge in a digression about Mul Raj,

whose ideas seemed to be better defined than those of most other leaders of the Samaj, and who, even though, keeping largely behind the scenes, made an intellectual contribution of special importance. He took care not to be loud, but he was certainly articulate, and he had a knack of making himself effective through influencing the key men of the movement. Without the ambition of political leadership, he played an effective role behind the scenes in various movements. He thought much about the political emancipation of his country. In later years Lajpat Rai used to say that Mul Raj had conceived the principles and programme of Gandhian non-co-operation when Gandhi must have been a mere schoolboy. But he was never known for bold action. He was himself in Government service, though he preached to young men who met him that they must never hanker after a career of that kind. He was an evangel of swadeshi—long before the swadeshi movement of the anti-partition days was born. He conceived industrial and financial reconstruction in the interests of swadeshi, combined with a political non-co-operation with the Government. Lajpat Rai in his autobiography had something to say about Mul Raj :

> "Rai Mul Raj--he was the Rai Sahib—had with him a history of the secret societies of Europe in two volumes which he had borrowed from some library. He read the whole book. I read a few pages then and there but Rai Mul Raj did not permit me to carry the book home with me...,"

Later Lajpat Rai got the book from England and satisfied his curiosity.

This early convert to swadeshism, though he wanted India to get rid of foreign rule, had no faith in Hindu-Muslim unity. His influence on Lajpat Rai's early outlook is revealed in a passage in the autobiography, without naming Mul Raj :

"The cause of my indifference towards the Congress after 1889 was the opinion of my Arya Samajist friends, After 1889 I had the privilege of being in the company of a respectable friend who was a staunch opponent of the Congress. The grounds for his opposition briefly were :

(1) The Congress has been founded by a few Englishmen; as Englishmen love their own country it is not possible that the Congress should win political freedom for India. The English derive great benefits from their rule in India; it is impossible that they should willingly restore India to freedom. Being afraid lest the intelligentsia should organise a deep political movement aimed at England's supremacy, they had provided this innocuous occupation for the intelligentsia so that they might gratify themselves by two or three days of 'speechifying' and by seeing themselves eulogised in the papers. In those days this gentleman looked upon every Englishman as an enemy of India.... He regarded the Congress not merely as useless, but even detrimental to the interests of India. What he then thought necessary was that Indians should make themselves stronger by education, by the spread of swadeshi and by the smuggling of arms, and then bide their time till they were strong enough to turn out the English.

(2) This gentleman had no faith in Hindu-Muslim unity. He believed that attempts at unity would harm the Hindus. The Hindus were void of internal solidarity, religious fervour and communal self-respect; the Muslims excelled in these virtues and would therefore always be the gainers in the attempts at unity. Also, the Islamic supremacy continued in Afghanistan, Turkey and elsewhere. So the attempts at unity would make the Muslims politically very strong. To him it appeared that the primary need was that the Hindus be strengthened and be shown the way to ultimate solidarity and that national fervour be instilled into them. The Congress movement, he argued, would divert energy from the work for Hindu solidarity and Hindu reform and set the Hindus a futile task.

(3) A further argument was that the political movement would make the Britishers suspicious of the Hindus, and they would therefore not only obstruct the progress of the Hindus, but harm them in all possible ways.

The Arya Samajist leaders generally shared these views which constituted the common credo of Mul Raj, Sain Das and Lal Chand (who later became a Judge of the Chief Court in the Punjab). All three of them were in Government service. Sain Das, we are told, clad himself in nothing but swadeshi, and preached swadeshi even in 1881. Mul Raj too believed in swadeshi, even though he did not practise it as rigidly as Sain Das. Of their younger colleagues Hans Raj took to swadeshi very early in life. Many of the leading men in the Arya Samaj were preaching swadeshi long before the *swadeshi* movement had been born in Bengal and Maharashtra. Not all of them had been converted to swadeshi by the Samaj; possibly some of them had become swadeshi and patriotic before they joined the Samaj; but there can be little doubt these people found an affinity between the teachings, activities and the whole atmosphere of the Samaj, and their own *swadeshi* outlook. Some of them had conceived the idea of non-co-operation with the foreign government nearly half a century before the Congress thought of it. We read in Lajpat Rai's autobiography :

"Lala Sain Das and Lala Mul Raj often regretted that the best Indian brains were being used to strengthen the rule by a foreign nation. They used to dissuade the most brilliant Indian students from entering Government service....Lala Sain Das felt it keenly that the pandits of Kashi should have brought Hinduism into disrepute by drawing the cart of Lord Ripon. The acme of public morality for Hindus, according to him, was that in their religious and social reform and educational affairs they should have nothing to do with the Government or with the Britishers, and should seek no help from them in the form of money, consultation, or guidance. Whatever the Hindus wanted, they must try to get by their own effort, and they must generate in themselves a spirit of self-reliance."

The nationalism of these worthies was primarily a 'Hindu nationalism'. The memory of the days when the Muslims were the rulers and the Hindus the ruled was as yet too fresh. The flame of patriotism in the heart of these Arya Samaj leaders was fed by a feeling for the degenerate condition of the Hindus.

Sain Das had more to do with the shaping of the Arya Samaj in the 'eighties than any other single person. You could say his religion was three-fourths 'political' and yet you could say his politics were three-fourths love of the Hindu nation, and if that be religion, his politics were three-fourths religion.

These were some of the men in the Samaj with whom youthful Lajpat came into intimate contact. Whatever their shortcomings, they were a dynamic group, determined to have a hand in shaping the events. They were just the company that Lajpat Rai's soul yearned for. And youthful, firm, earnest, dynamic Lajpal Rai was just the worker that the Samaj wanted. So he casts his lot with them to work with them and for them for long years to come; and even when he outgrows the Samaj and they part company, he will not altogether discard the Samajic impression on his outlook and on his methods of work. Whatever departments of public activity he chose in the later years of his career, he could never forget that he had received his early training in the Arya Samaj. It was there he first schooled himself into a public speaker, and as a journalist, as a pamphleteer and a compiler of biographies, as a writer in Urdu and in English, as a leader of movements and an organiser of big institutions, as a zealous social worker leading relief campaigns wherever famines or earthquakes wrought havoc, or when orphans, those 'waifs of the storm' of life, needed the establishment of a permanent home to turn them into capable citizens. It was in the Arya Samaj that he acquired the art of appealing to the hearts of his audience and making them empty their pockets for great causes and institutions.

2

Early Life and Career

Lala Lajpat Rai was the most prolific writer among his contemporary nationalist leaders of India. His literary activity started when he was still in his teens and he continued to write almost to the last day of his life. He was the author of a score of books in English and Urdu, besides numerous articles contributed to newspapers and periodicals published in India as well as abroad. He had a strong desire to write a complete autobiography, but this task could not be accomplished because of his sudden death in 1928. Lajpat Rai had, however, written his autobiography in fragments which mostly remained unpublished during his life-time. In this volume have been brought together three of his autobiographical writings—*The Story of My Life, The Story of My Deportation* and *The Indian Revolutionaries in the United States and Japan.* The three fragments put together provide an authentic and trustworthy account of a fairly large part of his active public life which was devoted to the political, social, religious and economic development of the country.

The first of these three works was written in Urdu in November 1914 soon after Lajpat Rai's arrival in New York. *The Story of My Life,* written closely on about one hundred sheets, was obviously not intended for publication at that time and the manuscript was sent in April 1915 for safe custody to his friend Mr. F.W. West brook in London. It was brought to India by Lalaji during one of his visits to Europe after the non-cooperation movement. This work was posthumously published in the *Bandematram,* the Urdu daily of Lahore founded by Lajpat Rai, and its English translation appeared in *The People* during 1929. Since the original manuscript is not available the English version, as published in *The People,* is being reprinted in this volume. I have, however, taken the liberty of making some changes in language to eliminate the ambiguities of expression in the translation which was too literal.

In the *The Story of My Life* Lajpat Rai has left a vivid account of his life and activities until the early days of 1907, a period during which the Punjab was in great ferment. Apart from furnishing a true account of his early life the *Story* forms an invaluable source for the study of religio-social movements in the Punjab, particularly the Arya Samaj, and the growth of political consciousness in the country. The closing chapters of this work contain an account of the conflict between the old leadership of the Indian National Congress and the new group of Nationalists of advanced political views, led by Lokmanya Bal Gangadhar Tilak, Bepin Chandra Pal, Arabindo Ghosh and Lajpat Rai himself. His account is of added significance as written by one who played an important role in shaping the events.

The *Story of My Deportation* has been reprinted in an abridged form. The original work, written in great haste, appears to be a piece of amateurish writing and is full of trivialities. The abridged version is entirely in Lajpat Rai's own words; but it has been shorn of certain trivial and irrelevant details in the original text. It has been my endeavour to retain all that can be considered of historical significance.

Lajpat Rai had a strong case in regard to the unjust action of the Government in deporting him to Burma and in the *Story of My Deportation* he gives his version of the episode. The facts related by him are substantially supported by the official records and the private correspondence of Minto and Morley.

Sir Denzil Ibbetson, who had succeeded Sir Charles Rivaz in the Office of the Lieutenant-Governor of the Punjab early in 1907, was able to convince Lord Minto of the 'exceedingly serious' and 'exceedingly dangerous' aspect of the situation in the Province with his 'weighty' Minute of April 30.[1] The Governor-General agreed to the local government's proposal for deportation without judicial proceedings, in spite of the opposition of two members of his Council. When Lajpat Rai was suddenly arrested and deported to Burma, he as well as his countrymen were kept in the dark as to the reasons which had prompted the Government to resort to such a grave action. In view of the tense situation in the beginning of May Lajpat Rai was apparently expecting to be arrested, but even he did not believe that the authorities would suspect him of "threatening the security of the British dominions" and creating "internal commotion" and resort to the special powers under Regulation III of 1818. A few hours before his arrest, amid the heat and passion of a popular agitation, Lajpat Rai summed up in a brief statement[2] with his characteristic-calmness in difficult situations, his views on the situation in the Punjab. He stated his case with frankness and showed how the discontent in the Punjab was not due to any political agitation, but was caused by certain unjust legislative measures of the Government, in particular the Colonization Bill.

To most of his countrymen—Moderates as well as Extremists—Lajpat Rai was innocent and the wild charges made in the Anglo-Indian Press against him were unfounded. The grave action of the local government was born out of panic in the ranks of the bureaucracy, caused by widespread discontent among the people. The Government wanted to make an impressive show of force and as Gopal Krishna Gokhale put it "they struck at Lala Lajpat Rai simply because he was the most prominent political worker in the Province."[3] Lajpat Rai's high reputation in public life and his popularity appear to have been chiefly responsible for his choice for the Government's-attack.

Though Minto had agreed to the deportation of Lajpat Rai and Ajit Singh, he recognized the reasonableness of the discontent and vetoed the Punjab Colonization Bill, in spite of the strong views to the contrary of Ibbetson's Government. It was soon realized that the trouble in the Punjab was essentially agrarian in character and the removal of the main grievance of the agriculturists was responsible for restoration of peaceful conditions in the Province. The Viceroy was also convinced that the action in deporting Lajpat Rai was hasty and unjust. He wrote to Morley on November 5, 1907, "Lajpat Rai is undoubtedly a man of high character and very much respected by his fellow-countrymen, and if when I was asked to arrest him, I had known what I do now, I would have required much more evidence before agreeing."

The autobiographical fragments in this volume leave a gap of seven years in the life story of Lajpat Rai. It is unfortunate that he has not left an account of the fateful Surat Congress held in December 1907 in which he was a key figure. He was perhaps so much distressed and disheartened by the unseemly developments there that he did not feel inclined to write the story of the schism in the national organization. Although he was virtually aligned with the Nationalists in regard to his political beliefs, he exerted moderating influence both at the Banaras Congress (1905) and the Calcutta Congress (1906). He held in high esteem both Gokhale and Tilak, who between them symbolized the conflicting ideologies of the Moderates and the Extremists; he could perhaps reconcile the irreconcilable. In return Lajpat Rai had the unique distinction of winning the respect and affection of both the Moderates and the Nationalists. When he was deported the two opposing factions were equally shocked at the unjust action of the Government against a man of Lajpat Rai's standing and high character. Gokhale, who was to lead the agitation for the release of his Punjabi friend, significantly exclaimed, "We certainly do not want any disorders in the land, but the reforms which the Viceroy and the Secretary of State are contemplating will lose their meaning for us, if they cannot be had without the deportation out of India of such earnest and high minded workers in the country's cause as Lala Lajpat Rai."[4] Gokhale's advocacy of Lalaji's case was in a large measure responsible for the latter's release.

Lajpat Rai was restored to freedom only a few weeks

before the ill-fated Surat Congress. The deportation had given him the halo of martyrdom and when he returned from Mandalay he was at the height of his popularity. The Nationalists, led by Tilak, put forward his name for the Presidentship of the forthcoming Congress in place of Rash Behari Ghosh, but Lajpat Rai strongly disapproved the idea. He was unwilling to take sides in the conflict, and asserted that he would be "the last person to allow himself to be made the reason or the occasion of any split in the National Camp."[5]

At Surat Lalaji fearlessly played the role of a peace-maker between the two camps. He tried hard to bring them together for a conference, but his efforts were not rewarded with success. When the split came, he, unmindful of popularity, decided to remain with the Moderates and to continue to strive for his country's cause under the flag of the Congress. At the same time he appealed to the Moderates not to give the Extremists over to the enemy and expose them to persecution by the Government. To his Extremist friends he appealed, "not to be impatient on the slowness of age and the voice of practical wisdom." His advice, however, was not heeded. The Extremists were completely isolated and fell a victim to the repressive policy of the Government. The Moderates became more 'moderate' without the Nationalists in the Congress camp and virtually turned to be the allies of the Government. The Congress unreservedly accepted the Minto-Morely Reforms Scheme along with the provision for communal electorates for the Mohammadens.

Lajpat Rai soon found that the Congress after the Surat split was a different organization from what it used to be during 1905-7. His sense of loyalty to the national organization and deep faith in the leadership of genuine patriots like Gokhale had swayed his decision to stay with the Moderates. But his interest in it began to wane because of the basic contradiction between his political ideology and the creed of the Congress. He drifted away from it, and voluntarily chose the path of political oblivion.

A leader of Lajpat Rai's political stature, however, could not remain silent for a long time and he had to take the public into confidence in regard to his non-participation in the Congress activities. In 1909 the Congress was to meet in Lahore, his own home town, and he had to make public his attitude in regard to this session. In a letter to *The Panjabee*[6] he recounted the circumstances in which he had attended the Moderates Convention and explained that his object in remaining with the Congress organization after the Surat split was to bring about a reconciliation between the two groups. But he soon found that his efforts were thwarted by both sides and there was little chance of achieving unity. He particularly disapproved the tactics of the Moderates in keeping the Extremists out of the Congress and making the split a 'settled fact'. In Lajpat Rai's opinion the persistent refusal of the Moderate leaders to agree to reconciliation materially contributed to the extinction of the Extremists and he considered "the extinction of the extreme left wing of the Indian National Party a grave menace to the Congress itself". He also questioned the right and the title of the Moderates "to sail under the name of the Indian National Congress" and the right of the Convention, to make a constitution for the Congress. The Congress, according to Lajpat Rai, had lost its representative character as a national organization under the exclusive control and management of the Moderates.

Lajpat Rai had another grievance against the Congress leadership who had given unqualified support to the principle of separate denominational electorates and excessive representation to the minority community as embodied in the Reforms Scheme. He was opposed to separate electorates and also felt, along with many other Hindu leaders of the Punjab, that the Congress had let down the Hindu community, particularly in his own Province where the Hindus were in a minority.

For these reasons Lajpat Rai kept aloof from the Congress in 1909. In fact he remained away from Lahore during those days.

During the months following the split at Surat he devoted himself whole-heartedly to famine relief work in the United Provinces. In the famines of 1897-98 and 1899-1900, the activities-of the Arya Samaj, under his leadership, had been limited to orphan relief work. In 1908, the scope of these activities was expanded to include general relief. The campaign was well organized and met with remarkable success. The depressed classes among the Hindus also received special attention from Lajpat Rai during this period. In the field of education too he made a notable contribution. In addition to his work for the Dayanand College, of which he was a distinguished founding father, he set up the Hindu Elementary Education League for the promotion of education amongst Hindus.

In 1911, Lajpat Rai made his second venture into the field of Municipal Administration; he was elected to the Lahore Municipal Committee with an overwhelming majority. The authorities were still suspicious of his motives; but he proved to be an asset in conducting with extraordinary zeal and honesty the civic affairs of the metropolis of the Province.

Lajpat Rai's interest in the Congress gradually revived. He attended the annual session at Bankipur (Patna) in 1912 and once again occupied a prominent place among its leaders. His most remarkable performance at Bankipur was the vigorous advocacy, in a speech delivered in Hindustani, of the cause of Indians in South Africa. At the 28th Congress held in Karachi in December 1913, he again had the distinction of speaking on the same subject.

In one of the resolutions (Resolution XVIII) the Karachi Congress decided to send a delegation to England to represent Indian views on the disabilities of Indians in South Africa and other Colonies, the Press Act, the reform of the Indian Council, separation of Judicial and Executive functions, and other important questions on which the Congress had expressed opinion. Lajpat Rai joined the delegation as a representative from the Punjab and reached England in May 1914. During his absence in England five out of nine Provincial

Congress Committees voted him for the Presidentship of the Madras Congress. Though the final choice lay with the Reception Committee there was every chance of his election. When informed of this significant development by a friend in India he decided without hesitation to decline the high office, if offered to him. He felt that he would not be very happy among the Madras politicians and other Moderate Congress leaders with whom he had fundamental differences on principles as well as the manner in which the Congress organization was being run by them. Lalaji emphatically pointed out that his opinions had remained unchanged and were substantially the same as before his deportation in 1907. By accepting the Presidentship he felt that he would put himself in a "wrong hole".[7]

Before Lajpat Rai's wishes were known in India some of the prominent leaders of the Congress set on foot a move to make a second reference to the Committees, with the object of reversing the decision. They feared that his election would not be expedient in view of Lajpat Rai being *persona non grata* with the Government and the Mohammadens. Two of the Committees reversed their decision under pressure and the Reception Committee declared Bhupendra Nath Basu as duly elected President of the Madras Congress. Lajpat Rai must have heaved a sigh of relief at this decision.

When Lajpat Rai left in April 1914 he did not expect to be away from India for more than six months. On the completion of his mission in England he intended to visit some of the European countries on his return journey. The outbreak of hostilities, just on the eve of his departure from London for Switzerland, brought about a change in his programme. He gave up the idea of travelling to Europe and settled down to writing his book on the Arya Samaj. In London he also engaged himself in writing for the Press on Indian matters and a number of his articles and letters were published in the Liberal and Labour Press.

In November 1914, after he had completed the writing of the "Arya Samaj" he suddenly decided to leave for the United

States in the company of his friend Shiv Prasad Gupta of Banaras. Lajpat Rai's first visit to the United States in 1905 had been for a brief period of only three weeks; during the second he did not expect to stay there for more than a few months. But circumstances forced him to extend his sojourn in the United States for more than five years, except for a visit of five months to Japan in 1915.

The third part of the "Autobiographical Writings" under the title of "Indian Revolutionaries in the United States and Japan", relates to this period of his exile. This short, but frank, narrative was written by Lajpat Rai in June 1919 as a memorandum, presumably for his future use. Since it was not intended for publication in that form, the manuscript was left by him in a sealed cover with his friend and publisher, B.W. Huebsch of New York.[8] In this memorandum, Lajpat Rai recounts mainly the activities of the Indian revolutionaries who were aiming to liberate India with the support of German arms and money and his relations with them. This account becomes very meaningful in the context of the Indian revolutionary activity abroad during the First World War and German attempts to exploit the situation to bolster their designs against the British. The movement in the United States had two groups of workers—one on the Atlantic seaboard who were totally dependent on German money, and the other on the Pacific coast, self supporting but also accepting German help. It is interesting to note that the agents of the Berlin Revolutionary Committee in the United States were practically all from Bengal. Lajpat Rai came into contact with both the groups and they made attempts to enlist his support in their cause. His reactions to these proposals and the German offers made to him are narrated candidly in Lajpat Rai's account.

The memorandum provides only one-sided picture of Lajpat Rai's life in the United States. The object of the visit, in his own words, was "to know more of that fascinating land and to study the social and political conditions that prevail there, to cultivate acquaintance with a few at least of its intellectual leaders, to get first hand knowledge of its system of education and to find out what opportunities we had of training young men there." With this purpose in view he travelled through the length and breadth of the country, visiting New York, Princeton, Boston, Washington, Atlanta, New Orleans, Chicago Urbana, Los Angeles and San Francisco. His observationson various facets of American life are to be found in his fascinating and illuminating work, *The United States of America—A Hindu's Impression and a Study*.[9] Lajpat Rai also carried on vigorous, but enlightened, propaganda for Indian independence throughout his stay in the United States and it met with considerable success, particularly among liberal circles. He made full use of the opportunities available to him to address American audiences, to remove their ignorance about his country. His vigorous pen was also called into service in India's cause and during this period Lalaji wrote several books and pamphlets of abiding interest, including *Young India, England's Debt to India* and the *Political Future of India*.

Lajpat Rai also founded, in October 1917, in New York the Indian Home Rule League of America with the object of supporting the Home Rule Movement in India and promoting intercourse between India and America. In January 1918 came out the first issue of the 'Young India', the monthly organ of the League. A year later he set up, with himself as Director, the Indian Information Bureau of New York, to serve as a publicity organization for India.

All these efforts were directed towards the sole object of creating a favourable opinion abroad towards India's aspirations. In spite of the success he achieved in this effort he, however, did not believe that the salvation of his country would come from outside. He was opposed to reliance being placed on foreign assistance—political or military.

At the end of the War, Lajpat Rai wanted to come back home, but the British authorities did not allow him to return throughout 1919. Finally he was given a passport and he was back in India in February 1920. The year proved to be a momentous one in his life and so also in the history of Indian's struggle for independence.

Lawyer in Haryana Towns

Valuable as this training was, it hardly helped solve the question of a living. His father had made great sacrifice and put the whole family to severe hardship to provide for him the benefits of education. He had qualified as mukhtar in 1881. He had passed no university examination in his arts course, having been too busy with other things. Meanwhile he had become a married man. He must earn his own living and must also afford some relief to his father who had to maintain a large family on a slender income. The father impatiently looked forward to the day when this badly needed relief would come. The son was haunted by a desire to serve the people, the miserable millions; yet he could not ignore the hardships of his own family, and he could not begin by being an ingrate to his own father. He lived in an agony, torn between these two opposing calls.

His heart turned away from his books. "My spirit wanted to soar higher, but poverty and the hardships of my parents made me despair. Again and again the Penal Code or some other law book might lie open before me while I finished in my mind the periods of a speech addressing people of a by-gone age." He thought of dedicating himself to the service of his people. He tried to train himself for this task and preferred self-devised tests to those imposed by the university. But, ah, the buts that chain poor mortals down to sordid earth when their spirits yearn to soar higher and higher! For the moment it was with sordid circumstances that the last word lay. He had to set up as a mukhtar and to begin earning.

He went to his small native town, Jagraon, to practise in the law courts as a mukhtar. He found both the profession and the town uncongenial. The place was too small for him. He was fast growing beyond it. He felt choked in that little town where nobody thought of the big problems, where he could get no contacts which would yield nourishment to his spirit. His soul felt frustrated. The mukhtarship too was uncongenial—much more so than Jagraon, for it was humiliating. He had fed his spirit on heroic stories about the Rajputs. Could a Rajput do all the kowtowing before all the arrogant petty officials clad in brief authority? Yet if he wanted to succeed with them, he had to get all the fool Rajput things out of his head.

He was fed up with Jagraon, and to improve things at least a little he shifted to Rohtak, where his father was now posted. Rohtak was a bigger place than Jagraon and perhaps his dislike of kowtowing would not be such a handicap at the headquarters of a district as it had been at Jagraon.

He felt keenly the humiliation of being a mukhtar, and if he must practise law this must be as a member of the higher hierarchy of vakils. He had made an attempt at getting through this examination in 1883, but because of his preoccupation with so many other things he had failed. His father goaded him to a second attempt as also did the humiliation felt deeply by a sensitive soul. But again he had been dividing his time between work as a mukhtar, and work for the Rohtak Arya Samaj and preparation for the examination—with the result that once again he was among the 55 unsuccessful candidates and not among the successful ten. Three more marks would have done the trick! The failure was disheartening but his father insisted that he should make yet another attempt.

He would not neglect his Samaj work. He had found the Samaj at Rohtak in a sorry plight and was working hard to infuse some life into it. Besides, the social work was taking him to Lahore very frequently, for committee meetings, and consultations at headquarters. The D.A.V. College had been conceived in 1883, and he was taking an active interest in the preliminary work and in the planning out of things. At Rohtak he kept busy finding support for the proposed college chiefly in the shape of funds. The college work interested him much more than did law.

Though he could not follow the example of Hans Raj he

might have envied his friend's B.A. degree, and his having an elder brother who had undertaken to maintain him. Lajpat Rai could look for no such support; on the other hand he had a family to maintain. Already as a mukhtar he was earning Rs. 200 a month. Not a princely income, but certainly a substantial one as compared with what he had ever seen in his father's house. His sensitive soul had for the moment to reconcile itself to the humiliation of a mukhtar's job.

During one of his visits to Lahore he made up his mind not to go back to the mukhtar's job, whatever the consequences. Yet he did not know what he should turn to next. His friend, philosopher and guide, Guru Dutt, discovering him in a state of spiritual agony, asked for the cause. Lajpat Rai laid bare before him his inmost heart. Guru Dutt, before he could advise him definitely, wanted to know whether he was having better luck in his third attempt at the law examination. The two of them, as was customary in such situations in those days, tipped a clerk to know Lajpat Rai's fate before the result was announced, and they were happy to learn that his third shot at vakilship had not gone amiss. When the result was published, Lajpat Rai stood second amongst the candidates. Guru Dutt sent him back to Rohtak to work as a vakil, telling him plainly that he could be more useful to the movement from there than by working as a second-master under Hans Raj.

At Rohtak he did some work in the local Arya Samaj and participated extensively in the Samaj and D.A.V. College deliberations at headquarters. He also wrote occasionally for the press. Sometimes he wrote in English but more generally he wrote for the Urdu *Rafiq-i-Hind* conducted by his young friend, Maulvi Muharram Ali Chishti.

He had patriotic impulses and an earnest desire to serve his people, but the raw youth had little to offer by way of serious study of political problems of his country. He was by no means a fire-brand—opposing Government for opposition's sake. Indeed in accordance with the fashion of the day he used to belaud the Government in his speeches at the Arya

Samaj. He had completely rid himself of the pro-Islamic bias that his father had fostered in him and had even moved away to the extent of feeling somewhat grateful to the British for having ended the oppression of Muslim rule. His political ideas were yet being formed. But he had started writing for public print. He and his friends felt that the Arya Samaj needed its own press. They decided on an Urdu journal to be named *Bharat Desh Sudharak* and an English journal, entrusted to Guru Dutt and Hans Raj and christened (at Lajpat Rai's suggestion) *Regenerator of Aryavarta*. The Urdu journal was to be Lajpat Rai's care but his absence from the headquarters prevented his carrying out this task. For the moment he had to be content with occasional articles in *Rafiq-i-Hind* and any other journal that cared to publish his stuff.

He had no reason to be dissatisfied with the progress he was making at the bar, but he does not appear to have struck root at Rohtak. On the whole the Rohtak days were unimportant as a formative period. He himself writes that his spirit was famished in the 1883-85 period. He had arrived at Rohtak in 1884. In 1885 he had qualified as a vakil. In 1886 he accepted a somewhat important brief in the adjoining district of Hissar and finding that place more congenial settled down there. For the first time he felt he was striking root. He remained at Hissar for about six years, and those years made considerable contribution to the maturity of his mind, and to his work for the Samaj, and above all to his initiation in politics.

At Rohtak the Arya Samaj had arrived before him but had shown no strong growth. At Hissar he had to enlist the help of his friends to prepare the ground, and sow the seed; but the soil was more congenial and the new growth was soon flourishing vigorously. In fact Hissar was soon reckoned among the most active of Arya Samaj centres in the province.

In his autobiography Lajpat Rai ascribes this achievement to the fact that the Hissar Arya Samaj was favoured with a set of leaders of calibre, and with tender delineation he has given us sketches of these leaders. Amongst them he contracted some of the most enduring friendships of his life. There was, for instance, Lala Chandu Lal, the "Sardar of Haryana". He was not associated with extremist politics. But a man more loyal to his friends could not easily be found. Even when Lajpat Rai was deported as an inconvenient extremist, Chandu Lal was one of the few friends who stood by him. His closest friends who had shared his political ideas and ideals disowned him but Chandu Lal stood by him openly as if nothing at all had happened. He had occasion to associate himself with officials, but he never tried to please them by disowning Lajpat Rai or even by trying to conceal the friendship. He openly said he was a friend of Lajpat Rai and firmly believed in his innocence. He wrote letters to Lajpat Rai in Mandalay and received the deportee's instructions about the conduct of his personal and family affairs. Of all the Hissar portraits done by Lajpat Rai in his autobiography, that of this loyal friend is drawn with the tenderest touch.

The Hissar leaders made the Arya Samaj a movement of the masses, instead of the vociferous intelligentsia. Here it was in genuine touch with the soil. Elsewhere the Samaj consisted of Babus; here it consisted of peasants. At Hissar, Chandu Lal and Lajpat Rai and Lakhpat Rai made the Samaj deeply vital. The experiment must be regarded as something unique in the history of the Arya Samaj.

At Hissar he was before long not merely a successful lawyer, but in many ways a leading figure, particularly known for his hospitality and for his being a voracious reader over a wide range. The self-schooling of the young man who had had to leave the Government College without a degree had started in right earnest. His was soon a notable private collection of books, something distinctive enough in such a place to attract occasional visits from the European district head. He was a highly respected citizen in the new locality which elected him to its municipal body—from a constituency with a preponderance of Muslim voters. This municipality he served for some time as its secretary in an honorary capacity. The Hissar days were important for him not merely because of the Arya Samaj work but also as the formative period in his civic and political training.

The Hissar Period

The Hissar period coincided with the earliest days of the Indian National Congress which held its first session in Bombay in December 1885 under the presidentship of W.C. Bonnerjee. Mul Raj, the shrewd and keen-eyed Samajist as we have seen, had declared the new movement suspect. However, Lajpat Rai was not guided very long by such mistrust in advance. In 1888, Ali Mohammad Bhimji was deputed to tour the Punjab on behalf of the Congress. The young lawyer at Hissar invited him to his town and arranged a public meeting for him. This was his first contact with the Congress, then hardly three years old.

When Hume started the Congress, Sir Syed Ahmad Khan opposed it in the name of the Muslim community. The Aligarh leader advised his co-religionists to keep aloof from the new movement. He wanted the Muslims to further their interests by standing behind the rulers of the land.

Lajpat Rai had already travelled far from the Syed-inspired teachings of his father. When he saw Sir Syed in this new and unpatriotic role, his respect for the Aligarh leader dwindled further. He wrote a series of "Open Letters" to Sir Syed in the press in which he showed how Sir Syed was going back upon all that he had preached in former days. These letters gave a copious amount of English translations of the earlier writings (in Urdu) of Sir Syed which went to show that therein he had been preaching just the reverse of his new gospel The "Open Letters" by "An Admirer" bore a Hissar date-line; and Hissar could not boast of many men in those days who could aspire to such polemical effort. Those who knew Lajpat Rai had no difficulty in guessing who the real author of the "Open Letters" was. He had no particular reason to conceal his identity; but he had not yet become much of a leader, and modesty impelled him to remain anonymous.

In an Urdu version the letters appeared in the weekly *Koh-i-Noor* over the name of Munshi Radha Kishan. In English the first of these letters dated Hissar, October 27, 1888 is subscribed "The Son of an Old Follower of Yours". When Sir Syed started his campaign against the Indian National Congress little could he have thought that his old writings would be flung in his face by one who had read with such care and thoroughness every word that he ever published in his books and magazines. Besides the proverbial short memory of his public, Sir Syed had the advantage that his writings had mostly been published in Urdu, and, therefore, Wedderburn and Yule and Hume and the Bengal, Bombay and Madras leaders of the Congress who dominated its counsels could not have been aware of their existence. The writer of the "Open Letters" at the very outset warned Sir Syed that he had been "a constant reader and admirer" of his writings.

"From childhood I was taught to respect the opinions of the white-bearded Syed of Aligarh. Your *Social Reformer* was constantly read to me by my fond father, who looked upon you as no less than a prophet of the nineteenth century. Your writings in the *Aligarh Institute Gazette* and your speeches in Council and other public meetings were constantly studied by me and preserved as a sacred trust by my revered parent"

The writer then reminded Sir Syed of the days when he had admired John Stuart Mill's *On Liberty,* and when Bentham's *Utility* was translated for his *Reformer* at his behest. Most telling of the quotations were those from Sir Syed's *Causes of the Indian Revolt* which had been written within a year of the "mutiny" and for the enlightenment of British M.P-'s had in 1873 been circulated in an English version. In this book Sir Syed had advocated the principles of representative government.

"Most men, I believe," Sir Syed had said, "agree in thinking that it is highly conducive to the welfare and prosperity of Government; indeed, that it is essential to its stability that the people should have a voice in its counsels. It is from the voice of the people that Government can learn whether its projects are likely to be well received. The voice of the people can alone nip errors in the bud and warn us of dangers before they burst upon and destroy us. This voice, however, can never be heard, and this security never acquired, unless the people are allowed a share in the consultations of the Government." Sir Syed had explained in his brochure how the conceding of the principles of representation would have averted a catastrophe like the fifty-seven "mutiny".

"If Hindustanis had been in the legislative councils, they would have explained everything to their countrymen, and these evils which have happened to us would have been averted."

This book of Sir Syed's had been rendered into English by Sir Auckland Colvin (at the time of the "Open Letters" Lieutenant Governor of the North-Western Province) and Lt.-Col. Graham, Sir Syed's official biographer. These worthies obviously had seen nothing 'seditious' in Sir Syed's insistence on some form of representative government—an offence for which Sir Syed was now denouncing the Indian National Congress as a body of sedition mongers. Home rule, self-government, *swaraj* had not yet been declared the goal of the Congress which spoke in much humbler accents—at the worst it made a demand that the principle of representation should be conceded and an elected element be introduced into the legislative councils of the Provincial Governors.

True, some "natives" had, in a patronising way, been nominated councillors. But, pertinently asked one of the "Open Letters" :

"Can men like Raja Shiv Prasad and yourself be properly considered as representatives of the people, and the method of selection by which you are sent to the Council Chamber be accepted as of any value? I think no reasonable man would contend that it would have been possible, if Raja Shiv Prasad had been an elected representative of the people of India, for him to have libelled the whole Indian nation, as he did, in his notorious speech on the Ilbert bill. Could Raja Pearey Mohan Mukherjee and other native members have consented to the raising of the salt tax if they had thought that their seats depended on the voices of the people, whose throats were, so to speak, to be cut by that obnoxious and inhuman measure?"

Nor was the young critic of Sir Syed Ahmad content with quotations from his writings thirty years old. He produced excerpts from his much more recent articles to show that till about seven years previously Sir Syed had been writing in the same strain. In 1881 when the question of raising the University College at Lahore to the status of a university was under consideration Sir Syed had written :

"Whatever may be stated by way of flattery, the fact is that in reality the relations of Hindustanis to their rulers are no better than those of slaves to masters."

A most pertinent excerpt on the question of representative government was dug out from an address Sir Syed Ahmad had delivered when laying the foundation-stone of the New Ghazipore College (later the Victoria College) which read.

"The appointment of natives to the Supreme Council was a memorable incident in the history of India. The day is not far distant, I trust, and when it does come you will remember my words, when that Council will be composed of representatives from every division or district, and that thus the laws which it will pass will be laws enacted by the feeling of the entire country."

Quoting this, the "Open Letter" commented : "Sir Syed, have the happiness to know that the day which you in 1864 said was not far distant is coming nearer and nearer and that you need no longer feel so much ashamed of your countrymen for not conforming to the age. Your prophecy is not fulfilled, yet. but we are certain that some time or other it is sure to be fulfilled, and then you will have the satisfaction of feeling that you did not prophesy in vain. Sir Syed, do you wish to withdraw this prophecy of yours?"

Sir Syed had criticised the Lucknow speech of the Hon'ble Pandit Ayodhya Nath of Allahabad and asked Congressmen if any of their agitations had existed when the Government "granted all the boons which we enjoy". Pat came the reply: "I have quoted largely from your own writings to show that such an agitation did exist, and that you yourself were one of the most prominent agitators." Then Sir Syed had written :

"I am afraid that a feeling of fear—fear that the Government or the district authorities would esteem you factious and discontented, were you to inaugurate a measure like this—deters you from coming forward for your country's good. Believe me that this moral cowardice is wrong, the apprehension unfounded, that there is not an Englishman of a liberal turn of mind in India who would regard with feelings other than those of pleasure and hope, such a healthy sign of increased civilisation on the part of its inhabitants.... Far better would it be for India were her people openly and honestly to express their opinions as to the justice or otherwise of the acts of Government."

Now as a critic of the Congress Sir Syed seemed to forswear all that he had stood for before.

Not so very long before, the Aligarh veteran had been known as an evangel of broad-mindedness and unity, and now he was raising a hue and cry that the interests of Hindus and Muslims clashed and that therefore the Musalmans must keep away from the Congress. It was Sir Syed who had contributed the beautiful classic image of national unity by visualising, the Hindu and the Muslim as the two eyes of Mother India. Could the right eye clash with the left? His youthful critic, who had once been his admirer, had no difficulty in confronting him with passages from his speeches which had preached the Oneness of Hindu and Muslim interests and which strangely contrasted with the new gospel that Sir Syed had started preaching. And these earlier speeches had by no means become ancient history. During his Punjab visit, justly regarded as a notable event for the Punjab in the 'eighties, Sir Syed had laid the greatest stress on a single Indian nationhood claiming Hindus and Muslims and Christians alike. At Gurdaspur he had said :

"From the oldest times the word 'nation' is applied to the inhabitants of one country, though they differ in some peculiarities which are characteristic of their own.... Remember that the words Hindu and Muslim are only meant for religious distinction—otherwise all persons whether Hindu or Muslim, even the Christians who reside in this country, are all in this respect belonging to one and the same nation.... They must each and all unite for the good of the country which is common to all."

And yet when soon after a common national platform was actually being created, he had gone over to the other extreme and started preaching a gospel of clash of interests. The Gurdaspur speech had been made in January 1884. Only a year later, Sir Syed seemed to have undergone an ugly transformation.

His speech at Lahore, on February 3, 1884, had been perhaps even more emphatic than the Gurdaspur utterance. In reply to an address by the Indian Association of Lahore, Sir Syed had said :

"Even granting that the majority of those composing this Association are Hindus, still I say that this light has been diffused by the same whom I call by the epithet of 'Bengalees'. I assure you that the Bengalees are the only people in our country whom we can properly be proud of, and it is only due to them that knowledge, liberty and patriotism have progressed in our country. I can thereby say that they are the head and crown of all the different communities of Hindustan.... I myself...heartily wished to serve my country and my nation faithfully. In the word 'nation' I included both Hindus and Muslims because that is the only meaning which I can attach to it (*i.e.,* 'nation' or 'qaum').... We inhabit the same land, are subject to the rule of the same governors, the fountains of benefit for all are the same and the pangs of famine also we suffer equally. These are the different grounds upon which I call both these races which inhabit India by one word, *i.e.,* 'Hindu', meaning to say that they are the inhabitants of Hindustan. While in the legislative council, I was always anxious for the prosperity of *this nation.*"

There was not a demand put forward by the then Congress nor a principle or policy advocated by it that Sir Syed had not himself advocated at one time or another. But when the National Congress came into being he seemed to have altogether changed his principles and policies.

The Congress was being condemned as "seditious" by narrow-minded critics, for daring to suggest the creation of Indian volunteers. When in March 1883 (*i.e.,* a short while before the Congress formally came into being) Hume had advocated the cause of "native volunteers" in India, and Lt.-Col. Graham (Sir Syed's biographer) had tried to rebut his arguments in the columns of *The Pioneer,* Sir Syed had taken up the cudgels not on behalf of Lt.-Col. Graham, but of A.O. Hume. He wrote to Lt.-Col. Graham :

> "I have perused your reply to Mr. Hume's letter advocating the volunteering of the natives of India. In not allowing the natives to become volunteers, the Government mean to say that they do not trust the natives of India. Its consequence should be judged *(sic)* from the saying : 'If you want us to trust you, you should also trust us.' There yet exists a wide gulf between Europeans and the natives of India and unless it be filled up," *"nothing can secure and improve the prosperity of the country."*

The last ten words were 'italicised' by the admirer turned critic, who did not fail to remind Sir Syed that the letter he was quoting had been written only about four years earlier. Lt.-Col. Graham, now "would be the selection, by the local authorities in 11 large stations in India, of a certain number of picked native volunteers—men of good family and well known for their loyalty—to be placed under the command of the officer commanding the European volunteers. I would let them select their own company officers; and once started, I would also permit them to select their own recruits as vacancies occurred. Give us this much, and we will be satisfied for a long time to come."

The strange contrast in the Syed of days before the

Congress and the Syed of the days subsequent to the founding of the Congress reminded his critic of the classic opening of the *Tale of Two Cities,* and the third of his letters opened thus :

"Well, may we say, that it is 'the best of times' as well as 'the worst of times'. Best, as the country is on the point of having a *nation, worst* as a particular section of the community wants to check the progress of the country and unfortunately is headed or at least is said to be headed by a man who has been a frequent advocate of representative government in India."

Quite forcefully the parallel continued through references to the 'age of wisdom' and 'foolishness', the 'epoch of belief and 'incredulity', the 'spring of hope' and the 'winter of despair' since 'we see her own sons deserting the cause of awakened India'.

The critic exhorted Sir Syed to feel happy that his countrymen were awakening, that his dreams and prophecies were about to come true, that the people had made up their minds not to be deterred by opposition—even if that came from Sir Syed himself!

The "Open Letters" were by no means a mere collection of excerpts from Sir Syed's writings and speeches strung together. The comments accompanying them were quite a castigation—combining taunt, irony, satire, sarcasm and downright tomahawking—though the craftsmanship was at times crude and the youthful hand struck rather relentlessly. Here and there, in view of the veteran's white beard—particularly in a country where respect for white beards is traditionally strong—the reader might even have been offended by what would seem the impertinence of a jackanapes.

Why there was this inconsistency in the attitude of the Aligarh veteran was the problem. At the end of the first letter, the author referred to insinuations by "some people" that "these writings which I have quoted came from an honest, uncorrupted mind, at a time when the author had no prospect of being raised to the Legislative Council by mere favour". He dismissed the insinuations, pausing for another solution of the riddle. The second letter once again dismissed as "childish" a possible claim to consistency "in the face of the above quotations" and Sir Syed's fall was likened to that of Adam :

"Just as Satan is said to be the cause of the fall of that progenitor of our race, this seeking after worldly honours seems to be the real explanation of your decline."

The jackanapes strain continues :

"It is nothing to you, because your term in this world must at no very distant date expire; but to us who are yet, we hope, to live long and to fight out the bloodless battles of liberty, it is destined to remain a permanent disgrace."

A footnote to the last of these letters carried an insinuation of a different kind : "Can it be that your once massive, manly intellect, succumbed to the feeble," school-girl-like sophistries of your shallow-pated employee; that, Merlin-like, the great heart that once beat true for India is now pulseless, and that you lie bound inextricably, by the treacherous spells of a modern Vivien?"

Here and there, the letters bore marks of callowness, but on the whole they were a creditable performance for a mofussil lawyer yet in his early twenties.

This was the first big polemic of his career. He made a promising beginning. He who would succeed in the rough and tumble called politics must needs know how to deal with his adversary in controversy. He must have an eye for the enemy's weak spot, and sharp tooth and claw to swoop down on it.

Even in his early twenties Lajpat Rai seemed possessed of sensitive political antenae for later developments have fully. "borne out his apprehensions of the dangers lurking in Sir Syed's new preachment of Hindus and Muslims being two separate nations. The seed sown then bore fruit in Jinnah's day. But his hard hitting on this occasion never blinded Lajpat Rai to Syed's great qualities. He even considered him pre-eminent amongst those who developed Urdu prose, and till the end he continued to command the Aligarh leader's advice to his co-religionists against the lure of Pan-Islamism and against looking for saviours in other Islamic countries. But weaning Muslims away from the national awakening and seeking salvation as a separate nation through the grace of the British rulers was bound to spell disaster, though no doubt even in such ill-advised or ill-considered doings Sir Syed had no personal axe to grind, for, as Lajpat Rai always fully acknowledged, he was a man of high character and dedicated to ideals and sought to serve his people in an unselfish spirit.

Mazzini Enthralled Him

The "Open letters" created a great stir, Hume who had been feeling nervous found them very helpful. It was suggested to the author that the letters should be put together and reprinted as a pamphlet. He readily agreed. Hume himself revised or edited the letters. Here and there the phrasing must have been improved.

The pamphlet, debunking the great Muslim leader with such deadly effect and confronting him with his own utterances, was issued on the eve of a Congress Session, and almost overnight it made Lajpat Rai a man of India-wide fame in political discussion.

The last of the letters to Sir Syed was published just a few days before the Congress met for its annual session at Allahabad. The ink of the letters had hardly dried when Junius emerged out of anonymity (unlike the original Junius whose identity continues to puzzle scholars to this day) and rushed to Allahabad to be received at the railway station with an ovation by Malaviya and Ayodhya Nath and to find that he had become a famous man in India's national politics. He was known as the controversialist who had so effectively exposed no less an adversary than the great Sir Syed Ahmad Khan of

Aligarh. He made two speeches at the Congress Session, one of them being a sort of continuation of the Open Letters. This he delivered as the seconder of the principal resolution of the day, the one relating to the expansion of Legislative Councils by the introduction of an elective element. In this speech he showed that Sir Syed, who was now seen as a leading opponent of the Congress, and in particular of its demand for elections to legislatures, had formerly spoken in different accents, and thirty years earlier in his book on the "mutiny" had himself made the same demand. The official historian of the Congress, Dr. Pattabhi Sitaramayya, commenting on the 1888 session, says :

> "Lajpat Rai was doubtless a man of true vision, for he spoke in Urdu at the Congress of 1888 and proposed that half a day be set apart for educational and industrial matters. The resolution was accepted and the industrial exhibitions since organised are a direct result of the recommendations of the committee appointed in that behalf."

Of his two speeches the first may have won more applause as topical controversy, but the second led to solid work. Even at that time when the Congress conducted its business entirely in English, Lajpat Rai addressed it in Hindustani. He gave a clear indication that if he played a role of consequence in the affairs of the Congress, he would strive to make it the real mouthpiece of the masses. His emphasis on industrial exhibitions showed that he was no mere politician, but attached great importance to constructive work.

The 1888 session of the Congress definitely threw Lajpat Rai into a movement directly political. With brief spells of comparative indifference he was to work for the Congress for the rest of his life, that is, for the next four decades. He had not attended any of the first three sessions of the Congress, but he had not been indifferent, although (mainly because of the influence of Mul Raj) he had entertained honest misgivings about the Congress. He had read the writings of A.O. Hume and been moved by them profoundly, but Mul Raj had declared the new organisation a trap set by wily. Englishmen who appeared in the dangerous guise of friends. By the time of the third session of the Congress (held at Madras under the presidentship of Badru-ud-Din Tyabji), Lajpat Rai had been converted into a Congressman. He has recorded in his autobiography that this session "impressed me greatly",

> "About this time," says he, "were published two pamphlets by Mr. Hume—*The Star of The East* and An *Old Man's Hope.* I have yet to come across in Congress literature another brace of pamphlets as good as these. A wave of liberty surged through their pages and they impressed me profoundly."

With his "Open Letters" and his speeches at the following session at Allahabad he had of course definitely cast his lot with the Congress though, as we have said, there were in his career brief intervals of comparative indifference both towards its organisation and its immediate policies. At Allahabad, the Punjab delegates deputed him to invite the Congress to hold its next session at Lahore, but Bombay was chosen. Though he attended the Bombay Session his enthusiasm began to wane. He felt that the Congress leaders cared more for name and pomp than for the interests of the country.

Till 1893 Lajpat Rai kept away from the Congress Sessions, and this was his first spell of indifference towards the Congress.

Even more than the Congress, his admiration for Mazzini urged him on towards the freedom movement. Perhaps if he had not adopted Mazzini as his guru the Congress might not have interested him so much. He had been led to the writings of the great Italian by Surendranath Banerjea's *Speeches of Joseph Mazzini* included in a collection of the Bengal orator's utterances which Lajpat Rai happened to come across at the beginning of the eighties.

"One speech," he records in the autobiography, "moved me to tears several times as I read it. It made a great impression on my tender heart and I determined that all my life I would follow the teaching of Mazzini, and serve my nation. I made Mazzini my guru, and so he continues to be to this day."

This was before he joined the Arya Samaj. His first 'guru', according to his own testimony, was Mazzini and not Dayananda. He had been soaked in patriotism before he joined the Arya Samaj. He felt drawn towards the Samaj because in it he saw a patriotic mission. No direct political movement had started as yet to which he might dedicate himself at the altar of his country. For a time he had to wait and hold his soul in patience.

He looked for the 'life and teachings' of Mazzini at bookstalls and eventually got a volume from England through a Punjabi friend of his. He read it avidly from cover to cover, "and I was moved by it far more intensely than I had been several years before by Babu Surendranath Banerjea's speech about Mazzini. The profound nationalism of the great Italian, his troubles and tribulations, his moral superiority, his broad humanitarian sympathies, enthralled me." He translated the *Duties of Man* into Urdu and when the manuscript was ready he sent it to a journalist friend in Lahore who, after giving it some touches, published it in his own name.

Later on, he was to produce in Urdu the life of Mazzini, and that of Garibaldi. These books, particularly that on Mazzini, were to be among the major influences that at this period affected the mind of the Punjab. We shall have occasion to speak of this later. Meanwhile, it is important to remember that Mazzini was the first guru that satisfied the longings of his restless heart. Before he joined the Arya Samaj and the Congress, his mind had already been formed. Both the Samaj and the Congress were to be the channels through which he was to work for the fulfilment of his mission, which had been formulated for him at its clearest in the writings of the great Italian teacher.

In 1883 Swami Dayananda Sarasvati died. The Arya Samaj was thrown into gloom on the Dipavali Day. The Samajists gathered to mourn the loss of their great master. Guru Dutt had attended upon the Swami during his last illness at Ajmer and had been profoundly moved by the death-bed and serenity that his eyes saw. He got up to address the Lahore gathering but his words utterly failed. Speaker after speaker failed; and the meeting was finally addressed by the young convert, Lajpat Rai, who spoke with fine feeling. For two hours he held the audience spellbound. It was this speech that made his reputation as a public speaker. He came to be regarded as the most effective orator of the Samaj. It is noteworthy that he made his reputation in public speaking first not as a stump orator, as is the usual thing with politicians or even such of them as later became dignified statesmen, but in the classic way of Greek orators, with what was practically a funeral oration.

After the death of Swami Dayananda, his followers and admirers gave much thought to the question of raising a befitting memorial. The Dayananda Anglo-Vedic College scheme was the final upshot of these deliberations and when they were to take practical shape, Lajpat Rai did more than his share.

By the close of the eighties we find him still at Hissar, as an active leader in the much wider field of the Arya Samaj with the established reputation of being its greatest public speaker, a fairly important figure in politics after the flutter caused by the "Open Letters" episode. He was giving a good deal of his time to public works now, and at the same time making quite a fine success of his job as a lawyer. He seldom made less than a thousand a month, and often doubled that figure. This was by no means a rare achievement in the profession but was sufficiently remarkable for a young man whose ambitions already lay largely in other nobler fields of activity. He commanded fees deemed handsome by any mofussil lawyer, and if he had given more time to his work at the bar he could certainly have made a good deal more, for by his able handling of briefs and his skilful advocacy he inspired confidence among his clients to the same extent, as he did by his sincerity and force of expression among the people at large. He now persuaded his father to give up his ill-paid teaching job. He set apart enough money for his father to retire and to provide for educating, bringing up and marrying off the young children. This was a mere precaution against emergency, for Lajpat Rai was himself meeting all the expenses, of the father and the household, and neither for the education of his children nor for their weddings was Munshiji called upon to touch his reserve. Lajpat Rai saw all three of his brothers properly settled in life. The money set apart for the father simply accumulated with interest.

In his Hissar days offers came of property that would be sure to appreciate and yield him sizable unearned increment at a later date. Those who availed themselves of such offers made goodly fortunes, but as his ambitions lay in other directions he shunned all such offers. Possibly he was all along thinking of leaving Hissar one day to settle down in the metropolitan Lahore, and did not want to be tied down to the provincial town by the shackles of real estate. He made no investments of that kind.

At Lahore

The Lahore to which Lajpat Rai returned to settle in life early in the 'nineties was vastly different from the Lahore of his student days. When he had got down at the railway station, the first time, for his matriculation examination, the most conspicuous sight had been the police constables bawling out warnings against pickpockets and swindlers, and the boy Lajpat as he trudged along followed by a porter carrying his baggage, had wondered all the time whether he would be led into a trap, done out of his small belongings and left stranded. Now Lahore was no longer so savagely insecure for the newcomer—no policeman could be heard shouting anyway; and he, of course, was neither a lad at school, nor a stranger in Lahore. He did not have to trudge along either. He could pay for a comfortable conveyance; and a horse and gharry would soon be his own as necessary paraphernalia for his professional and public activity.

The British Raj was already half a century old. The administration had had time to consolidate and it seemed to be expanding by its own momentum. Its offices were multiplying and this meant a continuous influx of a 'babu' population into Lahore. And of course the mills turning out these babus were working more and more vigorously. Scon they would have got into their full stride.

Though Lahore was growing rapidly, no factories could yet be seen sprouting up. Banking and insurance had witnessed no enterprise from Indians; but European commercial offices were a good deal in evidence, most of these being the remote ends of tentacles reaching out from Calcutta or Bombay or even the imperial octopus in London. These also absorbed some of the babus, but the majority were employed in State and railway offices. And with the growth of educational institutions, the student population too was swelling—babus and potenial babus. Lawyers also were increasing in number—not as yet very quickly, but steadily. Thanks to all those newcomers, Anarkali was developing into a prosperous bazaar. The sahibs and memsahibs did their shopping on the Mall at stores housed mostly in bungalows—all built essentially after the model devised by some unknown genius of the Public Works Department, beautifully innocent of all architectural sense and bold enough to think out a pattern that looked a complete exotic in the East, and had never been known in the West.

These hordes—babus, lawyers, students—had to be housed. And physically Lahore seemed to be expanding like a tapeworm—cell added on to cell of brick and mortar. Wildernesses could be built upon and made to yield substantial rents. Do hoarded fortunes come as 'unearned increment' or as 'the reward of abstinence'? Let learned economists wrangle over that.

Even more than the face of Lahore, its mind seemed to be undergoing a change. Whatever the causes, no one could help noticing that a ferment was at work. Vaguely, you could name education and religion, to some extent politics, as the ingredients of this ferment. The babus and the lawyers were the people it affected most of all.

A non-official purely Indian venture in education had not yet been thought of in Lajpat's student days, but the Christian missionaries with Dr. Forman at the head had been active in this field before Lajpat Rai had become a vakil; and in 1889 the Forman Christian College had been founded. The missionaries, of course, had vast resources behind their endeavour and they wielded unbounded influence with the rulers. Broad acres were theirs as a gift from Government for the manifold institutions they had planned or might plan. These missionaries certainly had a lot to do with the ferment in Lahore.

They indirectly provided the impetus for indigenous endeavour to raise institutions that would impart the new education. So, besides the haphazard houses for babus, the bungalows and Government buildings like the Dayananda School were sprouting up too. The site where the D.A.V. School had since sprung up, in Lajpat Rai's student days had been an unsafe—frightfully unsafe—wilderness. The ferment was manifesting itself in brick and mortar and in the conversion of what had been wilderness.

In his student days he had watched the University of the Punjab more or less in the process of being born. Dr. Leitner who acted in a miauctic capacity had his own notions about the baby. By now these had been definitely discarded and his experiments more or less liquidated. The university had set into a routine shaped after the accepted pattern of the universities at Calcutta and Madras. What used to be styled the University College had grown into the university, the college had come to be known as the Government College.

To this university were attached law and medical and oriental colleges (the last in a way a creation of Dr. Leitner's). The missionaries too had raised their college under the auspices of this university, and Indian leaders might follow suit now—leaders of the ferment.

In the 'eighties in Lahore the two rival channels for the ferment had been the Brahmo Samaj and the Arya Samaj Things had somewhat changed since the 'eighties,

Pandit Shiv Narayan Agnihotri, who as his father's friend had been a sort of guardian to the boy Lajpat, had now given up his job as a schoolmaster. He had also left the Brahmo Samaj, and founded a church of his own called the Dev Samaj. From Pandit Agnihotri he had thereby come to be known to his followers as "Dev Guru Bhagwan". He also weaned away many of the active spirits away from the Brahmo Samaj, thereby enfeebling it in the Punjab and making it easier for its rival, the Arya Samaj, to elbow it almost out of the field. To the new progressive element that was turned out by the new educational machine, the more dynamic and quite aggressive Arya Samaj could make a bolder appeal. And since education was a main activity of the day, the Arya Samaj had also set up a school and named it after its founder. This practically decided the issue against the Brahmos and in favour of the Aryas. Already their school had added on a college department. The head of this was a young man who after graduating had not sought a job and a career like other graduates, but had dedicated himself to the institution. He was the Honorary Principal a title that would not have been easily understood in Lajpat Rai's school days.

The Arya Samaj had definitely struck root among the intelligentsia. Its activity was expanding every year both at Lahore and throughout the Punjab. It professed to revive the Vedic religion. It harked back—like all revivalist movements. It compared the ancient glories of India with her present degenerate condition. It thus fostered sentiments of patriotism. That was one of it several facets. Another represented its activity in modernising Hindu society, of refitting it so that it might be able to tackle the modern problems with efficiency. It may be that all the evils in Hindu society had been unvedic; but the paradox remained that many of the Arya Samaj enthusiasts, paying homage to the Vedas, had more first-hand acquaintance with the modern writers. thinkers, historians and statesmen of Europe than with the Vedas and rishis. They wanted to equip the Hindu society for the struggle in the modern world. They wanted to eradicate child marriage, to abolish hereditary priesthood and to simplify all ritual, to lift the ban on the marriage of widows and on crossing the seas, to introduce (or reintroduce) an Aryan monotheism as rigid as the Semitic one. Most of these things they shared with the Brahmo Samaj, but they were more aggressive and had more of rough and tumble in them. They had not much use for an eclecticism that stressed the good points of all religions. They wished to give tit for that when the missionaries of other religions assailed Hinduism, and they wanted Hinduism to become aggressive and proselytizing like its rivals. They laid great stress on the removal of untouchability and started a 'reclamation' movement. They underlined the importance of Devanagari and Hindi, and here too their zeal perhaps outstripped that of the Brahmos. Their leadership may have lacked some refinement and culture, but it could put a more enthusiastic shoulder to the wheel. In the 'nineties the Arya Samaj seemed to promise a ubiquity that would pervade all walks in the public life of the Punjab. The dynamic and progressive element among the Hindus rallied more and more round its banner. The more the educated element concentrated in Lahore, the more grist there was for the very efficient mills of the Arya Samaj. The mind of Lahore was changing fast indeed. Revivalism and modernism alike were attacking the massive but lethargic forces of sacrosanct superstition.

Politics also was being talked about increasingly. A branch of the Congress had yet to be established, but that of the Indian Association existed. Politics was becoming the hobby of the lawyers. Law was a very lucrative profession. It meant money as well as respect. In it a man with brains could rise without an investment and once he had arrived in the upper hierarchy he could command big fees. True, the Punjab did not abound in big landlords and rajas who could conveniently be fleeced to the tune of lakhs, but successful lawyers could get decent fees from prosperous middle class people. A princely income at the bar was not possible but one ensuring comfort and respect certainly was to be had without too much drudgery. The lawyers dominated in politics as a matter of right, as they were the "independent" half of the intelligentsia (those who had received education and enlightenment), the other half being bound by the "rules of conduct" for Government services. The more '"Babus" there were in Lahore, the greater the number of potential Arya Samajists; the more lawyers there were, the greater the number of potential politicians.

Whilst the Brahmo and Arya Samaj activity among the Hindus made this stir, the Muslims too were hearing new voices—that of Sir Syed Ahmad Khan who had toured in the Punjab in 1883-84 and of a new sect called the Ahmadiyyas. In many ways the Syed school with its modernistic liberal tendencies resembled the Brahmo movement among the Hindus (or rather the resemblance was very striking till he started his narrow-minded campaign against the Congress); while the aggressive Ahmadiyyas resembled the Arya Samajists in their zeal and pugnacity. It was about this time that the Sikhs happened to become aware that they were distinct from Hindus. Hitherto most people had supposed them to be one of the several semi-autonomous units in the loose federation of Hinduism. It was in Lajpat's college days (as sometimes, reminiscing about those days, he once recalled) that the students noted in the admission forms of the examination that they had to enter whether they were Sikh, Hindu, Christian or Muslim. Before that, Sikh and Hindu had not been thus differentiated. Macauliff was persuaded in 1893 to give up his judicial career to translate the Sikh scriptures into English—the version then undertaken resulting in his six volumes on the Sikh Religion. Dr. Trump who had translated the Adi Granth for the Secretary of State had died eight years earlier. John Bull had begun to take an interest in the Sikhs. They had proved so useful in the 'mutiny of 1857' that imperialism wisely decided they must receive especial treatment.

The ferment seemed to pervade all communities alike and from Lahore it radiated to remote corners of the Punjab. Thanks to the ferment, Lahore was becoming more and more the metropolis of the Punjab, more and more the nerve-centre of its body-politic.

Ferment, public life, politics—in other terms, the nerve-centre of the Punjab, Lahore was giving an increased importance to the press. The "intelligentsia" ruled the roost. The "dumb millions" were as yet very very dumb. Naturally, prestige and power were with the press conducted in English. The *Civil & Military Gazette* had come into being soon after the annexation of the Punjab by the English. Indians wanted a paper too. The munificence of Dyal Singh Majithia resulted in the founding of the weekly *Tribune* in 1881.

In the mid-eighties the *Tribune* had begun appear twice a week. This was the principal Indian paper in English that Lahore then had. In the 'nineties it began to come out thrice a week with an editor Nagendranath Gupta who hailed from Bengal.

The mind and face of Lahore were thus changing swiftly when Lajpat Rai arrived there in the early nineties to settle down, to practise at the bar and to be at the nerve-centre of the public life of the Punjab. The ferment that was working the change gave just the opportunity that his talent sought, and just the sort of adventure that his spirit craved for—an adventure far bigger than was to be found, in a purely bread-winning career.

Arya Samaj Crisis

The Arya Samaj was now his principal field of activity. The Samaj was growing, undoubtedly, but at the same time it was passing through a grave crisis. Things seemed to be heading towards a split between the Little Endians and the Big Endians—with this interesting variation on the Lilliput theme that here one of the factions in its strict adherence to vegetarianism held as taboo the little end as well as the big. Sain Das and Guru Dutt, who had represented the two different trends of thought among the Arya Samajists, were now both dead. But the two schools of thought that they represented were ill at ease in each other's company. The D.A.V. managing committee had passed a resolution authorising the opening of the college department while Guru Dutt was still alive. Trouble started over it not long after his death. The causes that underlay these squabbles were thus described by Lajpat Rai, who in his autobiography has left a critical if not very detailed account of this split in the Arya Samaj :

"Firstly, Lala Hans Raj's personal unpopularity. People got the impression that he was haughty and conceited and grasping. His reserve, his aloofness, his sternness in administration, all went to make him unpopular."

Secondly, the question of vegetarianism. Underlying this was the question of the authority of Swami Dayananda Saraswati. Pandit Guru Dutt had in his last days become such a devotee of the Swami that he would not tolerate the smallest deviation from the doctrines laid down by the Swami. In his overzealous moments he often maintained that the *Satyartha Prakasha* of Dayananda was true in every syllable. The same spirit worked among the Pandit's disciples and followers. When they raised the controversy about vegetarianism, naturally the opposite group maintained that it was not binding on any Arya Samajist to accept Swami Dayananda's teachings in their entirely, and that the Swami was not infallible."

In the administration of the college differences became acute (soon after Guru Dutt's death in 1890) over the place of Sanskrit in its scheme of studies, and still more over the details of the Sanskrit syllabus itself. Dayananda's *Satyartha Prakasha* carried a chapter on education in which was set forth a detailed syllabus covering the entire range of elementary as well as higher teaching. In this puritanic scheme there was no room for Kalidasa or Bhavabhuti. In fact the Sanskrit drama was completely unrepresented, and in poetry only the epics of Valmiki and Vyasa tolerated, not as poetry but as history. The corner-stone of Sanskrit studies was to be Panini (with

Patanjali's great commentary), for the Swami vehemently condemned the later grammarians. It was a fundamental belief with Rishi Dayananda that between books composed by the rishis and those perpetrated by ordinary mortals lay an unbridgeable gulf, and the scholars to be prepared for realising the highest truths in the 'Vedas' were to be nurtured only on the sacred fare provided by the rishis. The literalists regarded the *Satyartha Prakasha* as infallible and as essential a part of the Master's teaching as any other doctrine or dictum found in his voluminous works. At least so their professions ran, for when they had to work out a scheme they too made concession and compromise. The more practical-minded people held that the *Satyartha Prakasha* curriculum was not meant for present-day conditions and that underlying it was the presumption of a Sanskrit-speaking Aryavarta. The Anglo-Vedic College raised by Dayananda's followers in his memory was from the beginning intended to be different from the master's ideal scheme. Its very name proclaimed its spirit of compromise. Guru Dutt had been a party to that name and to the original manifesto setting forth the promoters' aim and object which certainly were inspired by this spirit of compromise. Two years after the issuing of this manifesto nothing seemed to have materialised excepting a modest sum (considerably less than a lakh) but as soon as his friend Hans Raj offered his honorary services to the proposed institution he pressed for the starting of the school classes forthwith. Again when about three years later the Managing Committee decided (by a majority of one) to start college classes he (like Lajpat Rai) was amongst the six who voted for this step. He had served on the sub-committee of five appointed to implement that decision. As secretary to this sub-committee he had himself drawn up its report outlining the scheme of studies—still another compromise affair. Guru Dutt worked in a spirit of give and take; but there can be no denying that the trend of his own thought was different from that of Sain Das. The two trends produced a violent clash amongst the friends of Sain Das and the disciples of Guru Dutt, when both of them were no more. The doctrinaire group became more and more fanatical and began to condemn openly and vehemently the way the college was being run. Eventually this group broke loose from the college, and to translate the master's ideas into practice founded the Gurukula University. The other group worked to make the college a success by acquiring funds for it and tangible assets of brick and mortar, and by attracting a large number of scholars. Their Samajic conscience was quite satisfied if they felt that besides helping in the spread of education in a general way, they had created a most important agency for making Hindi popular in the Punjab and far inculcating a love of Sanskrit among some of the students that came to them even though they could not adhere to the ideal of compulsory Sanskrit and Sanskrit taught in strict accord with Dayananda's curriculm for all of them; that even if their scholars did not go through the strict *brahmacharya* enjoined by the Swami, their school and college served as useful recruiting-grounds for the Samaj; and that their institutions were helping the broad patriotic purposes dear to their hearts. If these things their college could achieve, they would not make it compulsory for all their students to study the intricacies of Panini's grammar, though Panini and Patanjali had been so much extolled by Dayananda. They were not willing to scare away all their students for the pleasure of a literal adherence to an impracticable scheme of studies.

When Lajpat Rai arrived on the scene, the cleavage was becoming increasingly marked. For a while he tried to remain non-partisan. But his own bent of mind soon asserted itself. He could not see the feasibility of converting the college into an institution that would adhere literally to what Dayananda had prescribed in Sanskrit curriculum or idolatry. He was rationalistic and valued intellectual independence too much to accept the 'infallibility' of the Swami or of anyone else. He was not able to see the sinfulness of his flesh diet. He had adopted Mazzini as his guru and he found that his ambition of patriotic service to his people was shared more by the 'cultured' section than by the 'vegetarian' faddists. The latter seemed to him too dogma-ridden, too unpractical, too other-worldly. Also he felt that his friend Hans Raj was being misunderstood and misrepresented, and was the aggrieved party. He cast his lot with the group led by Hans Raj. Once he had declared his partiality, he was called upon to do a lot of propaganda for the party. When the controversy raged over the Sanskrit curriculum, he produced a brochure in Urdu to show that the D.A.V. College had not neglected Sanskrit, as its 'Mahatma' vegetarian critics made out. He had to write to the press frequently to defend his party or to attack its opponents. He had to take his share of consultations and committee meetings. Like others he too violated at times the code decorous. He did not like all he had to do as a partisan but he did it.

How deeply he had been affected by these unseemly squabbles of his co-religionists may be gathered from : his reflections on the 1891 election of the Samaj, though they relate to the Hissar period.

"These scenes I saw with my own eyes. They moved me immensely and I used to keep awake at night pondering over them and wondering whether God himself could cure us of our national malady of disunity. To end dissensions and to unify the people we had put ourselves under God's own care, but even there we could not rid ourselves of our sins and the result of our dark deeds was that instead of being united we had begun to quarrel with each other, and that too in a manner the indecency of which knew no bounds. When I went back to Hissar after the '91 anniversary I was sick at heart and the condition of the Samaj and my own uneasiness over it compelled me to leave Hissar permanently for Lahore."

Discussing "the blackest episode" in this warfare, he comes to the conclusion that both the parties were equally to blame. "In my opinion," says he, "Lala Hans Raj's responsibility was as great as that of Lala Munshi Ram".

The actual split came about towards the end of 1892, at the time of the annual election of the Lahore Arya Samaj. On the evening previous to the election, the party with which

Lajpat Rai had cast his lot met at the house of one of their prominent leaders, Lala (afterwards Mr. Justice) Lal Chand. Their object was to decide what course of action they should adopt the next day, in view of all the irregularities and malpractices that the other section was supposed to have perpetrated to ensure a packed house :

"Some," chronicles Lajpat Rai, "wanted to take possess on of the Samaj Mandir with the aid of the police. Others wanted a decision, by a court of law fixing different timings for the meetings of the two parties. Still others would dispense with the police, capture the mandir by force of lathis at night, and give battle if there was resistance. A fourth group, in which I was included, was of the opinion that since it was impossible to co-operate with the mahatmas it was better to part company with them and for the time being to rent a house for our separate weekly meetings."

In a characteristic speech Lajpat Rai said at this meeting, memorable in the history of the Arya Samaj :

"Principles and not brick and stone constitute the Samaj. We joined the Samaj to reform our lives and to serve the people, not to take possession of houses or to quarrel over them..., I am entirely opposed to quarrelling or fighting or inviting the police or a court of law to our aid.

This sane and large-hearted appeal succeeded. The party passed a formal resolution of separation and founded the next day what came to be known as the Anarkali Arya Samaj. The idea of abandoning the original Samaj mandir in Vachhowali was very painful to Lala Hans Raj; even so he agreed."

Of this Samaj Lajpat Rai was chosen the first President.

Later he had to review his own conduct with severity as he realised that in the heat of his partisanship he had formed an uncharitable opinion of Mahatma Munshi Ram (Swami Shraddhananda), the leader of the other section.

"I must say," wrote Lajpat Rai in his autobiography, "that I have largely revised the opinion I had of him in 1892-93 and for several years after, that he was a mischief monger, and a hankerer after fame, and ambitious to become a leader. Now I believe it was unjust to pronounce upon Lala Munshi Ram's character on the basis of what he did in party spirit for party ends. Like all great men Lala Munshi Ram had his own failings and those who hung round him often exploited them. Those by whom he was always surrounded largely influenced his opinion and his actions...,

But I am certainly far from saying that he was a mischief-making or a vindictive person. In moments of heat I formed an opinion which I had to change afterwards and I am extremely sorry I should ever have done him such injustice. Lala Munshi Ram was by nature impulsive; lofty and noble impulses dominated him, and not the petty or ignoble ones. He was generous and hospitable and was actuated by a high sense of public service. He knew what it was to suffer and sacrifice. As a friend he was very loyal. As a man he was very frank and open and pious."

This was written in 1915. There is little doubt that Swami Shraddhananda rose still higher, very much higher indeed, in Lajpat Rai's estimation in the period beginning with 1919—days of Martial Law in the Punjab—and ending in 1926 with the Swami's martyrdom. How often did he envy the glorious death that crowned Shraddhananda's career!

Energetic and industrious as he always was, the work he had to put in in those days must have been pretty strenuous even for Lajpat Rai. He had to work hard in his career at the bar and to work harder in his dearer career in public life. Almost all his off days at the court he had to spend in touring about to raise funds for the college, for he was becoming not only its chief public speaker, but also its chief beggar. The split in the Samaj and the mutual hostility of the two groups made the burden peculiarly heavy. As a small instance, Lajpat Rai mentions that once he had to rush straight from Simla to Peshawar, for "had I arrived at Peshwar even a few hours later I would have got nothing. In two days I collected Rs. 3,000 in cash. Then the Mahatma deputation arrived and the college collection stopped."

Though the two groups in the Samaj had separated in 1892, the separation was not complete. The Samaj Mandirs were separate; but the "Mahatmas" who were on the College Managing Committee started wrecking tactics there, and from 1897 its was a period of severe struggle.

One day the fight took the form of an exchange of lathi blows. Sunder Das, eldest son of the late Sain Das, had his skull fractured and laid down his life for the sake of his party; somebody from the other side also paid the same heavy price."

There was hard work and there was this nerve-racking strife. No wonder that his health suffered badly, and at one time during this period he was at death's door from pneumonia. Both lungs were seriously affected and he went through more than one crisis, being confined to bed for about two months. "Doctor Beli Ram tended me with great affection and took great pains to save me. To him I remain indebted as long as I live," he wrote gratefully afterwards.

REFERENCES

1. The minute as representing the views of the Punjab Government in regard to the situation in the Province on the eve of Lajpat Rai's deportation is given in full in Appendix II. See below pp. 228-40.
2. See Appendix I, pp. 223-27.
3. Gokhale's letter dated May 22, 1907, published in the *Tribune* of May 25, 1907.
4. The *Tribune*, May 25, 1907.
5. The *Tribune*, December 17, 1907, Lajpat Rai's letter to the Editor.
6. *The Panjabee*, July 5, 1909.
7. *The People*, November 14, 1929.
8. In 1943 Mr. Huebsch deposited the manuscript in the New York Public Library, where the Editor of this volume first noticed it in 1958. It has since been transferred to the National Archives of India.
9. Published by R. Chatterjee, Calcutta, 1916.

3

A Nationalist Leader

Political Thought of Lajpat Rai—Nationalism

By character and temperament, Lajpat Rai was a man of action. In an environment congenial to his ideals he would have accomplished much in the service of his fellowmen. But British rule in the India of the nineteenth and early twentieth centuries did not take kindly to what he believed in, and he was the type of man who would make no compromise at the expense of ideals. So his life was one of constant conflict. His practical genius was frustrated by the necessity of having to fight constantly in the wilderness of opposition.

It is a tragedy of great national conflicts that immense constructive ability and energy are often dissipated in emotional struggles.

Lajpat Rai's ideal was Indian Nationalism; for this ideal he worked, suffered and ultimately laid down his life. He was not a mere worker in the cause of Nationalism. He gave the nationalist sentiment his own stamp and a new meaning. His thought coloured the Nationalist Movement and gave it a new turn. Exile and imprisonment afforded time for reflection and Lajpat Rai thought and wrote a good deal on India and her problems.

What is Lajpat Rai's contribution to the emergence of a new conception of Nationalism? To him patriotism meant an intense love of liberty and justice and was a matter of self-respect. It was a powerful feeling which emanated from the heart and its intensity gave it the loftiness of a vision. This feeling was supported by a convincing theory of nationalism, deriving its inspiration from India's past

History was interpreted to support nationalism. To Lajpat Rai, British rule in India represented almost the only period of subjection alien rule, and it was the most demoralising phase in the history of the country. Indian history, according to him rolled back to thousands of years before the Christian era. In spite of the mystery and uncertainty which concealed the true picture of ancient India, it was clear that India then possessed, "a marvellous civilisation, a wonderful literature, a well-organised social system, a conception of Government based on law and on the legal rights of subjects Interse, as well as against the ruling monarch." Democratic institutions and the idea of Universal Sovereignty over the whole of India were familiar to the Hindus. The Mauryan Emperors represented the greatness of the country. Chandragupta Maurya defeated the Greeks and completed the development of an elaborate system of Government which could compare favourably with modern institutions.

Asoka was indeed, the greatest and noblest Emperor of all times. India was practically independent upto the 12th century and then followed six centuries of Moslem rule, which, however, was not foreign domination. Like the Normans and Danes who conquered England, the Moslems settled down in India, "adopted the country, made it their home, married and raised children there and became the sons of the soil. Sher Shah and Ibrahim Lodhi were no more foreigners in India than were the descendants of William the Conqueror or the successors of William of Orange in Great Britain." The Muslim rulers spent, in India, every penny of the revenue they raised in the country. Their bias, if any, against the Hindus was purely religious, not political. There was no racial question which divided the Hindus from the Muslims. The Hindus served in the highest offices of the State; they were governors of provinces, generals of armies and rulers of districts and divisions. "The Muslims never attempted to disarm the population. They did not recruit their servants from Arabia or Persia or Afghanistan. They had no Lancashire industries to protect, and were under no necessity of imposing excise duties on Indian-made goods." Their Government was entirely indigenous.

Such was Lajpat Rai's interpretation of the History of India prior to British rule. He concluded : "History does not record a single instance of India being ruled from without, by a people of purely non-Indian blood and in the interests of another country and another people, before the British. India was always an Empire by herself. She was never a part of another empire, much less a dependency. She had her own army, her own navy, her own flag. Her revenues were spent for her own benefit. She had her industries and manufactured the goods she consumed.......There was no India office in Arabia or in Persia or in Kabul, to which the people of India looked for initiative in the affairs of their native land."

British rule in India, however, made an entirely different story. It made all the difference. "For the first time in history, India has been reduced to the position of a dependency. For the first time in her history she is ruled from outside, by a sovereign who does not live in India, who sends, at every five years, a Viceroy to administer the affairs of the country under the authority of a minister in a foreign land. For the first time her affairs are managed by people who come and go, under laws made outside India. All the chief offices of State, the direction and control of armies, the administration of revenues, of divisions, of districts, the coining of money, the administration of justice, the imposition of taxes, etc., are generally in the hands of foreigners, who have absolutely no interest in the country. These servants are recruited and appointed out of India. Indians, as such, are virtually ineligible for many of these offices." Not only did the character of Government undergo a complete change with the coming of the British rulers, racial cleavage also became acute and brought many social and political disabilities for the Indians. "The offspring of an Englishman, domiciled in India and married to an Indian woman loses rank and status by that fact; nor does the progeny of an Indian gentleman from an English woman gain anything thereby. The inferiority in both ways lies in Indian blood and Indian origin. The British officials come as rulers and till the end remain the same. Their sons and grandsons also may in their turn come as rulers but never as sons. The sons of India, who gain the rank of officials, are only servants of the British. Their position in the Indian service is generally that of hewers of wood and drawers of water for their British masters." These 'British masters' took every opportunity for showing mistrust of Indians. All Europeans, Eurasians including Armenians and Jews could carry arms, free of licence; not so the Indians.

Even outside India the Indian carried the badge of subjection with him. The British Colonies discriminated most strongly against him. He was a pariah all over the world. The British Government put many obstacles in the way of an Indian Nationalist, who wished to travel in Europe and America. No doubt many British statesmen, politicians, publicists and journalists, talked of the blessings of British rule in India and no one could deny a certain amount of material progress, born of technical advances in Science and Industry, which had extended to India. But to this Lajpat Rai replied that good Government could never be a substitute for self-government, even assuming that the British did give good Government. "Can it compensate for the loss of manhood which is involved in political bondage ? Chains are chains, no matter if they are gilded! Can the wealth of the whole world be put in scales against liberty and honour? What would it avail if one were to get the sovereignty of the world but lose his own soul? A subject people has no soul, just as a slave can have none."

It was this soul-force which Lajpat Rai introduced into the Nationalist Movement of India and thus elevated it to the level of an inspiration, which could move individuals and stir the masses to the greatest sacrifices in the cause of the Motherland—the cause of right and justice. The early Nationalist Movement of the last century was too mild, too intellectual and almost exotic. The gentlemen who founded the Indian National Congress and attended its annual sessions were liberals, not nationalists. Their liberalism was derived from the West, from a superficial study of British History and an intense admiration for British institutions. To them India's past was blank and, perhaps, bleak, and the salvation lay in the gradual introduction of parliamentary institutions under the guidance of the British rulers. These men basked in the warmth of the British rule which gave them some social status among their own countrymen and substantial incomes in the professions.

They made speeches, passed resolutions, and were quite thrilled, when they were invited to attend parties in Government House. They were loyal men essentially and from them no great sacrifices could come in the struggle for freedom.

Lajpat Rai was one of those who gave a new substance and a new emphasis to Indian Nationalism. It is true that the new substance and the new emphasis were already in the air and the various religious revivals had aroused pride and admiration for India's past. But it was Lajpat Rai who put the new tendencies into a coherent theory of nationalism supported by an appeal to a glorious past, an intense consciousness of existing wrongs and a splendid faith in ultimate victory.

His interpretation of history had an element of fanaticism in it, but it was substantially correct. The alien character of the British rule in India and its exploitation of India's economic wealth were new factors in History, which had no parallels in the period of the Muslim rule. The wrongs which British rule had directly or indirectly perpetrated on the soul of India were patent. A lover of justice, freedom and equality, Lajpat Rai hated the distinctions based on race and colour, which, Government continued to exert in India. His historical interpretation and his keen sense of wrong contributed to the transformation of the nineteenth century exotic liberalism into the 20th century indigenous nationalism. Nationalism became positive and confident, able to stand on its own legs and capable of bearing pain and suffering in the cause of freedom.

Above all Lajpat Rai inspired the country with a new hope and faith. The struggle was likely to be long and hard but there was no doubt as to the ultimate victory :—"A movement of this nature never dies. The battle of freedom once begun is carried on from father to son,—is as good to-day as it ever was. Success may come at once, or be delayed, or the issue may be confused, according to the wisdom or the folly of its advocates, or the amount of earnestness they put into it, or the amount of influence they have over the masses, as well as by the wisdom or short-sightedness or cunning of those who oppose it. All the world over, progressive political movements have had vicissitudes of fortune, stages of development, times of reactions, defeats and reverses. Governments always begin by ignoring such Movements. Then comes a period of ridicule, followed by repression. But their efforts are futile. The food on which the tender plant of liberty thrives is the blood of the martyr. The rope of the hangman, the axe of the executioner, or the shot of the gunner, extinguishes individual life, only to make the desire for corporate life keener and stronger. Banishments, deportations, imprisonments, tortures, and confiscations are the usual weapons of the tyrant to strangle liberty, to extirpate those that are after it, but they have so far proved ineffectual to kill it."

> *I admired Shri Lajpat Rai from afar from the time he was deported to Burma. My young heart was then stirred to the depths. Later I had the pleasure and honour of meeting him several times when he came to see my father. No one who met him could but be impressed by the zeal of this patriot for his country's freedom by his unflinching devotion to the cause he had espoused and by his supreme courage. Such as he must always live and inspire us to devote ourselves, heart and soul to win India's freedom.*
>
> *—AMRIT KAUR*

The Lahore Congress

We have seen that after attending its Bombay Session in 1889. Lajpat Rai's enthusiasm for the National Congress abated a good deal. He did not trouble to attend any more of its yearly Chrismas gatherings, till at last the 'mountain came to Muhammad' in 1893. The Punjab had invited the Congress at the suggestion of one of the D.A.V. College leaders, Bakhshi Jaishi Ram (father of Mr. Justice Bakhshi Tek Chand). Lajpat Rai too joined the Reception Committee, but he was not among its most active participants. Although the Congress had been invited at the suggestion of one of their important leaders, the Arya Samajists were rather lukewarm. There were others more willing, particularly Dyal Singh Majithia the philanthropist, and young Harkishan Lal, the latter by no means favourably inclined towards Bakhshi Jaishi Ram and his Arya Samajists. So the Congress session was the care not so much of the Aryas as of the Brahmos and so Nobin Chandra Roy, an outstanding Brahmo in Lahore, was Chairman of the Reception Committee.

Lajpat Rai made two or three speeches at the Congress session. "What was most worthy of note is," he records, "that Rai Mul Raj took a large part." This gentleman, as we have seen, was a Government servant, and, what is more, he was part of the judiciary. He was thus supposed to be doubly dead to politics. But as a matter of fact he was busy pulling the wires from behind the scenes and at informal meetings. He had drafted the Arya Samaj constitution for Swami Dayananda and he wanted the Congress to adopt one somewhat on the same lines. His suspicions about Hume still continued and the demand for a constitution was probably his way of putting these to the test, anticipating that Hume would not find it convenient to accept the suggestion. The anticipation was not falsified by events. Hume saw no necessity for any constitution and did not let the proposal materialise.

Today it may sound unbelievable that the Congress remained practically without a constitution all these years. Till the 1899 session in Lucknow it was without any constitution whatsoever and the one adopted that year hardly met the essential points of the proposals inspired by Mul Raj, *i.e.,* a representative character for the delegates and some sort of machinery for their election, and a standing organisation with regional branches for carrying on the work all through the year. Provincial Committees for such work were not thought of by the Congress leaders till 1908. The Punjab delegates insisted at several sessions on the Congress giving itself a constitution before it got the country one and the idea of course had originated with Mul Raj, that inscrutable man who always revelled in putting his ideas forward from behind a smoke-screen.

Even in 1904 the Punjab contingent headed by Lajpat Rai and his friend Dwarka Das urged in vain that the Congress should define its constitution. Now the high priest of the Congress was the grand and imperious Sir Pherozeshah Mehta. As Duni Chand (of Ambala) who was present at this Bombay Congress session says :

"Both Lala Lajpat Rai and Lala Dwarka Das pleaded in vain for a constitution for the Congress; the Parsee Knight coerced them into silence without much difficulty, Lala Lajpat Rai had not by that time developed that personality which he did only two years later."

This "two years later" is a reference to the memorable Banaras session, to the happenings of which we shall devote a chapter later. Here let it suffice that already in 1893 Lajpat Rai and his friends had realised the necessity of a proper constitution for the Congress, and the resistance they thus evoked must have impressed on them how hard they would have to struggle before a constitution could be wrung for India from the unwilling hands of her alien rulers, seeing that even the patriotic autocrats of the Congress were so unwilling to become constitutional rulers of their own organisation.

It was at this second session of the Congress at Lahore Lajpat Rai for the first time met the two leaders from Poona, G.K. Gokhale and Bal Gangadhar Tilak, acquaintance with whom in later years developed into the most valued friendships of his life.

Great Men of The World

The keen urge to share with those who had no access to books in English what he had got from Mazzini, more than anything else, impelled him to start, in 1896, a series of books in Urdu which he named the *Great Men of The World.* The first great man he picked on was his Italian Guru, Guisseppe Mazzini, whose teaching had so much moved and moulded him in his early youth. He had once attempted an Urdu version of the *Duties of Man.* Now he wrote out a small popular life of Mazzini and followed it up with another of Garibaldi. These sketches do not fulfil the demands made on the modern biographer as a portrait artist. It was not really the impulse to portray that moved him. And Mazzini and Garibaldi were not figures already familiar to his readers, so that these personal portraits clearly done would be welcomed by them. Lajpat Rai was working definitely on a utilitarian, call it a political, plane. The Italian movement of unification and freedom had appealed to him and he had seen points of similarity in the problem of India to that the Italian leaders had had to face. Besides, Mazzini's appeal was universal; his teaching was not addressed merely to his own countrymen. Lajpat Rai was one among the many admirers this teaching claimed in many lands. A sketch of Garibaldi was necessary as a complement. Without it the picture of Italian unification would not be complete for his reader. Garibaldi was the hand that executed the ideas which Mazzini as the head had thought out. Like Mazzini he too had loved freedom and not merely loved Italy, as his numerous and valiant fights in South America showed. He fought and won and with magnificent light-heartedness gave kingdoms to others, himself returning again and again to poverty or at best to the arcadian simplicity of an island home. Lajpat Rai's purpose in selecting Mazzini and Garibaldi had definitely been to infuse a patriotic spirit into the youth of his own land.

Naturally he had compiled these biographies from well-known books in English. He drew chiefly on the six-volume edition of *Mazzini's Life and Writings,* and on Countess Cesaresco's work. Bolton King's *Life of Mazzini* and most of the other popular books in English had not yet appeared. His task was neither to produce new facts nor to offer original interpretations. He merely wanted his countrymen to become acquainted with the life and teachings of the great Italian who had so profoundly impressed his own mind. And it is a fact that for decades afterwards patriotism was fed to young minds particularly in the Punjab from these Urdu booklets of Lajpat Rai's. The Mazzini sketch helped more than any other book by any man to infuse a new spirit and create a new awakening in the Punjab. The awakening made the political movement soon grow strong enough to the big events of 1906-07.

Mazzini dreamt of Italy's liberation, her unification, and her being a democracy. He was a nationalist, whose vision unfettered by parochial barriers embraced humanity, a revolutionist who believed in revolution "by the people, for the people" and denounced terrorism for it did not conform to this criterion. Ever giving a dynamic call, Mazzini was yet a teacher who laid great stress on moral values. All this to Lajpat Rai constituted an almost perfect gospel for his own people under alien rule. He greatly valued the unity that British rule had given to India, and wanted to liberate his country without jeopardising this unity. This was a cause for which he thought no sacrifice too heavy.

Meredith's summing up of the makers of Italian unity may here be aptly recalled :

"Cavour, Mazzini, Garibaldi : Three!
Her Brain, her Soul, her Sword...."

The Soul Lajpat Rai prized above all else, but his vision and his teaching never neglected. The other two in Meredith's Three—though (like Mazzini and Garibaldi) he may not have found all Cavour's doings in the name of expediency as commendable or even justifiable.

Some officials smelt danger in this small Mazzini book,

and Lajpat Rai often got reports of an impending prosecution; but probably the lawyers of the Government found it difficult to make out a case against him. His information was that "two or three times the officials had this book translated into English to get legal advice", and that "the official legal experts disagreed among themselves". The Education Department took very conspicuous notice of this new menace Circulars were sent out to all headmasters about it, and more than once the Principal of the D.A.V. College was asked by the Director of Public Instruction whether Lajpat Rai's books were being taught in his college or school. An Inspector of Schools discovered a copy with a student in the mofussil and the headmaster concerned was called upon to submit an explanation!

His next three Great Men were from his own country, Shivaji, Dayananda and Krishna. His *Shivaji'* came out soon after his *Mazzini* and *Garibaldi* had been issued. In fact all the three books belong to 1896. This was just the period when the reaction was beginning to set in against the "unfavourable picture of Shivaji presented by the Muslim historians who wrote mostly for the glorification of the very people whom Shivaji had fought all his life. The books by European historians on Maratha history were also at that time based mostly on Persian sources, Shivaji as a national figure had. yet to be presented properly. Tilak had about" this time begun his work in the 'Ganapati' celebrations and he was using this great festival for a political awakening in Maharashtra. It is possible that Lajpat Rai got his inspiration from Tilak's 'Ganapati' festival. Ranade's book on Maratha history may be regarded as the first serious attempt to utilise the Marathi sources instead of the hitherto prevailing exclusive reliance on the Persian histories written by Muslim writers. The tide turned, and Shivaji has since ceased to be a petty adventurer, brigand, "mountain rat" and all that. When Lajpat Rai brought out his little book on Shivaji, Ranade's work had not yet been published; but he had the advantage of seeing it in manuscript and he drew upon it a great deal. His was one of the early books that marked the swing of the pendulum from ridicule and condemnation to adoration and hero-worship. It was still scanty, work on Maratha records and chronicles having only begun. All the same, the author clearly took sides and defended Shivaji in almost every episode that had been used to tarnish his name. The Marathi archives had only begun to be studied and so the appraisal made had per force to be incomplete and tentative.

His own approach to Indian history he presented in a well-written introduction to *Shivaji* running into more than forty pages. In this he told Hindus why they should pay heed not merely to the history of their past glory, but also to the history of their decline and how their turning a blind eye to this period had given scope to interested misrepresentation which had made current false notions about the Hindu mind and character. The Hindus themselves seemed passively to acquiesce in this falsification of their character; this had infected the contemporary Hindu mind and the result was psychological effects that hampered its natural growth. In his preface he expressed a desire to follow up his account of the Maratha hero with that of "the great hero of the Punjab to whom the Punjab owed a rebirth in a period of crisis"—this no doubt referred to Gobind Singh, the last of the ten Gurus of the Sikh faith, for whom he was ever full of admiration. He definitely promised a life of Krishna as number four in his "Great Men".

The wish about the Punjab hero remained unfulfilled. The promise about the *Mahabharata* hero was made good, though *Sri Krishna* appeared not as number four but number five in his series. His number four was *Dayananda*. Dalpat Rai' Vidyarthi had published in Urdu Swami Dayananda's autobiographical fragment. After Dalpat Rai's death Lajpat Rai was working for two months on collecting other biographical material on the founder of the church he had joined. This book came out in September 1898. One would not expect a member of a church to be very critical towards its founder, but Lajpat Rai took good care to keep at a safe distance from hagiography. Its usefulness lay in the fact that it brought together not only the principal facts of the Swami's life and activities since his founding the Arya Samaj, but also all that could then be gathered of his little known early life, and that it presented the whole in the form of a readable story. That is why it remained for some decades the standard life of the Swami although the Arya Samaj set up a committee to produce an official biography with its own imprimatur. Lajpat Rai's book read quite well, as it avoided the language of excessive eulogy, and the dullness of official tones, and its pages were enlivened by small and clever touches of portraiture furnished by personal habits and mannerism and by pointed anecdote. But it could not be anything more than an interim sketch and was duly superceded by later attempts embodying later painstaking research in Kathiawar, Dayananda's homeland.

Sri Krishna is the last of this bunch of biographies and in certain ways the best written. Cut out a few passages of rhetoric here and there—in all these may amount to a dozen pages or so—and you have a "rattling fine yarn" in the best sense. The narrative shows the practised ease of a story teller. It might still be the best book for the young (of all ages) who want just the story of Krishna, provided you cut out those dozen pages intruding in the narrative, and the prefactory discussion. The Krishna of Lajpat Rai's story is mainly the Krishna of the *Mahabharata.* Later embellishment of the *Bhagavata* and some of the other puranas and of decadent Braj poetry he dismissed out of hand. To the rich poetry of the *Bhagavata* or to the elaborate artistry of the decadents he was perhaps not sufficiently sensitive: to their devastating effect on the mass mind which took all these embellishments rather literally (even for modelling ethical conduct on) he was certainly far more alive. In telling his tale faithfully he had every right to stick to the *Mahabharata* and that need not have compelled him to enter the lists against anyone. But he felt that to resurrect the *Mahabharata* Krishna it was necessary to nail to the counter the spurious Krishna of decadence. Once you accept the historicity of Krishna the task is not difficult either. For certainly, then, the authority of the *Mahabharata* outweighs all the legend and poetry of the subsequent millennia. Besides, once you start a historian's scientific scrutiny most of the poetic legends cancel each other, and many of them cancel themselves by their inherent contradictions. The poetic embellishments have helped hostile critics to make a facile accusation against Krishna of a youth rather wasted in escapades with the Gopis of Gokul. Yet, according to *all* legends (Puranic, poetic and other), Krishna had finally bid good bye to Gokul and cowherds—to assume duties that befitted his princely station—very early in his life, in his boyhood you might say. This single detail was enough to make Lajpat Rai throw out of the window all the legends, that lent support to the blasphemous accusation, as rubbish, of no value to a historian.

A Fighter

"Half wax, Half steel"—that is how an Urdu poet once dissected the heart of Lajpat Rai. The secret of his stubborn resistance against all odds, his indefatigable energy, his undergoing great suffering with dignity lay in the steely part, while the waxen half made him sensitive to suffering particularly of the poor and oppressed.

A fighter all his life, the 'steel' naturally looms large in his life story; but the sensitive wax can easily claim at least half his greatness.

The Arya Samaj made use of his head as well as of both halves of his heart. Besides editing or writing for the Samaj journals, turning out tracts, touring, lecturing, and raising funds, he was called upon to work in various capacities for the D.A.V. College and its off-shoots (like the Anglo-Sanskrit school at Jullundur which also later grew into a college). In fact his work for the college ranked next only to that of Principal Hans Raj. Yet his most important work under the auspices of the Arya Samaj lay in fields far removed from the academic, and from these fields it was the sensitive wax that first registered the SOS.

The closing years of the century were marked by severe visitations of natural calamities—drought, famine, epidemics.

In 1897 Tilak was sent to jail for 18 months for venturing to criticise the plague administration of the Bombay authorities. That year drought and famine seemed bent on doing their worst. Ghastly reports poured in from Rajputana among other places. Such misery anywhere was bound to affect the 'wax'; that the visitation should choose the land whose heroic annals had ever filled the boy Lajpat with a sense of glory and had continued to inspire him through youth and maturity was unbearable. Descendants of the brave and proud Rajputs were dying like flies and, struggling against dire want, they were even living and feeding worse than flies.

Stories from Rajputana spoke not only the acutest misery but what was far worse, of wretched exploitation of this misery. Many of the Christian missionaries in their proselytizing zeal seemed to have regarded the visitation as a godsend for them to collect a rich harvest. Ostensibly they were doing humanitarian work of giving food and shelter to those who needed it most. But at close range much of this activity took on a different complexion altogether. They were 'rescuing' not only babies, but even those who knew Hinduism was different from Christianity, and all means were being used that might be handy in seduction. The mission workers draped themselves in dhotis and even sported the sacred thread and the *tilak* on their foreheads to pass for Brahmins. Boys and girls were taken to the 'Panditji' by the agents sent out by Pandita Ramabai's Christian Orphanage at Poona. And sometimes the zealots would not stick at things much worse than this—for instance, the spiriting away of the starving wife of a starving husband and not restoring her to him though he happened to survive. These reports filled the sensitive heart with the anguish of humiliation.

Lajpat Rai felt deeply stirred in his inmost being. It was from there the words came to his tongue and his pen that imparted the wax quality to his hearers and his readers.

The 1897 famine and the 1900 famine taxed his entire energy, his gifts of eloquence and persuasion and his organising, administrative talent.

Lajpat Rai was a pioneer among the Hindu leaders. Though he started the work under the Arya Samaj he was soon addressing the entire Hindu fold, and he sought and got the co-operation of all Hindus—of the orthodox, no less than of the Arya Brahmo Samajists. He organised relief committees and raised funds for them. His personal contact with the student community in the D.A.V. College placed a strong contingent of volunteers at his disposal. He insisted that mere temporary relief was not enough and that permanent orphanages must be brought into being which would meet like emergencies in the future, and would train the rescued boys and girls in various crafts so that they might stand on their own legs and grow up to be useful citizens. He instructed his workers that in administering relief they must give the first attention to infants, to widows, and to minor girls—to those who could benefit least by the relief works started by the Government, and were the easiest victims of the unscrupulous sort among the Christian missionaries. In urging that 'relief should consist not merely of 'doles' but that as far as possible people should be made to work and earn their food, he specifically recommended hand-spinning, though not to the exclusion of everything else. It was his foresight and his insistence that brought into being the premier Arya Samaj orphanage at Ferozepore of which he was the General Secretary for several years, as well as the Hindu orphanage at Lahore and another at Meerut. Temporary orphanages were created at other places and some permanent orphanages also followed—some the direct, others the indirect results of Lajpat Rai's work. The example he set in the Punjab and at Meerut was soon being emulated all over India.

When the first batch of the famished orphans arrived at Lahore he could see that he had succeeded in infusing a fresh life, the pulse beat of which could be felt in the surging crowd that had assembled at the railway station. This batch, and the others that followed, found their first home under Lajpat Rai's hospitable roof. (He had already bought the house in Court Street after having lived in a rented house on Ganpat Road, off Anarkali, for some time.)

His workers had to fight the missionaries if they were at all to do their job. And the ardent devoted band that he had brought into being was quite equal to the task. He insisted that the official machinery must not take sides and his workers got their due share from the official relief agency wherever it decided to work through volunteers and non-official bodies. Several cases were taken to courts of law and there were inconvenient exposures for the missionaries. It was finally established that the missionaries could claim no Hindu orphans unless the Hindu agencies first declined to have them.

There were solid gains. Lajpat Rai looked upon them as moral gains rather than statistical ones. But measured in numbers, if you must so measure them, they were not poor showing. In 1897 when the entire machinery had to be created out of the void as it were, Lajpat Rai's volunteers were able to rescue some 300 orphans who were sheltered in the orphanages, besides of course administering relief to vast numbers. In the second famine they rescued about 2,000 orphans. The moral gain of course far exceeded that measured by figures. Hundreds of workers, particularly student workers, received sound training in civic and patriotic work. The whole movement was a vast venture in self-help by a community that had been prone to accept listlessly the official or the foreign missionary agencies as the only ones that could afford any relief what so in such dire calamities. Was not such self-reliance after all the quintessence of the D.A.V. College experiment too?

In the development of Lajpat Rai's own personality these two campaigns were of the highest importance. They gave him an opportunity to expand, and removed all apprehension of a parochial cramping that might possibly have resulted from routine Arya Samaj work confined for the most part to the Panjab. His name now became a password throughout the land and amongst the vast multitudes who politically still were a mere apathetic mass. Congress' speeches so far could affect only the intelligentsia; the relief work touched the neglected mass.

There was a debit side too. The missionaries active in the field resented encroachment on what they had regarded as their preserves and they did not at all relish the exposures they had to face in courts of law, before the famine commission and in public print. The dis-esteem of course was mutual.

Seeing these pseudo-Christians at close quarters in these campaigns did not fill Lajpat Rai with a sense of high regard for their moral and humanitarian standards, and when later during his stay in the USA he studied the tactics some of them employed in getting money for their work by misrepresenting and denigrating India to their wealthy fellow-countrymen, he saw no reason to revise his estimate. Anyway he had made enemies of the missionary bodies and they were certainly both powerful and vindictive. They could bide their time.

When a Famine Commission was appointed and witnesses were invited Lajpat Rai availed himself of the opportunity. Besides suggesting constructive economic measures he strongly urged effective redress against proselytizers with resources at their back regarding all the waifs as their prize booty. To what extent the fight against the explitation of human misery in the name of religion succeeded may be assessed from Section XXIII on "Orphans" in the Report of the Famine Commission (1901) which urged strongly that "the policy of the Government in regard to orphans should be formulated in Provincial Codes, beyond risk of misconception either by its officers or by the public". The Commission laid down that in the time of famine "the State should be... the tempory guardian of children whom it finds deserted, and should not, . . divest itself of the care of them, until a reasonable period has elapsed after the close of the famine, during which efforts should be made to discover the natural protectors of the children, or, failing these, respectable persons of the same religion who are willing to adopt them". For proper enforcement forules made in these principles the Commission urged "that every public famine orphanage should be periodically inspected by a non-official committee, comprising gentlemen of different religions".

The years 1897 and 1898 proved full of calamity for Lajpat Rai personally also. After strenuous work in the famine campaign which kept him busy till August 1898, in need of rest and escape from the sweltering heat of the plains he went to Abbottabad. There one day he got drenched in rain and developed fever which he could not shake off easily, and it lingered until it had inflamed his liver. He remained bed-ridden from September to April. Ever after his liver was a source of trouble. Probably the foundation for this trouble had been laid during the Rupar boyhood. This time the malady seemed so obstinate that many of his friends lost all hope of his recovery.

During his own illness his brother Dalpat Rai was found to be suffering from tuberculosis. When the elder brother left the sick-bed the younger's tuberculosis was already in an advanced stage. In June 1899 Lajpat Rai suffered the first sharp bereavement in his family. Lajpat Rai loved Dalpat Rai deeply and, of all his brothers he was the one most full of promise for public work. A staunch Arya Samajist, Dalpat Rai had great enthusiasm for Sanskrit. Probably that is why he styled himself Dalpat Rai Vidyarthi. "I had hoped that he would have better record of public work than mine," so writes Lajpat Rai in his autobiography.

The death at the young age of about thirty of the most promising of his brothers was a loss deeply felt by Lajpat Rai.

Two Jealous Mistresses

How did a busy lawyer find time for so much of extraneous activity? As lawyers are fond of putting it, law is a jealous mistress. Lajpat Rai's literary output was that of a wholetime writer and editor. His touring, lecturing, raising of funds, attending to office routine of the several institutions he was connected with, committee meetings and organising work in the Samaj, the college, the famine relief campaigns, the orphanages easily equalled the burden carried by two or three competent whole-timers. A host in himself one would say. Even so no one in his profession could have engaged himself in half that enormous amount of public activity without its affecting the number of clients who came to him, and without having to turn down some of the briefs. He was proving a great success at the Chief Court and was noticeably rising to the top. This seemed to happen in spite of himself, for Lajpat Rai's heart was not in these briefs. "My practice," he writes, "hampered my public activity, and my public activity hampered my practice." He was faced with the difficult situation of having to manage two jealous mistresses at once.

At times he felt impelled to make a choice. He could not think of deserting the mistress of his ruling passion with the other, it had been an affair of convenience or of sheer necessity for making a living to begin with, and that pressing necessity being no longer felt, he wondered if time had not come for ending the cumbersome bigamous arrangement. But of course this would have important consequences for his family, ana he was told he could not take a decision all by himself. He was now the father of three children—two sons and a daughter all born in the nineties, (The youngest of his children was to come early in the next decade). They were too young to have a voice in the family counsels, but a father's obligations were inescapable. His brothers had by now completed their education and were settled in life. His wife perhaps did not have very much of a say. It is not without significance that in his autobiography there are passages full of deep affection for his parents; there are tender sentiments occasionally expressed for some of his brothers or children. But there is very little said about his wife. The way Gandhi discussed, we might say dissected, Kasturba in his *Experiments with Truth* had not been to Lajpat Rai's taste. His autobiography refers but little to his wife, though that little is utterly frank writing.

His parents had married him off while he was still at school, but domestic life began some years later. It certainly remained free from rows and squabbles, but it does not seem to have been blessed with much of felicity of a higher type.

It may be a problem for psychologists whether his passionate zeal for reform, for creative work, and his *wanderlust* would not have been much less in evidence, if he had been more passionately attached to his wife and home. As it was, he had a sort of grievance that his partner in life could not take much interest in what life meant to him. His wife seems to have realised this fully, and was on the whole content with looking after her husband's comfort—which indeed she did devotedly. Perhaps she felt very justifiably that the husband was not always fair to his home and children and seldom did by them all that he could or should, judged by accepted standards. But she must have realised early that there was no mending his ways and kept her feelings to herself and must be given credit for thus adjusting herself to a way of life so little of her own choosing. If she did not make much of a contribution by an active participation in what he considered a richer life, she put no obstacles in his way, scrupulously avoided doing anything that might make for unhappiness or domestic tension. No jarring note, and taking the peculiar context fully into consideration, this was a considerable, even if not a positive, contribution. And thus by mutual consent (or her acquiescence) she had no effective say in the big decisions in Lajpat Rai's life, and the only members of the family to be consulted when the question of his retiring so early from the profession arose were his parents.

Munshi Radha Kishan was glad of the prosperity that his lawyer son's fees had ushered in. At the son's suggestion he had himself, long ago, somewhat prematurely, thrown away his teaching job. He strongly disapproved of Lajpat Rai's ideas of retiring from practice while still full of youth. Father and son disagreed. "Work at the bar," so the son wrote afterwards, "was not after my liking. I wanted to give it up and to devote myself entirely to the service of my country. But my father stood in my way. He wanted that I should make my pile and provide adequately for my brothers and my children. I used to reply that I had already discharged the obligation of educating my brothers and that I had with me enough to support my children.... In this noble resolve of mine my mother offered no resistance. Her sympathy was with me."

A tug of war went on for some time till on the occasion of the Lahore Arya Samaj anniversary in 1898 he announced his resolve to curtail his work at the bar and devote his time more and more "to the service of the college, the Samaj and my country". He now set up an office for himself in a room in the school building where, when not out touring, he would go every day to work for the college and the Samaj. His visits to the mofussil Samajas became much more frequent, for after the announcement every Arya Samaj in the province (owning allegiance to the college section) thought it had a right and a duty to invite him to its annual celebrations. He started lecturing on Indian history at the college though he could not keep this up beyond a couple of months. He wrote a small book in Urdu, mainly for the use of school boys, (but actually it was appreciated by grown up people as well) giving an account of the ancient Aryan civilisation. This was in a way a forerunner to something more ambitious dealing with ancient India which he may have conceived then, but which was actually written much later during his non-cooperation prison term. He compiled also an English reader for schools. For a while it looked as if he were setting up as a full-time teacher and educationist.

He was systematically reducing his work for his clients. To make his new resolve more effective he took a further step about two years later, by deciding to give away whatever he earned at the bar. This he announced in a letter to his friend Principal Hans Raj, and for several years he continued to offer his earnings, thus dedicated in advance, to the D.A.V. College (and the Samaj). He was generally understood to have earmarked his entire income exclusively for the college and the Samaj. As a matter of fact his resolve related only to his professional fees as a lawer, his main object being to take the edge off the temptation to be wasting time and energy in swelling his earnings. Adding to the pile must no longer come between him and his dedicated work. Although for a number of years he gave away this income mostly to the college and the Samaj, his pledge left him free to divert it to any other good cause at his own discretion. This kind of sacrifice was novel, perhaps unique, and it created a profound impression. It was this sacrifice, this utter disregard for money as a personal possession, as much as the eloquence and vigour of his speech, that made him such a dangerous beggar. His appeal for funds became a regular feature of the Arya Samaj anniversaries and, instead of scaring away people, it ever proved a great draw. His moving eloquence made the stingiest loosen their purse strings and helped in the collection on the spot of large amounts that were only too welcome to the yet scantily lined coffers of the Samaj and the college.

His Live Wires in Lahore

Amongst the live wires in Lahore of the 'nineties was a young Barrister, Harkishan Lala Lajpat Rai was bound to come in contact with him at the Chief Court. A scoffer at the expense of Arya Samajists, he delighted in dubbing them 'humbugs'. All the same, the two soon discovered they had much in common and the contact grew into collaboration and even friendship.

Though fresh from England after completing his education, Harkishan Lal seemed already aware of his own importance. He had had a fairly distinguished career at Cambridge as a student of mathematics. He qualified for the bar as did most other Indian students in England. But unlike them he had to some purpose watched the ways of Lombard Street and the working of the stock-exchange. He arrived in Lahore early in the 'nineties, carrying a massive head on sturdy shoulders choke-full of ideas and with a perfect understanding of finance—high finance—as well as the crook business of a bucket-shop—with scant respect for convention and a cynicism that would usually ill comport with youth. He seemed sure a big career awaited him somewhere—he did not quite know whether at the bar, in politics or in industry or finance. At the bar a bright man had bright chances in those days. In politics he could see rudimentary beginnings already made and an ample scope for talented and daring leadership. In industry and finance the Punjabis had as yet nothing to their credit. Harkishan Lal had set up as a barrister, but was undecided whether taking a firm root in the profession was worthwhile. He seemed to be looking round to see how the land lay, spying out the tortuous business contours as well as the spacious political terrain. He was too much of a scoffer and a cynic ever to join the Arya Samaj. He could laugh too much and in too loud guffaws for the all-too-earnest Samajists. To him they were a pack of low-pated killjoys. He treated them with ill-concealed contempt and found them a handy topic for his sharp tongue.

Despite admiration and esteem for Harkishan Lai's talent and profound acquaintance with the ways, including the by-ways, of the business world, the question dimly shaped itself in the listener's mind : were these wizards of high finance the models of conduct Harkishan Lal had chosen for himself?

After the rejoicing in the enemy's camp over Harkishan Lal's crash—the celebrations by Britishers when his bank failed—one was disinclined to be censorious towards him. And the splendid manly way in which he comported himself during the martial law ordeal in 1919 made every true Punjabi feel proud of him. When Lajpat Rai returned after years of exile, the two could meet with mutual esteem much enhanced and both anxious to undo the vast injury Michael O'Dwyer had inflicted on the Punjab. O'Dwyer had hated Lajpat Rai and Harkishan Lal alike, and thus forged a fresh bond of friendship between them. As soon as he had settled down to work in the Punjab after his years of absence in America, Lajpat Rai started his Urdu daily, *Bandemataram,* and founded his Tilak School of Politics. Harkiṣhan Lal came forward with a generous offer of help. He became an important shareholder and a director of the paper and promised a handsome donation of Rs. 10,000 for the School of Politics. Yet this collaboration was" short-lived. The non-co-operation movement found them again in different camps—one a member of Government, the other a prisoner in one of its prisons. Harkishan Lal's holding in the *Bandemataram* had to be bought by Lajpat Rai and the promise of a Rs. 10,000 donation remained unredeemed. When Lajpat Rai sent a reminder Harkishan Lal, about to set sail for

Europe, wrote back from Bombay that he did not believe in the Tilak or any other School of Politics and that it was no use asking him for money unless his friends could first convert him. Thus till the very end this friendship ran its erratic course!

To get back to our narrative of the 'nineties.

Mul Raj had for some time been insisting on an Indian joint stock bank as the first step in constructive swadeshi. At his suggestion Lajpat Rai had sent round a circular to selected friends and the response had been satisfactory. But Lajpat Rai made up his mind that the bank must be somebody else's care; his own hands were too full and he did not want his work for the College and the Samaj to suffer. Meanwhile Harkishan Lal's talent was emerging fast and attracting attention. In spite of the ridicule that he poured on the Arya Samajists he had come to realise that in the Punjab their co-operation would be necessary for any venture to achieve success. He had often exchanged notes with Mul Raj. He enjoyed the confidence of Dyal Singh Majithia and had got the Sardar's Editor, Nagendranath Gupta of the *Tribune,* by his side. The Punjab National Bank was floated. Lajpat Rai was not on the Board of Directors, "but Mul Raj and Harkishan Lal chose his brother, Dalpat Rai, for the post of Manager-cum-Secretary. From this experiment came the first blow to Lajpat Rai's friendship with Harkishan Lal.

"As Secretary," he records in his autobiography, "my brother had done something under Harkishan Lal's orders in which another director was concerned. The transaction brought a loss to the Bank, and the Board asked the manager to submit his explanation to Lala Harkishan Lal. My brother showed Lala Harkishan Lal his own signed instructions under which he had acted. Lala Harkishan Lal wanted Dalpat Rai to destroy the document. By refusing to do so, he incurred Lala Harkishan Lal's displeasure, and resigned."

Harkishan Lal, it seems, made the unpleasantness more acrimonious by deferring refund of the ten thousand rupees that Dalpat Rai had had to deposit as security.

Says Lajpat Rai : This amount was not paid back by the Board till after my brother's death, although this occurred more than a year after his having resigned the bank job. This amount my brother had borrowed from me and he left unhappy about it even in his last moments."

The second blow to this friendship came not long after. Harkishan Lal found that the Punjab National Bank Board did not suit him. He floated the People's Bank but when his term as Director of the Punjab National Bank expired he sought re-election. The Arya Samaj group put up Lajpat Rai against him. This was the first direct duel between the two, and Lajpat Rai won.

"I was elected in his place," says Lajpat Rai in his autobiography, "but lasting unpleasantness was left behind; and it became further accentuated by the squabbles over Congress funds. In the Bharat Insurance Company too, differences with an ugly aspect, arose between Mul Raj and Harkishan Lal. In fact Mul Raj was so embittered that the ruination of Harkishan Lal seemed to have become the mission of his life."

Harkishan Lal and the Arya Samajists did not get on well together and this rather tended to wean the Samajists from the Congress movement. Dyal Singh Majithia, who founded several philanthropic trusts and started *The Tribune,* took keen interest in the affairs of the Punjab Congress. The 1893 session had been invited to the Punjab by Bakhshi Jaishi Ram, a leading light of the Lahore bar as well as of the Arya Samaj and a prominent leader of the D.A.V. College group. But the Arya Samajists as such took little interest in the affairs of the Congress. The 'Mahatma' group on principle was opposed to all dabbling in politics, particularly under 'disloyal' auspices. Mul Raj, though anxious to play the part of a leader from behind the scenes, had clearly expressed his hostility to the Committee. Dyal Singh and Jogendra Chandra Bose, a leading Brahmo Samajist, remained prominent figures in the Punjab Congress. Harkishan Lal became a great favourite with Dyal Singh, and identified himself completely with his politics. In the 1893 session as during the years that followed Congress affairs in the Punjab were mainly in the hands of Dyal Singh and Harkishan Lal.

In 1900 Lahore was privileged to have a second Congress session. Dyal Singh had died in 1898. Bakhshi Jaishi Ram had kept up a consistent interest in politics and by 1900 he had built up good influence in his own circle. In this session, therefore, the Arya Samajists evinced more zeal than they had done on the previous occasion. They were methodical, trained hands and the suggestion came from them that instead of wasting money on a temporary *pandal*, they should erect a large hall in which the Congress session might be held and which would remain a permanent structure. It was thus that the Bradlaugh Hall came into being, though some of the Arya Samajists did not quite like the hall being named after a foreigner.

Differences arose again between the Arya Samajists and Harkishan Lal amongst other things over the accounts of the Congress session. Bakhshi Jaishi Ram died a few months before the session, much mourned by his numerous friends and by the D.A.V. College. The Chairman of the Reception Committee, Babu Kali Prasanna Roy, referred to him as "the light and life of the Congress movement in this province". By Jaishi Ram's death political life in the Punjab received a great setback.

Did Harkishan Lal share the misgivings of some of the Samajists regarding the Congress ? Later when some of the Arya Samaj leaders, in the difficult days of 1907, protested in the name of 'Hindu interests' and dissociated themselves from "all 'disloyal' activity, Harkishan Lal was seen with them, and not with those under a cloud. Lajpat Rai possibly has these loyalty' deputations of 1907 in mind when he says that "Harkishan Lal's political outlook was the same as that of the Samajists, but ostensibly he was a Congressman."

When the Congress met in Lahore in 1900, two opposite camps had already been formed in the public life of the province—Harkishan Lal's camp and that of the Arya Samaj.

The founder of the Tribune Trust, Dyal Singh, had nominated Harkishan Lal as a trustee in his will. In Dyal Singh's life-time the Arya Samajists had no grievance against the paper, but things changed when Harkishan Lal began to control it. At the time of the Lahore Congress (1900) the *Tribune* was already Harkishan Lal's paper.

The Arya Samajist leaders began to think whether they had not better start a paper of their own. Political life in the Punjab had been completely snuffed out, as it were, after the 1900 session in the Bradlaugh Hall. There was not much work being done by the Punjab Congress at any time, but now even the little that it did was far from smooth.

"The disputes about the accounts of the 1900 Congress session," we read in the autobiography, "were never properly settled. Therefore, whenever the Committee met, these controversies came to the surface. At last Lala Harkishan Lal stopped calling any meetings. Besides, Harkishan Lal himself fell out with the Congress leaders. ...The Indian Association had already gone to slumber. The Punjab was left without any political life whatever and took no conspicuous part in the agitation seen in other provinces during the early days of Lord Curzon's viceroyalty."

The administration grew utterly indifferent to public opinion and before long the Punjab leaders realised that if they were not to be trampled upon in contempt, they must bestir themselves and revive politics in the Punjab. Again and again during 1903 and 1904 the Arya Samaj leaders took stock of the situation. The political movement must be revived. The question was : how? The Congress Committee was moribund and in the hands of Harkishan Lal; the Indian Association was almost, dead; the *Tribune,* entirely under Harkishan Lal's dictation, was unfriendly and its politics were becoming execrable. What seemed indicated in their many consultations was a political paper of their own. An honest vigours journal for the Punjab would not be a bad corollary to the Harkishan Lal problem.

The Punjabee

Lajpat Rai entered on the new century with horizons very much widened, and still widening every day. The Arya Samaj and the Punjab were beginning to look too small to utilise fully the new energy that he felt surging within him and seeking appropriate outlets. The Punjab was coming to know him more as the author of those booklets on Mazzini and Garibaldi that were stimulating a new national awakening and a passion for freedom than as a leader in a socio-religious movement. The smaller things were all right in their own place but his spirit yearned for a big epic theme.

The Congress seemed too tame as yet to serve this purpose, but it had potentialities. There seemed to be no hot blood coursing in its veins. But given such a galvanising force, it could certainly serve.

After the 1900 session of Lahore the Punjab, as we have seen, was experiencing one of its periodic lapses into apathy. Even Harkishan Lal who was supposed to be running the Congress seemed to have had enough of it. All this was not much to the liking of Lajpat Rai. He began to devote his time and attention more and more to work directly political, and ere long he realised that the first and supreme need for making such work effective was a newspaper. He and those of his way of thinking did not believe that the existing press was willing to do its share in laying those sound foundations of popular education without which no political superstructure worth the name could be built up.

One day a situation arose which was simply unbearable. The editor of the leading Indian paper of Lahore had shown himself unworthy of any confidence and ignorant of the fundamentals of journalistic ethics by handing over to the Principal of the Government College the original manuscript of an anonymously published communication from some of his students. The students were victimized. Following this, Lajpat Rai and his friends could no longer resist the conclusion that a paper of their own must be started at once. Ten of them met and agreed to put in if need be and to lose a thousand rupees apiece in the venture. They lost nothing in fact, for they chose for manager a man with a sound business instinct, Jaswant Rai, a lecturer, at the D.A.V. College, *The Punjabee*—so the paper was named—was launched in October 1904. From its very first issue it confirmed the public expectation that it would take a bold stand. The policy of the paper, it was well known, would be generally guided and controlled by Lajpat Rai. He appointed K.K. Athavale as editor, at the suggestion of Tilak, and himself wrote signed articles quite frequently, besides almost regularly writing unsigned editorials. *The Punjabee* was not meant to be just one more newspaper. It was definitely intended to work week after week, and in a variety of ways, for the creation of a new political consciousness in the Punjab. Whatever it may have appeared to be to other people, to Lajpat Rai it was no doubt a weekly continuation of the work started years ago by his *Mazzini* booklet. The task in both cases was the same: journalism was just one more medium of preaching the same gospel. And an effective one too, for it dealt in concrete terms with the day-to-day application of that gospel. He started. *The Punjabee* because it was necessary to whip up a lazy public opinion that had steadily grown more indolent during the past three years. He felt too that the time was at hand when it would be proved how salutary and timely this castigation had been.

Judged by the standards of today, *The Punjabee* was not a great newspaper. Judged by the standards of tomorrow, it will appear to be a poorer thing still. It was an eight-page weekly, turned out by an insignificant press. It had no resources for news 'stories'—in those days such journalistic signification of 'story' did not seem familiar in Indian newspaper office—nor an elaborate staff to prepare a varied banquet. What are called 'features' were then unknown. A half-tone block was a rarity, for to get one made you had to go to Bombay or Poona or Calcutta. Typography and make-up tricks had not yet been mastered by many news editors, and the readers were none too fastidious in these matters. *The Punjabee* might appear crude in its ways; but it was alert and effective. It knew what to say and how to say it with its real purpose ever in view—preparing the Punjab for the big battle inevitably coming and already instinctively being anticipated, if not so much by the older Congress leaders, certainly by some of the younger ones, and by Lajpat Rai who always seemed to sense in a mysterious instinctive manner the coming on of big events. For this object *The Punjabee* worked most effectively; week after week, the local grievances, police high-handedness and race arrogance were dealt with in its columns. Then there were India-wide issues like the Universities Bill of Lord Curzon, and foreign and international events which could be used to further the same end. From the very beginning *The Punjabee* devoted great attention to the lessons of the Japanese victories against Czarist Russia. These victories were going to affect the awareness of the entire East and *The Punjabee* saw to it that its readers did not escape the invigorating influence.

The big battle that Lajpat Rai and *The Punjabee* were preparing for soon came—perhaps sooner than they expected. In Bengal it arrived with proconsul Curzon's bureaucratic act in cutting up the Presidency into two; in the Punjab it came with the Lieutenant-Governor Ibbetson's Land and Canal Colony laws. *The Punjabee* played an important role both in creating public opinion on these issues and in giving a true and bold expression to it when the agitation had become a swelling, onward rushing tide.

Bombay Congress Session

The Punjabee Group decided to renew contacts with the Congress and accordingly they sent a contingent of delegates to the 1904 session in Bombay. Lajpat Rai and his friend Dwarka Das (after whom Lajpat Rai named the library he presented to the Servants of the People Society) were amongst the prominent leaders of this group in the Congress session. The Congress did not yet have much fight in it and it did little 'constructive work'. It held a sort of an annual festival at which its orators gave excellent account of themselves. Its chief purpose till then seems to have been to give a public expression to the year's grievances (in addition to the stock or standing grievances). It remained a somewhat amorphous body. The Arya Samajists, used to well-nit organisations and well-planned public work, did not much admire the ways of the Congress. They urged again, with Lajpat Rai and Dwarka Das as their spokesmen, the need for a constitution that would set up machinery for sustained work throughout the year. But in this second attempt they were easily snuffed out by Sir Pherozeshah Mehta, who at that time was the grand potentate of the Congress.

However, this session proved of some consequence to Lajpat Rai in another way, as we shall presently see.

Immediately after it he took a boat to Sri Lanka, looked at and admired the landscape and the seascape of the Malabar coast; and on his way back made a pilgrimage to Rameshwaram, and visited the famous temple of Madurai. This was his first visit to the south. For three days he stayed at Madras as the guest of G. Subramania Iyer and then proceeded to Calcutta.

It was in the course of these wanderings after the 1904 Congress session that he had his first significant meeting with Gokhale, who happened to be in Calcutta for the Supreme Council. Gokhale took him as a visitor to the Council which was that day discussing a validating bill in regard to the irregularities of Curzon's University Act. He heard Gokhale speak from the non-official side. He heard other speeches too and recorded that "the mockery of the whole thing made a great impression on my mind"!

Feeling sore at the policies initiated by Curzon, the Congress leaders decided on sending a deputation to the Viceroy. Curzon refused to see the Congress President and thus "slapped the Congress in the face". The leaders "felt offended, they fretted and fumed... resolved to appeal to the British public". To place the grievances of India before the British public, therefore, the Bombay session decided to send out a deputation at the time of the impending general elections in England. Gokhale suggested that Lajpat Rai should be one of the proposed deputation to England, and Lajpat Rai readily agreed, feeling that he could be of use to the deputation, and that the experience abroad would certainly be worth his while. The contact with Gokhale he valued highly, and soon a friendship based on mutual esteem grew up between the two for the sake of which Lajpat Rai later made sacrifices without ever regretting them. The political outlook of the two was not identical, and in days that soon followed the difference became accentuated, but that never meant a clash.

Through Gokhale he made certain other notable contacts in Calcutta, and he esteemed that with Sister Nivedita as a rare experience. Possibly he was already acquainted with her writings on "aggressive Hinduism" and kindred subjects. The Arya Samaj was nothing if not "aggressive Hinduism" and by now his Arya Samaj had become a good deal liberalised. In interpreting Hinduism the emphasis in his outlook too was on the underlying genius of Hinduism rather than on this or that sectarian dogma. In action, the emphasis was on an all-round liberation of the people, particularly political liberation. He had not accepted Vedantism as his father had done, but he had now culture and understanding enough to be able to appreciate the beauty of that philosophy. Nivedita was working in the cultural and spiritual fields; he more and more in the political and active sphere. But they could understand each other well. The contact developed into one of two kindred souls. They talked politics also and talked without reservation. On their way to the office of Mr. S.K. Radcliffe (who was then editing *The Statesman)* they had a frank exchange of views.

"I can never forget," he wrote afterwards, "the things I heard on the way from her lips. She was a great hater of British raj, and a great lover of Indians. In politics she stood for the just principles that Mazzini had expounded. In short, this interview further confirmed me in my own convictions and gave me profound joy."

It left behind sweet memories. When in later years he sometimes recalled them, he did so in a joyous mood and they came forth fresh and fragrant like treasured things perennially laid up in lavender.

With Gokhale in England

The general elections in Britain were delayed. The British voter, supposed to be the ultimate master of the British Parliament, could not thus have the pleasure of conveniently receiving in audience the delegation from India for the next few months. Gokhale changed his plans. The day (May 10, 1905) Lajpat Rai was starting from Lahore, he received a telegram saying that Gokhale had been advised by Sir William Wedderburn, head of the British Committee of the Indian National Congress, to put off his visit till July and had done so accordingly. Lajpat Rai found this extremely awkward; he had completed his preparations for his first visit to Europe and his friends at Lahore had already given him a grand farewell. All that might now appear to have been much ado about nothing. General elections or no, he was not going to alter his plans.

As Lajpat Rai found out subsequently. Wedderburn had merely intimated the election schedule—which was misunderstood in Bombay as suggesting a like change in Indian delegate's schedule!

He kept his schedule. On his way to Bombay he halted at Poona where during his brief stoppage he was the guest partly of.Gokhale and partly of Tilak and the next day he set sail.

He could not continue the unsigned editorials for *The Punjabee,* but he took the earliest opportunity of sending it letters about his travels and activities abroad. His travelogue detailed his impressions of Port Said and of Naples and Rome and Milan—places that he visited *en route.* On June 10, 1905 he arrived in London.

Some propaganda on behalf of the Indian National Congress, which was already a 20-year-old organisation, was being conducted in London by an India Committee of which Sir William Wedderburn was the chairman. This committee issued a small monthly about Indian affairs called *India.* The Congress was annually voting substantial sums for this journal. Dadabhai Naoroji too was in England most of the time. He lived in South Kensington and devoted much of his time to canvassing support for the Indian cause. He had already presided over a Congress session in 1886 and again in 1893. Dadabhai had a pathetic faith in the Englishman's "instinctive love of justice and fair-play" and most of his time was spent in appealing in vain to this "instinctive love" on behalf of India. Dadabhai and Wedderburn were the chief spokesmen of the Indian National Congress in England.

Younger and keener men were very much dissatisfied with the tame and staid politics of Congress leaders and of their India Committee in London. Shyamji Krishna Verma was the moving spirit and leader of this younger group. Shyamji had started as a disciple of Swami Dayananda, at whose recommendation Professor Monier Williams, the renowned Sanskritist, had taken him to England for help in his researches. After qualifying there for the bar, Shyamji had returned to India, tried his hand at a few odd jobs in the course of a few years and then finally left India, finding conditions in this country too uncongenial for a lover of freedom. He seemed to have settled down in London. He had been deeply influenced by the writings of Herbert Spencer and when he started a journal in England he called it the *Indian Sociologist.* Sociology owed is vogue largely to Herbert Spencer and the name of the journal was intended to proclaim the Spencerian leanings of its editor in social thought. This journal made vigorous attacks on the Congress leaders, on Gokhale and Dadabhai and on the British friends of the Congress. It was a sort of counterblast to *India.* Shyamji was a difficult man to get on with, and though he was initially considered the brain and the chief inspirer of the Indian revolutionary movement abroad, he made no lasting friendship and attracted no loyal disciple. For one thing, his stinginess was a serious limitation. He could make money always, but was ever loath to part with it. All the same, he acted as a very potent influence in creating discontent against the sober and staid politics of the Congress leaders.

> "To say that Har Dayal and Savarkar were his 'disciples' would be to belittle these two great men, but there can be no doubt that Shyamji's ideas did influence them," writes Lajpat Rai, and the implication clearly is that since Har Dayal and Savarkar are known to have influenced the entire revolutionary movement, Shyamji's role may not be dismissed lightly merely because of this lack of devoted disciples.

In 1905 Shyamji was very active with his *Indian Sociologist* and with his India House, a hostel intended to attract Indian students. He called on Lajpat Rai at his hotel and exchanged notes with him and invited him to stay at India House—an invitation availed of somewhat later.

The India House in Highgate was formally opened about this time, and Lajpat Rai was present on that occasion.

For about a month Lajpat Rai toured about visiting the English counties and Scotland, addressing meetings for the cause he represented, and when he got back to London in August responding to Shyamji's invitation he put up at the India House.

However, his stay at the India House could not have found favour in the eyes of some of the members of the India Committee of the Congress in London. When one day Shyamji and Lajpat Rai addressed a Labour or Socialist meeting in Holborn Hall in favour of Home Rule, a flutter could be seen in the India Committee dovecots. Lajpat Rai had not yet moved in to Shyamji's India House. The meeting had been called by a labour organisation and Lajpat Rai invited by Dadubhai Naoroji, its Vice-president.

Lajpat Rai Writes :

"When Sir Henry Cotton learnt that Shyamji and myself had made speeches from the same platform in favour of Home Rule, he felt greatly annoyed and brought a motion before the British Committee to the effect that as I was in England as a delegate such conduct on my part was objectionable."

Sir William Wedderburn, however, did not support Sir Henry and Lajpat Rai himself "made it plain that by becoming a Congress delegate I had not bartered away my liberty, that though my speech contained nothing to which a Congressman could take exception, if it was suggested that (being a 'delegate') I had no liberty to express my views in that country, I was quite prepared to resign from the delegation, but would in no case sacrifice my freedom."

Sir Henry Cotton at last put the blame on the inaccurate reporting of the speech and the incident was closed.

Lajpat Rai would not lightly let his freedom be taken away, and he exercised it fully. He addressed meetings in Manchester, Edinburgh, Liverpool and elsewhere. Gokhale had also arrived. Often they spoke from the same platform. Sometimes they toured about and spoke separately. They delivered their message to the British voter leaving, of course, the decision to his good sense.

In an article on India and British party politics, contributed to *The Punjabee,* Lajpat Rai wrote that there was nothing to choose between Liberals and Tories and the only people from whom some friendship might be expected were Labourites. (Till then the Labour group was only a part of the Liberal party). Through Shyamji and Lajpat Rai made some friendships in radical circles. He particularly mentions the British socialist writer, H.M. Hyndman and some of the Irish leaders.

The Gaekwad of Baroda who also happened to be in London, gave a reception at the Cecil where he was staying. The guests included Lajpat Rai and Shyamji, these constituting two-thirds of the entire number of Indian guests. They were introduced to Her Highness the Maharanee. The Gaekwad whispered to them asking them not to hurry away when the reception broke up. They stayed on after the English guests had departed and had a talk "in which the Maharaja laid bare his heart before us", to render Lajpat Rai's Urdu literally, "the blisters of a scorched heart".

Before returning to India Lajpat Rai made a brief trip to the United States, in the company of Dewan Badri Nath, the scion of a well-known family of Punjab 'chiefs', at that time a young man with progressive views.

In October he was back again in London and Sir William Wedderburn had drawn up the programme of another lecture tour for him : Both he and Gokhale addressed a large number of meetings, several of these, particularly Lajpat Rai's, arranged under Labour auspices.

Gokhale's choice of Lajpat Rai as a fellow-delegate to England had been readily endorsed by the Punjab branch of the Indian Association and it had sent round an appeal for money for the delegate's expenses. On his return to Lahore Lajpat Rai announced that the three thousand or so thus collected had remained intact to be used for other public causes. It may be that his earnings at the bar for this year went to political work abroad instead of the D.A.V. College.

The New Spirit

Early in November 1905 Lajpat Rai left the shores of England, at Marseilles taking the very steamer *S.S. Peninsular,* by which Lord Minto was coming to India to take over as Viceroy, landing in Bombay on November 17.

At Lahore an unprecedented welcome awaited him. A huge crowd had collected on the platform and outside the railway station and just as he stepped out of his compartment, a very distinguished citizen, the Brahmo leader, Babu Jogendra Chandra Bose lifting him up put him on his shoulders. He could thus be seen by the eager crowd and at the same time be spared the jostling. As he got into his carriage, the students unharnessed the horses, themselves drawing the carriage for the three km. and more right into his Court Street house. The students simply adored Lajpat Rai and when the round of parties and addresses of welcome started, they by no means lagged behind—even those of the Government Colleges came forward with their address of welcome.

As he looked round, he could immediately read the portents foreshadowing big events. For the Arya Samaj anniversary he had of course been announced, and that had drawn such an unexpectedly big crowd that the meeting had to be adjourned to improvise adequate arrangements. He addressed the crowd later in the D.A.V. College hostel. It was at this meeting that he said that the credit for whatever was good in him belonged to the Samaj. However, the speech became more memorable for certain other passages in it. For, it was in this speech that later on the official apologists sought justification for his deportation. In concluding the speech he foresaw "blood raining down from the Indian sky. At the moment it was a seemingly clear sky but tiny red specks were already visible."

The Lajpat Rai menace in C.I.D. records was obviously swelling. The "blood raining" speech was followed soon after by this one threatening "unpleasant consequences" and, besides, perpetrating the dangerous heresy of "conditioned loyalty" Lahore, where a short while before the officials had thought all was so quiet, had galvanised of a sudden and become so dangerous. That the very first meeting of protest against a lathi charge in far-off Barisal would be held at Lahore must have seemed incredible to the official mind. Shocked and bewildered, officialdom had to wake up to an intolerable "state of affairs, and to the new phenomenon of Lajpat Rai's Lahore, Lajpat Rai's Punjab.

And it was not all imported or vicarious resentment. The Punjab had its own grievances in the new land measures.

A measure restricting the alienation of land had been enacted. This evoked much hostility, but it was supported by the classes which it sheltered in its ample schedules as "agriculturist". Lajpat Rai and *The Punjabee* opposed the bill. At the next Congress session a resolution was passed against this measure. Later on when the Congress saw that a large body of Muslim landholders supported the measure as affording just protection to their rights, it dropped its opposition.

Far more intense was the opposition to Ibbetson's Land Colonisation Bills. Here Hindu, Sikh and Muslim, urban and rural, agriculturist and non-agriculturist joined hands, and soon the Punjab was in the grip of a whirlwind agrarian agitation. We shall have to speak of this agitation in a later chapter.

A few days after the Barisal conference, the Congress met for its annual session at Banaras. For the first time "left" and "right", then styled "extremists" and "moderates", openly clashed.

In Bengal the new spirit had been visible in the columns of Aurobindo's *Bandemataram*. In Maharashtra Tilak's party decried the moderate methods of Gokhale and his followers. In the Punjab Lajpat Rai was already the idol of the people, especially of the younger generation, and he had left little doubt in anybody's mind that he was with Tilak and Aurobindo and Bipin Chandra Pal, rather than with Gokhale and Dadabhoi Naoroji, and Pherozeshah Mehta.

At Banaras the new spirit loomed large; all round there was far more of fervour than had been witnessed at previous Congress sessions. The presidential procession with its enthusiastic scenes was a flattering homage to the moderate leader, Gokhale; but the fervour was engendered not by moderatism but entirely by the new spirit. In the presidential carriage with Gokhale was his colleague in England, Lajpat Rai, and he recorded afterwards :

"The citizens of Banaras gave a splendid reception to Gokhale. I was sitting in the same carriage with him. On the footboard stood a volunteer whose shouts deafened the ears. Looking at this reception one thought that the nation's evil days were coming to an end. Gokhale was joyous. 'If only we had worked, there would be enough appreciation and fervour amongst the people,' observed he, and tears were seen in his eyes. It was a wonderful sight indeed."

4

The Swaraj Party

"Now, which of you three is going to make room for Lalaji?" was the somewhat abrupt question with which Shamlal Nehru greeted the three Swarajist Assemblymen from the Punjab—Duni Chand (of Ambala), Raizada Hans Raj and Dewan Chaman Lal whom he found chatting in the Assembly library. Shamlal obviously looked full of important news. He had just come to know that the rules for eligibility to the Legislative Assembly were about to be amended, and that it had been decided that the existing rule which disqualified anyone who had been in prison with a sentence exceeding six months would go.

"Anyone of us, and willingly," was the Punjab trio's reply to Shamlal's query. They were all delighted that Lalaji would become eligible.

This unofficial forecast came early in 1925 during the Delhi session of the Assembly. Lalaji had hitherto been ineligible not merely because of his sentences of imprisonment, but also for his having been disbarred by the Chief Court. In 1917 during his war-time exile in the States the authorities had banned the circulation of some of his books and on the strength of this arbitrary ban, the Chief Court, without hearing him, had removed his name from its rolls. Of this additional disqualification few even among his close friends seemed aware and the term in prison was generally believed to be the sole obstacle. The question naturally arose whether a seat could be found for Lalaji if the obstacle disappeared.

The very day Shamlal had brought the news, Raizada Hans Raj sent a letter to Lalaji offering to make room for him.

During the next few months he repeated his offer several times, leaving it to Lalaji to avail himself of it at the right moment.

In the course of that very session the amendment in rules was notified and it did not go quite far enough. The six months' limit was raised to one year, and as Lalaji had served an aggregate sentence exceeding that period, it did not seem quite sure whether he would be eligible. Raizada himself consulted some of the eminent lawyers in the Assembly—amongst them M.A. Jinnah—and they could not give a reassuring reply. Later on, during the Simla session, Sir Alexander Muddiman, the Home Member, was informally asked, and his interpretation made clear Lalaji's way to the Assembly; for, according to Sir Alexander it was not the aggregate of the different sentences but the length of each single sentence that was to be taken into account. None of the sentences awarded in Lalaji's case went beyond a year and he might therefore be deemed eligible.

Shortly after, Lalaji was taken ill at Solan. On his recovery he told Raizada Hans Raj that he had satisfied himself about the interpretation of the amended rule and made sure that he was eligible. The Raizada wrote out his resignation and came down to Lahore to place it personally in Lalaji's own hands.

About his other disqualification, some of Lalaji's friends sounded the Punjab authorities and ascertained that they had no intention of obstructing Lalaji's return—possibly it was presumed that in any event the disqualification could easily be removed by a representation to the High Court. Since it could be taken as a certainty that there would be no rival candidate to dig up this inconvenient fact and bring it to the notice of the returning authority, Lalaji felt sure that his way to the Assembly Chamber was now clear. So Raizada Hans Raj resigned and in bidding farewell to his constituency through the press, he thankfully recalled that he had been returned un-opposed, and he confidently hoped that Lalaji would be returned in like manner. Thanking his colleagues in the Assembly the Raizada expressed the hope that Pandit Motilal would find in Lalaji his "best friend and a true colleague".

When the dates for a by-election were gazetted Lalaji had to be summoned from Delhi telegraphically to Jullundur to file his papers. Lalaji and the Raizada were the only ones to file nominations. Lalaji had to preside over the Hindu Conference being held on December 6, 1925 in Bombay and thither he proceeded on the withdrawal day. That day (after Lalaji's departure) the Raizada withdrawing, Lalaji was returned unopposed. In *The People* (December 13) he offered his thanks to Raizada Hans Raj and to the constituency; even to the authorities for "having put no difficulties in my way".

His concluding words were :

"As to my programme in the Legislative Assembly, I must take some time to, formulate it."

We have deliberately given a somewhat detailed recital of these minutiae, for in the subsequent controversy the question loomed large whether Lalaji was pledged to join the Swaraj Party by assurances given at the time of his election. In strict accord with the party code the correct thing for Raizada Hans Raj would have been to place his resignation in the hands of his leader and not in those of Lalaji. The fact is that in his repeated offers to Lalaji, during the best part of a year, the Raizada never laid down any conditions and never demanded any assurances. In correspondence as well as in talks his offer to resign had all along been entirely free from even a remote suggestion of any accompanying conditions. When he finally desired the Raizada's resignation, Lalaji. did so in the full assurance that the seat was being vacated for him without any conditions for him as "Lalaji", and not for a member or prospective member of this or that party. On the Raizada's side the only public statement was the one in which while thanking his fellow-Assemblymen and his constituents he expressed the hope that Pandit Motilal would find in Lalaji his "best friend and a true colleague". The hope that he expressed conveyed his own desire and not an assurance extracted from or given by Lalaji; and, even so, he did not explicitly say that he expected Lalaji to join the Swaraj Party. Was the "hope" in any way based on any "assurance"? For an answer we should record two further details—a little talk that preceded Raizada Hans Raj's statement, and a letter written in the sequel. After Raizada Hans Raj had written out and signed his resignation and placed it in Lalaji's hands he begged leave to say something—that he held Pandit Motilal in very high esteem and that it should pain him if he (Lalaji) should in any way inconvenience Panditji. Lalaji in reply said that Motilalji should find in him his best friend and true colleague. The talk was all too brief and in broad and rather vague terms. Later on when Raizada Hans Raj issued his statement to the press, he sought really to repeat Lalaji's own words—though he did not explicitly say so. Seeing in this a possibility of misconstruction and misunderstanding, Lalaji wrote to Raizada Hans Raj that if in any way it was suggested that there was any condition or obligation accompanying his offer or his own acceptance thereof, he was quite willing not to avail himself of the offer, and though the vacancy had already been caused he undertook to have the Raizada re-elected, and to foot the bill for these proceedings. Raizada Hans Raj does not seem to have taken any further steps one way or the other—neither withdrawing his press message nor explaining it to Lalaji, nor availing himself of Lalaji's offer to have him re-elected. Shortly after they had to meet at Jullundur for the nomination ritual; both filled in the papers and filed them but neither said anything about the press statement or the letter. After Lalaji's departure, Hans Raj filed his withdrawal and secured for Lalaji an unopposed return.

Lalaji was returned early in December 1925. He attended the Congress session at Kanpur at the end of that month without having committed himself to joining the Swaraj Party—in fact at Kanpur he was very near parting company with Pandit Motilal. In *The People* for January 17, he said :

"I am not a member of the Swaraj Party; I need not become one, as being a Congressman I am a Swarajist for all practical purposes."

When he was sworn in, he had not yet joined the party. In fact before joining the party on January 25, he had already attended several sittings of the Assembly. Five years prior to his formally joining the party he had accepted Pandit Motilal's invitation to join the Swaraj Party, and in doing so, had written to him as leader of the party:

January 20, 1926

My dear Panditji,

I have to thank you for the invitation you have extended to me to join the Swaraj Party in the Legislative Assembly. Last time when I met you I said that personally I had made up my mind to accept your invitation; but that before giving my final consent I would consult my Lahore friends and would give you a final answer on Monday next. Since then, I have consulted my friends, and this letter is the result of that consultation. While joining the party, I would like to make my position quite clear, so that there be no misunderstanding about it now or hereafter. As I read the rules of the party, I do not think my position is in any way inconsistent with them.

(A) I believe in council work. I am opposed to the boycott of councils and the assembly. I am not in favour of the Swarajists accepting offices in the gift of Government.

(B) I don't believe in wholesale obstruction and have never believed in it.

(C) I wish to retain my freedom of action on communal questions.

I understand that communal questions shall not be decided by a party vote.

(D) In disputes between labour and capital, I am a labour man; but as I understand, the majority of the Swaraj Party is also of the same way of thinking.

Subject to these observations, I shall be glad to be a member of the party.

Yours sincerely,

Lajpat Rai.

He told Motilalji, besides, that his joining the Party would not make his newspapers, *The People* and the daily *Bande-mataram,* controlled organs of the Party; these were to remain as independent of party affiliation as they had hitherto been.

The assurances and formalities apart, what was Lalaji's political stand about the time he joined the Assembly? In July 1925, he had started his weekly *The People* and though even before that he was writing frequently for the press and airing his views, now he was doing so every week and there could be no room for anyone to say that it was not known where he agreed and where he differed. When the withdrawal of non-co-operation started with the Chauri Chaura anti-climax, he had begun to re-think politics and even from jail he had sent out articles (his authorship of which was not much of a secret) giving the trend of his thoughts. This was clearly a Swarajist trend—that is, he desired Congressmen to capture the legislatures. Even from prison he had helped C.R. Das in laying the foundations of this party. When he came out even while convalescing, he had done his bit for the Swarajist candidates. In the Punjab the entire campaign had been his care. After that, when he went to England he had been in the closest-contact with Motilalji, and had carried on talks with the Labour Government on behalf of the Swaraj Party. But he had not joined the party, had never been subject to its discipline and had valued and exercised his freedom to criticise it wherever he thought fit. He was an unofficial Swarajist in the sense that :

(1) he believed in a council programme and was not with the "no-change" school; and

(2) he did not believe in acceptance of office, and therefore was not with the Responsivist school.

To a hurried lumper he might easily appear to be nothing but a Swarajist, and yet to one rather scrupulous about essential detail his differences with Swarajism were clearly expressed, and you might even say, underlined in his writings, week after week. Starting as a heresy, and for a while being treated as such by the 'no-change' orthodoxy, Swarajism had in turn settled down into an orthodox church and developed its own Athanasian creed which demanded that "whosoever will be saved" must swear by "obstruction, continuous, uniform and consistent." This formula Lalaji had at no stage been able to accept Like "Swaraj within a year" and by a named date it seemed to him obviously much too unpractical and to his ears almost had a ring of insincerity about it. In practice the Swarajists had often strayed far from the letter of the formula. They had installed V.J. Patel into the Speaker's chair and and their everyday practice in the legislature was by no means consistently governed by the obstructionist canon. Obstruction in fact was just one of the weapons in their armoury. But they put certain rather severe limitations of their co-operation—they would not accept 'office', and in its original wide signification this had meant that even committees of the house were under taboo. By the time, however, Lalaji arrived on the scene, the taboo was already slackening its grip, for the Swarajist leader himself, quite wisely (as Lalaji thought), had accepted a seat on the Skeen Committee on Indianization of the Army. This was a significant departure from the Swarajists' avowed creed—a serious violation of the taboo, and one that many expected would inevitably lead to other violations. In fact some feared (others hoped) that this might be the thin edge of the Responsivist wedge.

At times Lalaji felt that the Swarajist leadership was becoming too exacting in the name of discipline, that it was forgetting all too soon the indulgence it had asked for its own 'heresy', that of late there had been too much talk of "amputating the diseased limb", whilst the orthodox non-co-operation still could not convince himself that the entire Parliamentary limb calling itself the Swaraj Party was -anything but a malignant growth on the body-politic. In criticising what seemed to him the intolerant attitude of the leadership, Lalaji seemed at times to be taking the side of the Responsivists though he was so little in sympathy with the quintessence of responsivism in the 1925 context, *viz.,* the desirability of accepting office in a dyarchical constitution.

He himself had expressed misgivings about his having chosen the wrong moment for his parliamentary debut. For, as he put it, the "situation was uncertain and obscure". In 1925 the discipline and solidarity of the Swaraj Party was being sapped by dissension, and an over-stressing of discipline was only making matters worse. Things came to a crisis with the Tambe episode. Shreepad Balwant Tambe, the Swarajist Speaker of the C.P. Legislative Council, was offered an executive councillorship and he accepted it. His action was trebly open to objection. It was wrong of a Congressman to accept office in the dyarchical system. It was a bad parliamentary precedent that a Speaker should be thus seduced by the Government. And it was beyond doubt a clear act of gross indiscipline, for Tambe had never cared even to inform the national executive of the Swaraj Party about the offer and of his own intention. Pandit Motilal was naturally much upset. What made matters worse was that Jayakar and Kelkar and certain other important Swarajists offered, if not exactly an apologia, at least an extenuation of Tambe's conduct. To them it was practically on the same level with V.J. Patel's appointment to the Speaker's office and Pandit Motilal's nomination to the Skeen Committee. It might be that the conduct of Pandit Motilal and of V.J. Patel was not censurable technically as a breach of the party's rules, but the crux of the whole thing (the two dissenters urged) was that the rules had not kept pace with the real evolution of the party's principles and tactics. These had been in a flux and from obstruction simpliciter the party had, without openly admitting so, already travelled a considerable distance towards responsive co-operation and it was high time the party rules and leadership gave due recognition to the fact.

L'Affaire Tambe filled the political forum all through October. On November 1, the national executive of the Swaraj Party met at Nagpur. Pandit Motilal maintained that Tambe's was not an isolated action but that it had the backing of many others and that in the Central Provinces—where the Swarajist successes at the elections had outshone those in all other provinces, the leader of the party himself had encouraged attempts at securing office. It was plain that the C.P. Swaraj Party was not of one mind regarding the Tambe episode, and a goodly part were in favour of the Responsivist heresy. In Bombay, Kelkar and Jayakar set afoot a move to get responsive co-operation accepted by the local Swaraj Party. The death of C.R. Das a few months earlier had been a severe blow to Swarajist leadership. Motilal had to face the storm so soon after. He must have missed in counsel the uncanny intuition of C.R. Das, and in action his gigantic dynamic force. The A.-I.C.C. met at Nagpur and the meeting ended in a patched-up truce. But, within a few days this was followed by resignations of Kelkar and Jayakar from the Executive, because they complained that the leader had violated the truce by persisting in attacks on Responsivists. They resigned so that they might be free to air their views.

Thus the storm still continued to rage when Lalaji was returned by the Jullundur constituency.

Though he was himself opposed to experimenting with offices. Lalaji's sympathies lay very largely with the Responsivist'group. There were ties of personal esteem—a legacy from Tilak's days, and Kelkar and Jayakar and the Maharashtra group in general more or less shared his outlook regarding the need for a Hindu organisation. But more strictly relevant to the questions at issue was the fact that the talk of "uniform continuous and consistent obstruction" was to Lalaji even more abhorrent than that of office. Besides at a time when a big campaign like that of non-co-operation was not in progress, when the leaders themselves were groping in the dark and policies and principles seemed to have been thrown into the melting pot—at such a time he felt it was not wise to. stifle all difference of opinion in the name of 'discipline'. Rather, freedom for a cold scrutiny of all doings seemed more than ever needed so that a clarification might be possible. Jayakar complained of the 'hectoring' tone of the leader of the Swaraj Party and there were many who, whilst not sharing Jayakar's responsivism, felt that the leader was invoking 'discipline' too often and all too readily, and who did not like to see him set up in the role of a political sawbones ready to lop off whatever he suspected of being a "diseased growth".

The Responsivists were thus getting a certain measure of sympathy and support from Lalaji even though he himself was neither enamoured of their label nor convinced that the acceptance of office under the dyarchical constitution would be a wise step. In fact he was not completely reconciled even to the acceptance of the Speaker's office, though here experience soon allayed his apprehensions for which the credit we suppose should go to the genius of V.J. Patel who filled the office with dignity and yet made himself useful to the cause to an extent beyond the best expectations.

This feud inside the Swaraj Party was thus leading to an internal crisis when Lalaji arrived in the Assembly. Not being a partisan, and in fact not being even a member of the party, he was for a while of use as a moderating influence. After filing his nomination papers he had proceeded to Bombay to preside over the Hindu Conference, for which M.R. Jayakar had been chosen Chairman of the Reception Committee. Pandit Motilal and the President-elect for the next Congress session, Mrs. Sarojini Naidu, were also present in Bombay, and after much discussion in which Lalaji's was an effective role a truce was arranged.

But the "cease-fire" did not mean a settlement. It afforded an armistice"; whether a settlement was possible could only be decided at the Congress session at Kanpur at the end of the month.

And a settlement formula seemed as far away as ever when the Congress assembled at Kanpur and Sarojini Naidu took over from Mahatma Gandhi. At the end of his term, the Mahatma retired from the political arena devoting a whole year to his ashram and to the direction of his pet constructive programme. The Congress organisation he now handed over to the Swarajists—completing the surrender he had started some months earlier. This surrender had begun with a bare tolerating of the Swarajist heresy of a parliamentary programme; and even for their being tolerated within the pale, the Swarajists had had to pay a price in the form of especial support of the khadi programme. At Belgaum, when Gandhi presided, they effected a settlement with him by accepting the 'khadi franchise' for membership of the Congress. When a few months later the A.I.C.C. met at Patna, it was clear that the Swarajists regarded the franchise as unworkable, to put it bluntly, as a nuisance, and some of the no-changers indulged in plain-speaking and said that the Swarajists had never been sincere in accepting the franchise. Gandhi himself was in the mood to yield further, and even waiving aside the question whether the A.I.C.C. had any jurisdiction to tamper with the resolution passed by the plenary session, sacrificed his pet, the spinning franchise, as a peace-offering and as a gesture of generosity. At Kanpur he completed the surrender by handing over the Congress machinery to the Swaraj Party. Hitherto the Swaraj Party had managed the elections on its own, with the barest sufferance from the Congress; now the elections were to be run fully with the Congress imprimatur. The parliamentary programme had hitherto been an affair of the Swaraj Party only; now it became the care of the Congress as such. The Swarajists thus got the entire Congress prestige, machinery and funds at their disposal. The Congress now accepted the responsibility of whatever they did as a parliamentary party, and of course, this also meant in a way that for their doings they were now accountable before the entire Congress. The Swarajist camel was now in possession of the Arab's entire tent. The surrender completed, Gandhi retired to Sabarmati to devote himself to the charkha and the promotion of the homespun.

But the principal resolution of the Kanpur session not merely installed the Swarajists in power in the Congress, it also laid down a programme for them. . And here controversy again popped its head : will it be an obstructionist programme or a responsivist one?

All attempts at finding a via media failed Pandit Motilal would not tolerate the Responsivist label, nor would he brook any formula that might expressly or by implication tolerate acceptance of office. Within the limitations thus set it did not seem possible to satisfy Kelkar and Jayakar.

As in 1907 at Surat and in 1920 at Nagpur, Lalaji was the question-mark of the Congress session. He had not even joined the Swaraj Party; for his unopposed election to the Assembly he had not had to ask for party nomination or to appeal in the name of that party or its programme, and in his writings in the press since his election he had quite freely criticised some of the Swarajist doings and doctrines. The Responsivists got a certain measure of support from him, but he was not attached to their group and had not accepted either their label or their faith in capturing office. In his home province there was no question of office for the Swaraj Party; nor were there any Responsivists among his Punjab lieutenants and friends. In fact, their full pressure was exerted in favour of a settlement with Pandit Motilal. The Responsivists, on the other hand, were bound to feel let down by him should he settle with Nehru.

When the Swarajists, first went to the Legislative Assembly, with the support to the Independent Party, they had offered terms of settlement to the Government. This had happened on February 13, 1924 and all the "innocent souls" in the Congress believed that the Swarajists would just present that demand—an 'ultimatum' as some chose to call it—and be done with the Assembly for good. The demand had been presented and for the best part of two years there had been no indication that it was going to be accepted; meanwhile those who had been anxiously waiting for the final exit of Congressmen from the Assembly had with surprise and with misgivings watched the progressive dilution of the original obstructionist programme, till it had come down to acceptance even of a nominated seat on the Skeen Committee. Now that the next general election was in sight, the Swarajists once again began to think of the much deferred break over non-acceptance of the "National Demand". The draft resolution for the Kanpur Congress laid down that they should walk out of the Assembly and go to the country and devote themselves to the furtherance of the constructive programme. Such a gesture, it was believed, would impress the voters' imagination and thus secure for the party even more glorious triumphs at the polls than those of the 1923 elections.

Such a programme was not much to Lalaji's liking. It seemed he would rather go with Malaviyaji and Jayakar and Kelkar, and then there break with the Swaraj Party—which would now mean with the majority party of the Congress itself. But pressure was brought to bear upon him, particularly from his Punjab friends, to avert such a happening. Within the framework of the draft resolution Pandit Motilal was willing to consider modification of detail, and friends urged that Lalaji must come to a settlement with Motilalji. At Nagpur too the Punjab contingent had insisted that he must settle with Gandhi. But there was this difference—he himself was anxious to arrive at a settlement with Gandhi; for, he accepted the principle of non-co-operation, and was all for starting a big non-co-operation campaign; only certain details were unacceptable to him. His own inclinations and commitments led him much further away from the Nehru programme in December 1925 than they had done from the Gandhi programme four years earlier. Negotiations led to a breaking-point again and again, but common friends tirelessly ran to and fro and again and yet again brought Panditji and Lalaji together to arrive at a settlement. At Lalaji's insistence the draft resolution was changed in several of its provisions; in particular it was provided that the Swarajist members of the Legislative Assembly and the Council of State shall vote for the rejection of the Finance Bill and immediately after leave their seats. Till then they could function as they had hitherto done under their party rules. Also it laid down that

"It shall be open to the Special Committee to allow the Swarajist members ... to attend the legislatures when such attendance is in its opinion essential for some special or unforeseen purpose".

In other words, of the budget (or New Delhi) session only the fag-end was being risked, though the brief, much less important session at Simla would be under interdict, and if in all likelihood the special committee deemed it of unusual importance it would ask the Swarajist Assemblymen to attend it. This was the compromise resolution that Pandit Motilal moved and Lalaji supported. Malaviyaji moved a briefly worded amendment which reads :

"That the work in the legislatures shall be so carried as to utilise them to the best possible advantage for the early establishment of full responsible Government, co-operation being reverted to when it may be necessary to advance the national cause and obstruction when that may be necessary for the advancement of the same cause."

Jayakar, while seconding the amendment, announced his own and Kelkar's resignations from the Assembly and Moonje's from the C.P. Legislative Council.

A break had thus come—not with Motilal Nehru, but with Kelkar and Jayakar--and this was no small wrench to Lalaji. Perhaps if his own Punjab lieutenants had not been so keenly insistent he would have acted differently. But Lajjavati and Santanam and Achint Ram had in beseeching him done their utmost and it was not so easy for Lalaji to ignore their earnest entreaties. Perhaps if these lieutenants had fully taken into consideration their leader's commitments with Jayakar and the Poona group, or realised how ill at ease he would feel after a break with them, they might not have been so insistent. The Kanpur resolution in its final form had enough elasticity to be deemed not completely inconsistent with his own assessment of what the political situation required, but he would not have liked to break with Jayakar and the Poona group. On the merits of the resolution he wrote in his paper that the Kanpur session had "brought back the Congress into its own" as all political work was henceforth to be done "in the name and under the guidance of the Congress. The Swaraj Party had been dominating the legislatures; outside it had no organisation worth the name." On the anomaly of such a self-contained party with no one except the electorates to give account to, his comment ran : "A good many Swarajists did not care at all for the Congress Committees, they paid no subscription, attended no meetings and did nothing to further the cause of the Congress. The only authority they looked to and cared for was their leader. In fact, the Council Swaraj Party had members who were not Congressmen. The Kanpur resolution has changed all this."

In current controversy the two concrete recurring issues were—obstruction and office. On the first of these he reiterated his stand : "I am very strongly opposed to the boycott of Councils and also to the policy of wholesale obstruction in the Councils. I believe that the Councils should be worked for what they are worth in the same way in which they have been worked by the Swaraj Party during the last two years."

And on the acceptance of offices : "I am still of opinion that Nationalism requires that there should be at least one party of Indian politicians who would not accept any high office in the gift of the Government. In doing so, Indian Nationalists are only following the historic example of Irish Nationalists."

The Kanpur resolution was in no way opposed to such an approval. But it could be asked, "What is the meaning of that part of the resolution which requires the Swarajists, after the next session, to come out of the Councils and appeal to the country?"

Lalaji's interpretation (and justification) of this provision was: "As I understand it, the object is to make a striking demonstration. A helpless people like ourselves who have no material sanction behind their demand cannot altogether banish demonstrations of this kind from their programme. In the history of Indian Nationalism this has been done several times, even long before Mahatma Gandhi's movement was born. Sir Pherozeshah Mehta once left the Council with all his followers as a protest against the Government attitude . . . Mr. Shastri left the Council after the Viceroy had rejected his resolution about the administration of Martial Law in the Punjab. The Swarajists are going to the country for the new elections. Their chief work in the existing Assembly has been to unite with other parties in putting forward their minimum demand for the change of the Constitution. I see no objection on principle to the course contemplated by them. They want to show to the Indian public, and to the world in general, that they have done everything possible to come to terms with the British Government and the Government has invariably treated their advances with contempt."

Assessing the gains of the Congress, Lalaji wrote : "I think the one permanent gain of the Congress session has been that the Congress has come into its own. So far as political work is concerned, it has been non-est for the last three years. The whole of the political work was done by the Swaraj Party. Consequently the latter loomed large and the Congress was overshadowed by it. The Swaraj Party will now be practically abolished. "The Congress Executive will control and guide the policy of those who seek election to the Councils and the Assembly in its name and under its prestige. This is a decided advantage" both from the tactical and practical points of view;" and he added "though it is not entirely free from risk."

However convincing this might have sounded, the fact is that the leaders of neither of the two schools in conflict were satisfied, and, on neither side could be seen the requisite good will and trust needed for making a compromise a success Lalaji himself had been pressed rather overmuch by his own Punjab lieutenants—particularly by Santanam and Lajjavati not to part company with Pandit Motilal, and somehow to evolve or accept a compromise. The sequel showed that such pressure had not yielded an enduring settlement

One notable little event was an innovation at this session—the ceremonial hoisting of the national tricolour. Hardiker's Hindustani Seva Dal was by now regularly functioning and Lalaji was chosen for unfurling the flag and taking the salute.

But as could have been anticipated, the Maharashtra

group were sore. And not long after Lalaji had to complain about the scur comment he was getting from them. He wrote in *The People* :

"My Mahratta friends appear to be very angry with me. Ever since the Kanpur Congress, the *Mahratta* has been at me in some way or the other. In every issue it has some fling at me. I have never replied and do not intend to do so now. My respect for and attachment to Messrs Jayakar and Kelkar has not in any way been affected by the differences in our policy. The Poona Maharashtrians and myself have been lifelong friends and it will pain me immensely if ever I have to say anything unkind about them. I must resist that temptation to the best of my capacity. I am confident that we shall work on the same platform and with the same mutual goodwill as we have always done in the past. The present differences are only temporary. I do not think sarcasm and ridicule ought to be employed against friends and that is my only reply to the last fling in the *Mahratta*."

He was being invited to preside over a Hindu Conference in Burma. He accepted the invitation but asked the organisers to put off the conference till after the New Delhi session. But (as he wrote later on in *The People*) "the desire to see Burma, and be finished with it prevailed." This was somewhat natural as he had never been to Burma after 1907, and then, being kept in captivity had only aroused his curiosity about Burma without an opportunity to satisfy it. Possibly also he wanted to work off the rather melancholy effect produced on him by the Kanpur developments and on second thoughts he hastened compliance with the Burma summons. Accompanied by Achint Ram from Kanpur, he proceeded to take the steamer that was leaving Calcutta on New Year's Day.

He met his old Burmese friends, and made new contacts among them and of course he met and heard the Indian settlers there and gave them what advice he deemed fit regarding their problems. Above all he visited Fort Dufferin and the P.W.D. Bungalow inside that Mandalay fort in which he had been kept a prisoner.

He saw the pagodas and the images, the ancient ones as well as the new shrine, then being built for the relics that the British authorities at Peshawar had presented to the Burmese priests.

His jottings published in *The People* had some interesting observations about the Burmese manners and morals, the picturesque costumes even of men and the extraordinary long hair of the women folk—streaming down to the ankles—"and are even longer than that" He heard that when some time ago the patriot priest Uttama was released from prison... "young Burmese ladies, made him pass through a double row of themselves on a path covered by their hair, which they stretched along the path." This beat all the emotional doings of crowds for their leaders that he had witnessed in his own country!

The Indian community were rather perturbed over the legislation then pending regarding expulsion of non-Burmese. With his keen sense of realities and his customary candour he summed up the situation facing them : "The Indian has had his time. He is no longer essential. The country can be governed and managed without his help and co-operation. In fact, the Anglo-Indian rulers, merchants and manufacturers would be happy if the Indian is eliminated from Burma altogether." He frankly said that "the problem of Burma must be decided in the interest of Burma and the Burmese and not of anybody else." He advised the Indian community therefore to "remain there only as Burmans", completely identifying themselves with the Burmese, so that they would not have to ask for special representation and the Burmese not to treat them as aliens. This counsel of perfection was never adopted and the result was seen in the sufferings of the Indian community when in 1942 they were forced to flee to India before the onrushing tide of a, Japanese invasion.

From Burma he returned to New Delhi to attend the Assembly session which started in the latter half of January 1926. A few days later, as we have seen, he formally joined the Swaraj Party. During this session he made a notable contribution by participating in several important debates—when the first Indian Trades-Union Bill came up, and when a resolution on employment came up, and yet another (Mr. Shafee's) regarding political prisoners and exiles. The last-mentioned touched the personal chords, recalling what he had undergone and claiming that no one else in the House was better qualified to speak on the motion out of personal experience.

"Practically, all the three clauses have applied to me at some stage or other of my life. In 1907 I was deported under Regulation III of 1818. In 1921 I was convicted of a crime which the Government of India afterwards declared was not a crime. The same year I was again convicted of a crime which the Government Advocate said had not been proved. When I wanted to return from America I was treated as an exile by the refusal of a passport."

While yet this session was on, the Hindu Mahasabha met at Delhi under the presidentship of Raja Narendranath. Lalaji took a leading part in its proceedings. In fact, the Mahasabha policy was then being shaped mainly by Malaviyaji and Lalaji Raja Saheb as President had been, in the first place, their joint choice. A strong section in that organisation favoured the idea that the Hindu Mahasabha should run candidates on its own ticket in the general election due in a few months. Laiaji (and Malaviyaji) opposed this policy, and following his lead, the delegates decided against the proposal except to a very limited extent, that is, where the local contingencies absolutely demanded that the Mahasabha should be represented by its own nominees.

In March while the Assembly session was still in progress, the A.I.C.C. met at Delhi, and substantially altered the walkout provisions of the Kanpur resolution. The course now decided upon was that the walk-out should not be put off till the rejection of the Finance Bill. The Kanpur Resolution was sought to be amended. Lalaji objected that the A.I.C.C. had no jurisdiction to amend the resolution passed by the plenary session. The objection was accepted but the sponsors of the new move thereupon shifted their ground and said that they 'interpreted' the Kanpur resolution as laying down the latest date and that an earlier walk-out was not contrary to its text. Lalaji took exception to the 'interpretation', but was outvoted. At Kanpur he had insisted that the walk-out should be resorted to only after the throwing out of the Finance Bill. That provision now having been abrogated, he was in a way free to absolve himself of the Kanpur commitments. In actual fact the A.-I.C.C. resolution cut short the party's attendance in the Assembly only by a few days—it was already near the fag end—Lalaji wrote in his paper that if he had his way he would have put off the walk-out till the August session—but "the die has, however, been cast."

Geneva Conference

"Simplification of inspection of emigrants on board the ship" might be a very fit problem to figure as the chief item on the agenda paper for an international conference at Geneva called by the International Labour Office in May 1926; but what exactly was Lalaji's interest in the details of inspection of emigrants? Perhaps these interested him even less than the clauses of the India Bill for which in 1914 he had gone as a Congress delegate to London. Then as now he was far more interested in the bye-products. Above all, at such a conference workers' delegates from all over the world would assemble, and whatever the agenda, he did value a comradely handshake with some of them.

Lalaji's active participation in the Indian trade union movement had started, as we have already seen, in 1920 when he presided over the first session of the Indian Trade Union Congress at Calcutta. After that he continued on the national executive of the Trade Union Congress and he did his bit in important consultations. He took some interest in the organising of trade unions in the Punjab and the N.W. Railway strikers received guidance and support from him, but on the whole he did not find conditions such that with the limited time that he could find because of his other commitments, he might be as useful to the movement as he would like to be.

Also as he thought "non-co-operation" could not at that stage suit the working class, he resigned his AITUC office long before completing his term. It was, however, his heart's desire to lend a helping hand in the building up of the trade union movement. When an opportunity presented itself, he sent of his U.P. young men from among the Servants of the People to Kanpur to work for the Mazdoor Sabha there. Both of these, Harihar Nath Shastri and Raja Ram Shastri not long after became important trade union leaders. From his newspapers, particularly from *The People,* the Labour and Socialist movements in those early stages received valuable support. When he arrived in the Assembly, he was soon thinking of a parliamentary labour group. That is why, in his letters to Pandit Motilal accepting the invitation to join the Swaraj Party, he specifically mentioned that he would keep himself free to voice the workers point of view. His idea was that a labour group for certain specific purposes might be formed in the Legislative Assembly, even though for purposes other than those specified, its members might belong to different parties, Congress, Liberal, Muslim League or Independent. N.M. Joshi and D. Chaman Lal and he himself were to be the nucleus to get things started. He had several talks with them and with Tarini P. Sinha, but somehow the plans were deferred and the labour group was not inaugurated.

The setting up of the ILO as a League of Nations offshoot had been one of the important reasons given in Lalaji's presidential address for creating without further delay a national trades union body in India. C.F. Andrews, though he did not participate in the inaugural session in deference to the wishes of Mahatma Gandhi, who thought the time not yet ripe for this, had also felt likewise. When a couple of years later he presided over the AITUC, he too emphasised the importance of the ILO to the Indian working class, and it was under his presidentship that Lalaji was named the workers' delegate for the conference in Geneva.

The question was raised by doctrinaire non-co-operationists whether the nomination to the International

Labour Conference could be accepted by a Congressman, and if it could, whether after the walk-out from the Assembly it could still be availed of with propriety. In fact, at the A.-I.C.C. meeting in March at Delhi the question was raised whether V.J. Patel, the Speaker, should also not leave the Assembly, and whether Pandit Motilal could be permitted to continue on the Skeen Committee, but since discussion on Lalaji's nomination as workers' delegate for the International Labour Conference was disallowed by the Chair, the House decided that Patel should continue in the Assembly as Speaker, and that Nehru could retain his seat on his own. Both the President of the Congress and the leader of the Swaraj Party were quite clear that Lalaji's selection for the International Labour Conference was clearly outside the purview of the ban on offices, etc. Lalaji himself was absolutely clear that he was going as the workers' accredited delegate and not as a nominee of the Government and that the opportunity offered him of serving the Indian workers and of making useful international contacts was too valuable to be thrown away.

In Bombay, a couple of days before his scheduled departure, he received a telegraphic message from the deposed Maharaja of Nabha, Ripu Daman Singh, then living at Dehra Dun, and the telegram was followed by a special messenger. The deposed Maharaja was not in the Government's good books, largely (at least partly) because he was suspected to be not as loyal to the rulers as he was expected. The Maharaja received sympathy from many Nationalist leaders (apart from rather widespread Sikh sympathy). He was at that time seeking redress from the India Office by having his case represented mainly with the help of his solicitors in London. Lalaji's help also he sought so that his case might be properly represented Lalaji made it clear to the Maharaja's emissary that as a public man he did not feel interested in this kind of errand but that if the Maharaja wanted to engage his services as a lawyer he could accept the brief. This he made very clear to the Maharaja himself through a letter written before his departure from Bombay in the course of which he said : "I have taken up your case as a lawyer-agent of yours, and not as a public man."

He was going this time by a P.&O. steamer, S.S. *Ranpura,* one of their largest and most up-to-date liners. He noted that the food served was by no means up to the pre-war standards, in fact was inferior even to what he got on the Italian boat that had taken him to Europe two years ago.

It was the racial exclusiveness of the P.&O. that had made Jamsetji Tata, the father of Indian industrialism, realise the need for an Indian shipping industry. Things had changed since then, but "racialism was still far from having completely disappeared from the P.&O. atmosphere."

Lalaji landed at Marseilles early in the morning on May 7, 1926 and left immediately for Paris. The International Labour Conference which he had to attend in Geneva was to meet in the last week of May. Britain was in the throes of a general strike—the big strike that someone dubbed as Britain's only civil war since Cromwell; and so, though he had booked his heavier kit direct for London, his proceeding straight thither did not seem feasible. In fact, H.S.L. Polak advised him by telegram to stay on in Paris for the time being. So he did, and did not proceed to London till after the strike had been settled.

In Paris he stayed with S.R. Rana, the pearl merchant, and many old friends. Amongst the interesting new contacts was that with Jean Longuet, "one of the two topmost leaders of the French Socialist Party", and a grandson of Karl Marx, through his daughter who had married a Frenchman. Lalaji had an interesting interview with this "very good-looking, strongly built, tall Frenchman with a fine forehead, extremely polite, extremely well-informed and extremely balanced in his views"—for he did not swear by the communist creed and was expecting that before long the peasants would come into power and overthrow the communists in Russia.

He was in London for barely a week—to see friends, to collect impressions about the very recent general strike, to have a preliminary talk with his solicitor-friend, H.S.L. Polak, regarding the Nabha brief, leaving over any tangible steps till the relevant documents arrived, and to see the *Light of Asia,* the first Indian enterprise in film-making in England, with Devika Rani as a star and produced by Niranjan Pal in whom he was interested because of his father Bipin Chandra Pal.

And then he left for Geneva.

The eighth session of the International Labour Conference opened on May 26, 1926 for the "simplification of inspection of emigrants on board the ship". On the very opening day Lalaji handed in two resolutions, one demanding an inquiry into the conditions of native and coloured labour in Africa and America—which was agreed upon after some amendments, Lalaji accepting the amended form as a first instalment. His second resolution called the attention of the Governing Body to a previous resolution sanctioning the appointment of a correspondent in India which had remained in cold storage for about four years. He was told that the year's budget arrangements having been settled, nothing could be done immediately, but was given an assurance that his reminder would prove effective the following year.

But his main speech was delivered on June 2 when the Directors presented their report. He had received a cabled representation from Kanpur urging the enforcement of an eight hours' day for India. But here he was well aware that (at that time) the eight hours' convention had not yet been ratified even by some of the principal European countries and that year there had been a conference in London regarding this subject. He knew too that India could not go ahead of her competitor, Japan, and he exhorted the Japanese to show the way. He spoke of a "skeleton in our cupboard", the existence of *begar* or forced labour in British India and the Indian states. This was resented by Sir A.C. Chatterjee, who, representing the Government of India, was deemed India's principal delegate Lalaji addressed a letter to the President of the conference the next day and challenged an inquiry and promised that "as soon as I return to India I shall send to the International Labour Office proofs in support of my statement". This letter, at Lalaji's request, formed part of the record of the conference. It seems hardly necessary to say that on his return to India he made good his promise.

Lalaji was rather struck by the continental atmosphere of the conference. The British no doubt dominated the League; but the Labour Conference at any rate was permitted to develop in a different way, and the British were far from ruling the roast. This to Lalaji was an added reason why India should pay more attention to the ILO and why she must send a full and truly Indian complement to its conferences To the conference that Lalaji attended, India had sent just four delegates, Sir A.C. Chatterjee and Sir Louis Kershaw to represent the Government, Sir Arthur Froome to represent the employers and Lalaji to represent the workers. Just the minimum number of delegates and just one Secretary for the Government representatives; not a single substitute and not a single adviser for employers or for workers. And of this delegation Sir Atul and Lalaji, only two, were Indians. S.N. Haji, Manager of the Scindia Steam Navigation Company who was present in Geneva, in fact addressed an ably prepared representation to the authorities of the conference, challenging the credentials of Sir Arthur Froome who had been chosen by the European Chamber of Commerce, the Indian Merchants' Chamber having had no chance. Lalaji felt handicapped for want of expert advisers to assist him. Perhaps at the whole conference at which more than 30 countries were represented, Lalaji and Sir Arthur were the only delegates who had no advisers attached to them. In contrast to the two Indians he noticed the delegation from Japan were fifteen strong—delegates and substitute-delegates and advisers—the maximum number laid down and a few extra too! He noticed the Japanese were making excellent use of all international opportunities that came their way.

Lalaji had looked forward to the conference somewhat avidly as it was the first international gathering for him since his return from the United States. He used the occasion as best he could for developing international contacts. Of the informal events on this occasion, Lalaji's dinner on June 3 was a notable one, workers' delegates from almost all the important European and Eastern countries having attended it. These included Jouhaux, the French Socialist leader, Duffy and Suzuki from Japan, the British Trade Unionists, Pugh and Ben Tillit, and Margaret Bandfield (who later became Lady Chatterjee), besides the delegates from Switzerland, Norway, Sweden, Denmark, Holland, Germany, Bulgaria, Australia and South Africa.

Jawaharlal Nehru who was in Switzerland at the time because of the illness of his wife, Kamala, was amongst the Indian visitors who watched the proceedings of the conference. Other Indian visitors included Dr. Taraknath Das and the sugar technologist, Sarangdhar Das, and his American wife (Freeda, who afterwards left Das and wrote a book which she called *Marriage to India)* and S.N. Haji (the shipping expert then with the Scindias) and Mrs. Haji.

At Geneva Lalaji had occasion to meet his old friend Shyamji Krishna Verma and found him a sad, forlorn figure, and in certain respects very unlike the more famous rebels—Rousseau, Mazzini, Kropotkin, Lenin—who had found asylum in Switzerland, and for long had lived in poverty and endured hardship. "Shyamji has plenty of money but he also prefers to live a life of poverty. He carries on no propaganda and simply lives." Somewhat surprisingly Shyamji was attending the international conference as a pressman, on the strength of his *Indian Sociologist* which had ceased regular publication some time after his leaving England about two decades earlier and of which he had brought out an edition in 1920 when the Lokamanya died.

Romain Rolland lived nearby, and Lalaji paid several visits to his villa.

Lalaji was in Geneva for about three weeks during which he attended one or two international gatherings (besides the one for which he had undertaken the voyage), in particular one styled the World Parliaments Union.

Then he went again to England, meeting his numerous friends there in a stay lasting nearly two months.

At Geneva, the centre of so many international bodies, he came in touch with certain other organisations too. In particular the World Parliaments Union solicited his interest in their work. Just a short while before the ILO Conference, they had been in session in London, with Sir Purushottamdas Thakurdas representing India.

The World Migration Congress was being held in London and Lalaji had been invited to represent the Indian working class. Lalaji spoke on the colour question with his usual vigour, and perhaps some of the British and colonial "labourites" did not much relish the home-truths and home-thrusts from India's representative.

These two conferences provided him with excellent contacts among the labour and socialist movements the world over.

An internationally signed manifesto was issued from London during Lalaji's stay there demanding the abolition of conscription. Its signatories included Romain Rolland and Henri Barbusse, and from India Tagore, Lajpat Rai and Gandhi.

Talking of international organisations we might mention one more body, though of a different type, for it had no workers' delegates and did not concern itself with labour or leftist movements, Lalaji evinced some interest in it about this period. This was the Empire Parliamentary Union, in which Lalaji and some of the leading Swarajists began to take interest. A local branch was formed in India, and next year two of the Indian Swarajist Assemblymen went on its behalf to Canada and Australia. There was nothing in the Swarajist creed or policy then to preclude such interest in the Parliaments of the Empire, but we fancy the Swarajist leaders interest owed a good deal to the persuasive diplomatic personality of Sir Howard d'Egville, the Secretary of the organisation, who during a short visit to India made friends with many of the Indian leaders.

A Royal Commission on Indian currency, presided over by Sir Hilton Young, was busy drafting its report about the time of Lalaji's stay in London. It was on the recommendation of this commission that a little later the Government decided to fix the exchange ratio by statute at 18 pence to the rupee. This was generally condemned in India as manipulation in the interests of Britain, a 16-pence ratio being regarded as fair by most Indian economists. Sir Purushottamdas Thakurdas who was in London as a member of this Royal Commission regarded the ratio suggested by his colleagues as disastrous to Indian interests and had misgivings about certain other suggestions favoured by them. He took counsel with Lalaji and at repeated meetings with him spoke of his many doubts and difficulties. While not presuming to teach the Bombay expert on the technical side, Lalaji was of great help to him by his firm insistence that he must not be overawed by the opinion of the majority or permit himself to be persuaded or cajoled into signing recommendations that in his own judgment would adversely affect Indian interests. Lalaji could not give expert knowledge to Sir Purushottamdas but he certainly could give him moral support which he seemed to need. Lalaji thus made an indirect contribution by insisting that Sir Purushottamdas must write out a minute of dissent. He may also be said to have contributed something to the firm tone of this minute.

Lalaji had to overstay in London, more than once putting off his departure because of his Nabha brief. One of the Maharaja's men had accompanied Lalaji, but he did not have the necessary record with him and this, it was understood. would follow soon after by post. In London Lalaji had a consultation with his solicitor friend, H.S.L. Polak; but before being able to take any effective steps the solicitor wanted certain documents which Lalaji and the Maharaja's agent accompanying him did not have. Letters and cables seemed to have no result in expediting things. In the end Lalaji cabled to the Maharaja that he could not wait indefinitely in London and returned. The Maharaja felt much annoyed; but afterwards when he saw that in the circumstances Lalaji was justified, he expressed regret to Lalaji for his earlier annoyance, made up with him and next year when Lalaji again happened to be going to Europe requested him to get legal advice for him on certain minor things, which Lalaji gladly agreed to.

An India debate came off in the Commons during stay in London and Lalaji attended some of the sittings.

A week before he started on his return journey, the *Times* published a letter from Lajpat Rai on certain points raised in correspondence being carried on in its columns regarding "communal tension in India". This earned him a rebuke of a rather unusual sort. He had joined the National Liberal Club; and even before he had yet been elected or confirmed a member, he was guilty of a breach of its rules; the letter, as it appeared in the *Times*, bore the writer's club address. Promptly, the Secretary called his attention to the rule that laid down that no member could use the name or the address of the club in communications to the press without the previous sanction of the General Committee.

For two whole days he was with his old friends, the Webbs, and wrote in *The People* that though he had had the privilege of their (Webbs') friendship over a number of years, "he never knew them so well as he does now after having lived with them for two whole days under the same roof and after having read Mrs. Webb's My *Apprenticeship* from cover to cover."

Lalaji was much impressed by this book, and when he returned, for several days it seemed to be his chief enthusiasm. He not only wrote enthusiastically about this book in *The People,* but had brought a number of copies with him which he presented to his friends, one to Lajjavati, another to his own daughter-in-law Saraswati (Mrs. Amrit Rai) commending it in glowing terms.

On the return voyage Acharya Prafulla Chandra Ray, the scientist, was amongst the company. Acharya Ray was then writing an autobiography and he would very fondly read out to Lalaji the chapters he had already completed, inviting his opinion or criticism sometimes, but as was his habit, all the time asking him "You follow?" Lalaji sometimes felt amused by his mannerism and sometimes even irritated and then he would say: "I follow all right, for heaven's sake don't make me repeat again and again that I do."

On August 13, 1926 he landed in Bombay.

Communalist

I

The gods and the Titans joined hands in churning the ocean, in quest of the draught of immortality. The churning threw up many precious boons and also noxious by-products, and eventually the gods and the Titans fell out, each wanting to grab the goblet of ambrosia. In their quest of freedom the Hindus and Muslims started an epic churning under the Mahatma's direction. The scheduled year of toil came to an end without securing the boon; though the churning was called off soon after, the noxious by-products had already started mischief—the worst of these being the lurking suspicion that the other party might grab the boon, though this seemed still a long way off, and though wise men warned that if the two did not pull together the churning could not be resumed, and without this the boon could not materialise. Though news of the Punjab happenings in the last year of his exile had given Lajpat Rai agony, Swami Shraddhananda's appearance on the Jama Masjid pulpit was something unprecedented and inspired new hope. In his "message" to his countrymen before he left the American shores he had emphasised with utmost force the supreme need for unity. He asked them to follow the lead of Gandhi, because above all this seemed to promise unity. On landing in India he uttered grave warnings against communalism particularly warning his own community. He denounced the Khilafat wrong, both on anti-imperialist grounds and out of sympathy for Muslim susceptibility. Out of the unspent funds that had been placed by friends at his disposal when in the U.S. he made a donation to the Khilafat fund. He toured about with Shaukat Ali in the non-co-operation campaign. When the Ali brothers' Karachi trial started, he was amongst the 17 signatories to the statement for which the Alis were being prosecuted. Even though he had his doubts about certain things he considered the Mahatma's leadership invaluable, because he had been able to secure Muslim support.

II

Whilst he was still in jail, things changed and Hindu-Muslim riots seemed to become the order of the day. The need for unity was as great as ever, but the Gandhian handling had clearly failed to achieve it. The prison-term leisure was devoted by Lalaji above all to a much-needed stocktaking—the results of which were given out in several series of articles smuggled out and published over fictitious names. As part of this stock-taking and of pondering over the problem of unity, Lalaji undertook quite an intensive study of Islam and Muslim history, and of modern movements in Muslim lands, and became rather enamoured of Shibli's writings—his lives of the Prophet and of Omar and his other biographical and historical writings.

Very naturally he discussed things with some of his fellow-prisoners. One such discussion left behind abiding misgivings and therefore has to be taken note of here. This particular discussion was with Maulvi Habib-ur-Rahman (of Ludhiana), a prominent Khilafatist and notable divine, and a fellow prisoner. Drawing the Maulvi into a frank exchange Lalaji desired to be enlightened about the limits within which, in strict conformity with religious injunctions, Muslims could co-operate with Hindus. The reply (in effect) was that the Believers could certainly remain in partnership with Infidels in turning out the alien Christian rulers, but not beyond the achievement of that objective. In a letter to C.R. Das Lalaji spoke of the misgiving thus engendered—suggesting that he might pursue things for an authoritative interpretation, and in the light thereof, determine the implications for the nationalist programmes. Lalaji had indulged in loud thinking in a confidential letter. Das seemed uninterested in what the divine said and he could not treat the letter as confidential for he wanted to use what was said in other paragraphs regarding the need for re-thinking on boycott of legislatures. At the Gaya session, Das shared that letter with all and sundry! And, unheeding the implied warning it was at Gaya he let himself be led by another Maulvi into accepting the Kabul scheme—which we shall deal with later in this chapter.

Some nationalists thought it improper to raise such awkward questions or to express such misgivings. The people who had most reason to feel perturbed were, of course, just those who in their hearts shared the theological dictum though they thought the Ludhiana Maulvi's candour had been devastatingly inexpedient.

That letter to C.R. Das has to be mentioned also because of its contribution to Lalaji's assessment of his colleagues. Das he esteemed very highly—and yet Das seemed interested only in what had relevance to the immediate political context, not in giving serious thought to what Lalaji regarded as a matter of fundamental import.

Lalaji mentally made note of this and kept quiet. He could not help thinking that such nonchalance on the part of the leadership was a perturbing symptom.

Soon after his release Lalaji found himself on a panel of two set up by the Congress Working Committee to draft a "National Pact". Before the Ansari-Lajpat Rai draft could be considered, news came from Calcutta that C.R. Das had entered into a local pact there! The Bengal Pact at best had a short-lived initial success; in the long run it only created complications and dissensions in the Bengal Congress, and it blighted the chances of a National Pact. Das seemed to care too much for immediate dividends.

Lalaji was convalescing at Solan, and some other Congress leaders including Abul Kalam Azad also happened to be there for a holiday in the hills. A short while after that holiday came C.R. Das's Bengal Pact like a bolt from the blue Lalaji wondered how Azad who had spoken to him in vastly different accents from those of the new Bengal document could possibly endorse that Pact, and yet how was it possible for

Das to have made the Pact, if Abul Kalam did not approve of such a move? He had no facts as to what had happened behind the scenes; but the superlative tribute to Das's statesmanship as evinced in this Pact, in the Maulana's posthumous book *(India Wins Freedom)* goes to confirm Lalaji's suspicion. Gandhiji's strategy of the "blank cheque" had not worked. And the national leaders in negotiating a concrete settlement seemed too prone to be lured away by what seemed the local requirements of the moment, instead of working for a lasting arrangement based on fairness and mutual accommodation!

III

How far did the Hindu-Muslim riots affect Lalaji's attitude? The 1924 happenings deserve special consideration here—particularly the Kohat holocaust.

1924 witnessed outbreaks of communal frenzy, in quick succession and at places far apart—"specially at Delhi, Gulbarga, Nagpur, Lucknow, Shahjahanpur, Allahabad, Jubbulpore, and worst of all at Kohat".* At Kohat the Hindus formed a microscopic minority—less than 5 per cent, the toll was enormous, but a far more perturbing symptom was the complete exodus of the entire Hindu population who sought shelter at Rawalpindi, 320 km away.

Of all communal rioting, that at Kohat in September 1924 was the most perturbing. Lalaji did whatever he could to arrange relief for the afflicted people, but he could not endorse the idealist advice that came as Gandhiji's first reaction Gandhiji soon after took out the most powerful weapons in his armoury—agonised prayer, a 21-day fast, which brought in its sequel a Unity Conference which started in real grand style with a fanfare and raised high hopes, but the promise came to naught. As the Congress *History* puts it pithily, Kohat broke India's backbone.

Gandhiji had the utmost faith in the Ali brothers. Apart from the Unity Conference, he tried to work with their help

* *The History of the Congress,* Vol. I, p. 275.

to retrieve things and to create conditions for the Kohat evacuees to return to their homes. This attempt proved a bitter disappointment. Acharya Kripalani has summarised this episode in his life of Gandhi :

"Gandhiji along with some Muslim leaders wanted to go to Kohat to enquire into communal incidents there and to bring about peace. The Government did not permit him to go there. After a few months, however, he was allowed to go. He and Shaukat Ali were asked by the Working Committee to make an enquiry and send in a report. The work did not proceed smoothly. The Muslims were willing to come out with the facts. They were, however, tutored by Shaukat Ali not to do so. The result was that Gandhiji and Shaukat Ali were unable to submit an agreed report. This was the beginning of the estrangement between Gandhiji and the Ali brothers. It had been manifest earlier at the Unity Conference."*

Some interesting details of the rupture may be found in Mahadev Desai's *Diary.* It seems the Mahatma had in his anguish been getting up at 3 in the morning to pray for divine guidance—till on the 16th September the response came in a flash, a call for a 21-day fast. The resolve was straightway made and announced. Many of his friends and followers (including Mahadev) pleaded that since he had in no way been responsible for the holocaust, no penance could be due from him; to which the reply was :

"My error! Why, I may be charged with having committed a breach of faith with the Hindus. I asked them to befriend Muslims. I asked them to lay their lives and their property at the disposal of the Musalmans for the protection of their Holy Places. Even today, I am asking them to practise *Ahimsa,* to settle quarrels by dying, but not by killing. And what do I find to be the result? How many temples have been desecrated? How many sisters came to me with complaints? As I was saying to Hakimji yesterday, Hindu women are in mortal fear of Mussulman *goondas.* In many places they feared

* J.B. Kripalani, Gandhi : *His Life and Thought,* p. 102.

to go out alone. I had a letter from....How can I bear the way in which his little children were molested? How can I now ask Hindus to put up with everything patiently? I gave the assurance that the friendship with Mussulmans was bound to bear good fruit. I asked them to befriend them, regardless of the results. It is not in my power today to make good that assurance....And yet I must ask the Hindus even today to die and not to kill. I can only do so by laying down my own life. I can teach them the way to die by my own example."*

The Unity Conference which started in the second week of the 21-day fast was a very impressive gathering, and its appeals for and assurances of harmony made many think that it had made the fast a real success. Actually, the National Panchayat Board that it gave birth to proved only a still-born babe. Towards the close of the year Gandhiji visited the Punjab. (Gandhiji wanted to go to Kohat in the company of some Muslim leaders—but the authorities forbade this). Other leaders including the Ali brothers, Hakim Sahib and Dr. Ansari joined him. There were lengthy discussions at Lalaji's place; everybody had his say, and the special stress on this occasion seemed to be on finding an acceptable formula of apportionment (in legislatures; etc.). No agreement could be reached. What is relevant here is that in these discussions, as on all like occasions (whether a large Unity Conference, or a small National Pact sub-committee) Lalaji patiently and earnestly strove for finding an agreement in a rational (as distinct from a purely sentimental) way, but fully taking into consideration the realities of the situation, however irrational or uncongenial some of these might be. Even when he addressed a purely Hindu audience he laid the utmost stress on the need for communal harmony and exhorted his people to strive for this in a spirit of accommodation. He did commend courage and strength but all suggestions of retaliatory goondaism or of insults to Islam or the Prophet he condemned with all the force he could command. At the Hindu Mahasabha meetings at Belgaum (when the Congress met there under

* Mahadev Desai : *Day-to-Day with Gandhi*, Vol. 4, p. 195.

Gandhi's presidentship) Kohat naturally loomed large. But Lalaji's speech there (as also that from the Congress platform on the same topic) was found unexceptionable by Gandhiji—though when Lalaji opposed his "spinnning franchise" at the Congress meetings Gandhiji taking exception to some of his remarks ascribed them to the Kohat tragedy having cost Lalaji his sleep and his health! But Lalaji's addresses on Kohat, particularly that at the Mahasabha meeting, clearly showed that whatever the damage to his health he had not lost his poise.

Lalaji's attitude and his message were in no way different from those of Gandhiji except that for his message Lalaji made full use of the Hindu platform and that though Gandhiji declared himself against the "dole" Lalaji even though, on principle, fully appreciating Gandhiji's stand did not want to be a stickler and collected funds that were used for the "dole".

IV

The way the Ali brothers reacted to Kohat affords a contrast that disillusioned Mahatma Gandhi about them. As we have noted in the leaders' discussions at Lalaji's place (December, 1924) Shaukat Ali's chief contribution had been a clamour for a *"holi"* which Lalaji treated as a piece of buffoonery, but Gandhiji still relied on the Alis and valued them us "pure gold". (In another discussion when one of the Alis talked about the flowing Ganga of Hindu-Muslim bloodshed flowing in the Punjab, Lalaji's spontaneous retort was—"Gangotri in Rampur", from where the Alis hailed!).

The progress in Gandhiji's disillusionment regarding the Alis can be traced in Mahadev Desai's *Diary*. We would content ourselves with a couple of extracts. In the last week of December (1924) at Belgaum Mahatma Gandhi formally took over from Muhammad Ali, the outgoing President of the Congress'. There was no indication of divergence between the two in regard to the Kohat happenings, though these were naturally a major topic and one of grave concern. But barely a couple of days later the Muslim League met in Bombay and passed a resolution on Kohat which upset Gandhiji a great deal, particularly because this had been proposed by Muhammad Ali. The very next day (January 1, 1925) Gandhiji sent a letter to the Maulana full of rebuke and sore disappointment. After the text of the letter we read Mahadev's own noting :

"Bapu at first would not let me take down a copy of this letter but agreed afterwards. When I talked of Shaukat Ali's shamelessness, Bapu said : 'The cat will be out of the bag by the end of the year.' 'Rather by the end of two or three months, Bapu!' I said. 'Still better then,' Bapu returned."*

The revised time-limit proved nearer the mark. Whether Shaukat Ali's "shamelessness" had also been exhibited at the League is not clear. The younger Maulana who had been a party to the Congress resolution on the subject moved at the League meeting one widely divergent therefrom, and Muhammad Ali had moved this in substitution of a motion which Gandhiji found decidedly less offensive—the less offensive motion had come from none other than the redoubtable Zafar Ali Khan who had frankly expressed dissatisfaction at Belgaum with the Congress resolution!

Still appearances were kept up and early in February Gandhiji accompanied by Shaukat Ali arrived in Rawalpindi for the Kohat Inquiry which the Working Committee had entrusted to these two. This inquiry resulted in ah open rift—the cat was out of the bag, and in about one month rather than in two!

The *Diary* for 10-2-1925 bears the heading—A *Shocking Disclosure.* We cannot quote *in extenso,* but by way of samples would give a few bits. Under Gandhiji's cross-examination the two leading Muslim witnesses "unconsciously gave revealing but truthful answers"—and this proved inconvenient to the Maulana. The *Diary* reports that Shaukat Ali "had pre-warned the Peer and all others" against betraying their internal

* Mahadev Desai : *Day-to-Day with Gandhi,* Vol. 5, p. 112.

differences in the evidence. But the tutoring notwithstanding the Peer came out with shocking disclosures :

"Every year the figure of converts to Islam [at Kohat] goes up to 150. There are sure to be a few of them on every Friday. Even married women are converted. But the difficult question then arises as to whose wife a converted woman should be. According to the Shariat she cannot be allowed to go back to her husband."*

On this "shocking" statement which the witness gave "in a casual and nonchalant manner as if there was nothing, wrong in it"—Gandhiji wanted Shaukat Ali's own "candid view".

"It is really a shocking affair. It is preposterous if a man like you, too, goes to an Ulema (a Muslim Divine) for the interpretation of the Koran's and the Shariat's texts."**

And the Maulana pleaded ignorance of Arabic for consultations! "And he (Gandhiji) said many other prodding things besides this. Shaukat Ali gave evasive and halting replies." The next morning (February 10) Gandhiji began a "heart-stirring discourse" thus—

"I am now in the position of a man who is shocked to find a snake under his quilt and gives it a thorough shaking and sweeps his whole room clean. I came to learn amazing things about Kohat which I had never known before."***

When Gandhiji spoke of the enormity of conversion through abduction the Maulana just "squirted and kept silent".

And there were further shocks too—unconnected with Kohat —the news from Afghanistan of fanatical mobs pelting heretics to death, and Shaukat Ali's approval of this.

Lalaji's touchsome had done better assaying than Gandhiji's which had declared such dross to be "pure gold".

---

* *Ibid.*, p. 262.

** *Ibid*, p. 262.

*** *Ibid*, p. 264.

The Nehru Report finally showed up the Ali brothers in their true colours—open opponents of democracy and nationalism and of the basic principles of the National Congress. Perhaps death intervened too early for the full blossoming to have come into view.

In retrospect it may seem surprising that the fanatical Alis could be accepted as the spokesmen of Congress nationalism and permitted to brand not only Shraddhananda, but even Malaviya and Lajpat Rai as "communalists" As long as the Alis wielded power in the Congress, they successfully created a hiatus between Lalaji and many other Congress Leaders Gandhiji understood Lalaji well enough not to be completely misled by the Alis, but the fact remains that there was far better rapport between Lalaji and Gandhiji after the unwholesome Ali influence had disappeared. For a proper assessment of Lalaji's stand in regard to nationalism and communalism the story of Gandhi's relations with the Alis is a very relevant factor.

V

About the Ali brothers Lalaji had come to the right conclusion—that they were too fanatical to be accepted as nationalists—much earlier than did Gandhiji.

Once during a halt at Delhi, on his way back from a rather extensive tour of many provinces, Lalaji called! on Hakim Ajmal Khan. Dr. M.A. Ansari was present and probably Abul Kalam Azad also. Talk inevitably drifted to the growing Hindu Muslim tension. "There must be four or five persons from the Hindu side and four or five from amongst the Muslims, who, however awry things might go, will be able to talk things over with mutual trust and perfect candour, and place before each other their doubts and difficulties without mincing matters." From the Muslim side Hakim Sahib named Azad and Ansari and himself and the two Alis. With his usual outspokenness Lalaji forthwith said, "I must make it plain I put the Alis on a very different plane from that of Ansari and Ajmal Khan. I do not think I could trust them so implicitly."

Things came to a head with Munammad Ali's presiding over the Congress session at Kakinada (1923-end) and in the presidential address making an outrageous proposal, at the instigation of the Aga Khan, as became known afterwards, that the "untouchables" should be divided amongst Hindus and Muslims. The cold impudence of this suggested share-out hurt Lalaji deeply and, as we have seen, it was this proposal from the presidential chair of the Congress that made Lalaji decide on an immediate nation-wide drive for the removal of untouchability and making such a drive the number one item of his programme. As narrated in our chapter dealing with that campaign, the treatment that Lalaji's offer to the Working Committee received from the Maulana (as Congress President) was by itself enough to create a wide gulf between Lalaji and the Alis.

Muhammad Ali had amongst his many gifts a vitriolic pen and a vitriolic tongue and a waspish readiness to use both against those who did not agree with him. When Lalaji began to criticise certain aspects of Congress leadership, Muhammad Ali hurled missiles at him from his oratorial catapult, and in lampooning him in the columns of his *Comrade* dipped freely his pen in the rich assortment of his vials of slander and satire. This sustained lampooning was taken scant notice of by Lalaji who dismissed it as 'billingsgate', but in certain quarters it was bound to work mischief.

For attacking Lalaji Muhammad Ali very often chose Lalaji's heresies in respect of programmes sanctioned by the Congress or carrying the Gandhi imprimatur, but not many were deceived by such alibis. Lalaji gave mortal offence to the Maulana by his publicly denouncing his suggested fifty-fifty deal regarding the Depressed Classes (later designated as 'Harijans'), and his launching in all earnestness a drive to counteract that move. Perhaps none amongst the front-rank Hindu leaders of the Congress could endorse the Maulana's proposition but whilst most others listened to the mischievous proposal from the presidential chair in discreet silence—Gandhiji, it must be mentioned, was still in prison—Lalaji though not present at the Kakinada session had the temerity to start effective action to frustrate the mischief. The Maulana could not resist his proselytizing zeal, but that he should thus exhibit it from the Congress presidential chair and simply walk away with it was a symptom profoundly perturbing betokening a debasement of values. In such a topsy-turvy context Lajpat Rai no doubt was seen in the role of a "communalist".

VI

An ardent nationalist, Lalaji had not abjured his duties towards the Hindu community, mainly of the nature of social reform or of uplift of backward sections, and wherever the Hindus faced a calamity, man-mads or act of God, they expected Lalaji (and Malaviyaji) to rush to their help. Because of these activities Lalaji was dubbed by some a "communalist". We may here briefly examine Lalaji's "communal" activity to see if it really ran counter to his professions of nationalism.

Foremost among Lalaji's "communal" activities was of course his work for those treated as untouchables. He had been interested in this from the very start of his public life, and he attached the highest importance to it as a Hindu reformer, as an Indian nationalist, and above all as a believer in man to man equality. His work here, in its objectives and in its methods, in no way ran counter to nationalism. Under Gandhi's leadership the Indian National Congress adopted this work as part of its "constructive programme"—and it has so continued, in spite of a deplorable lapse or perversion, in Muhammad Ali's presidential speech.

Lalaji started his nation-wide campaign in this field nearly a decade before the founding of the Harijan Seva Sangh. After suspending civil disobedience the Congress was supposed to have taken to constructive programme, but the all important anti-untouchability part of the programme remained neglected for many years so far as the Congress was concerned. Lalaji who earnestly took it up had to create his own medium and also to make use of "communal" bodies for this national work.

In all essentials Lalaji's work here was but an anticipation of Gandhiji's work through the Sangh. For Lalaji the immediate provocation had come from the Aga Khan inspired proposal made by Muhammad Ali. This perturbed Lalaji just as Ramsay MacDonald's Award which too (like the Kakinada proposal) was calculated to treat the Harijans as no part or at best a detachable part of the Hindu community. In his agony the Mahatma resorted to fasting and prayer and achieved an agreed formula of representation and started the Harijan Sangh. Lalaji, deeply perturbed, sought inspiration from what he deemed a sacred day—the day sacred to Guru Gobind Singh—and announced his resolve, following this up with the launching of a drive through the Achhut Uddhar Committee.

The only other "communal" item that figured in Lalaji's activity was his association with the Hindu Mahasabha. Lalaji's earliest association with such a body was in the first decade of the century when the Punjab Hindu Sabha was started. The date is significant, for to Lalaji such communal bodies seemed a sort of corollary to certain communal provisions in the constitution. Minto had then introduced the communal electorate, which even Gokhale, much to Lalaji's chagrin, had found acceptable. We have called attention to this early fact because Lalaji regarded the communal electorate as poisonous in its effect on the growth of Indian nationalism, but if perforce we had to woo the voters in communal compartments we may have willy-nilly to set up some sort of communal organisation, without losing sight of our nationalist goal. A British friend of the Indian movement put Lalaji's thesis very tersely thus :

". . . .If could have avoided communal representation, democratic institutions could have been used to unite the two communities, would have brought them together on planes of economic interest. But with communal electorates in full swing and in the absence of any overriding class interest we have got to put the clock back"*

* Josiah C. Wedgwood's letter of October 8. 1926 to Lalaji, published in *The People,* November 7, 1926.

It is necessary to remember that the Hindu Mahasabha has passed through many phases, and Lalaji could not possibly have approved of *all* its policies and activities. (Even in the Punjab Sabha Lalaji's active interest had been short lived as he did not approve of much of its doings.) Anyone wanting to adjudge Lalaji's Mahasabha activity will have to restrict himself to what that body did during the period when Lalaji had a decisive say in its counsels.

Thus viewed, a very noticeable thing in the Mahasabha, under the Malaviya-Lajpat Rai leadership, is that it had little to do with hustings. Thus there was no confrontation with bodies like the Congress, nor any question of its in any way weakening the fight for liberation. Lalaji's association with the Mahasabha could thus indirectly prove to be of help to the Congress party. A significant admission of this came from Pandit Motilal himself, and just in the course of his high polemic against Lalaji :

"Up to the time you left India you were a stout champion of Congress candidates and *put up a brave fight for them in the Hindu Sabha**. You do not say what particular incident in the last four months has revolutionised your ideas." (Pandit Motilal's reply dated 30 August to para 3 of Lalaji's letter of resignation from the Swaraj Party.)

Lalaji's hold over the Sabha was useful to, perhaps greatly needed by, the nationalist cause. (A "particular incident" also there was as we shall see. Motilalji may have had a shrewd suspicion about this and about Lalaji's unwillingness to come out in the open.) Even when Lalaji left the Swaraj Party, for the hustings he joined hands with Malaviyaji to create the Independent Congress Party still keeping under check the enthusiasts who wanted the Mahasabha to run its own candidates.

At a Hindu conference in Bombay someone objected to the presence of a "non-Hindu", the noted Parsi scholar, G.K.

---

* Italics ours.

Nariman. Lalaji straightway brushed aside the objection, saying (as Nariman himself recalled*) that anyone—Hindu, Muslim or Christian—could, be included in the conference provided he loved India. Such was the broadmindedness that ever characterised Lalaji's Hindu Sabha Work.

Always he took good care that his work for his own com- .munity was carried on so as to make a wholesome contribution towards the bigger cause to which he had dedicated himself—that of India's liberation and of building a great Indian nation. Even for the furtherance of Hindu-Muslim unity he thought work through a communal body—of course with his own nationalist approach—was helpful, even necessary, his approach and his methods being clearly different alike from those whose thinking could not transcend the sectarian or communal barrier, and from those Hindu leaders who, ignoring the realities of the Indian context, shunned all Hindu bodies lest the contact sully their pure nationalism! Many of these worthies in private assured Lalaji of their full support, but their public stand was different! At Belgaum Srinivasa lyengar told him in effect: I am in agreement with your stand but would like to be left alone for one year!

VII

Like many others Lalaji felt that too much of religion had been let loose in the wrong handling of the Khilafat movement. He supported the Mussalmans in their Khilafat demand whole heartedly, but he would not keep quiet when some enthusiasts began to sing songs inviting Enver Pasha's hordes or those from Afghanistan to India—and, characteristically, Lalaji chose a Khilafat platform to speak out what he felt! Sir Tej Bahadur Sapru who was no Hindu Sabhaite wrote to Lalaji :

"I was much pleased to hear an account of your spirited and straight speech at the second sitting of the Khilafat Conference. I think it is up to us to tell Shaukat Ali and his friends that we cannot possibly contemplate the prospect of

* *The People : Lajpat Rai Number,* April 13, 1929.

our friends the Afghans coming to 'rescue' us; all that is nonsense and mischief pure and simple and I am afraid the non-co-operation movement as understood by some of our friends in the Mohammedan community is very much different from the non-co-operation movement of Mr. Gandhi—though even with his view I do not at all agree. But though one may differ from Mr. Gandhi, one can respect him and his view. It is entirely impossible however to agree with Mr. Shaukat Ali and his friends who dream of Afghanistan as the redeemer and saviour of India. I was much pleased to hear that you told them what Hindus thought of it."

When one of the young muhajireen from India met Enver Pasha somewhere in Central Asia, about the first question the valiant Turk asked him was a polite enquiry about Lajpat Rai—the only Indian leader in whom he evinced interest! Lalaji had friends amongst the young Turks and amongst Egyptians. Whenever their delegations came to India, he felt proud to act as their host as in their country he had gratefully accepted their hospitality.

VIII

The Kohat tragedy apart, the one act of communal madness that Lalaji felt with the keenest poignancy was the murder of Shraddhananda. Neither of these events however turned him away from attempts at a rapprochement whenever an opportunity for this arose. Not even threats to his own person. Some time after the Shraddhananda murder, he received one day an anonymous letter threatening him that he shall pay with his life for his "Sangathan" activities. He sent on the letter in original with the cover in which it had come to the District Magistrate of Lahore. About this time a stranger one day tried to get at him in a rather suspicious way, at the Court Street house. When questioned, the man could give no satisfactory explanation of the purpose of his visit and seemed to have got into a blue funk. This much seemed clear that he was a Mussalman and that he had come on no normal errand. Lalaji had him sent away, refusing to call in the police to hand him over. Lalaji acquired a new habit in these circumstances

—of going about with a revolver in his pocket. Those around him besides began to insist that as far as possible he should not stir out unaccompanied. But no fuss was made about either happening—the threatening letter and the suspicious visitor. So far as I can remember, neither was mentioned in the press.

IX

Lalaji felt that Gandhiji's stress on religion, which to the Mahatma connoted tolerance above everything else, was in the long run likely to create complications since it ignored what had often been a strong trait of the fane. Not for nothing is the *fanatic* a derivative of *fanum*.

Lalaji always strove after a concrete and well-defined settlement based on considerations of equity and of mutual accommodation by the two communities. He could not be persuaded that high gestures about offers of a 'blank' (Hindu) cheque to be filled in by the Muslim leaders, or that professions of implicit faith in the Musalman's *khandani* (a favourite phrase with Gandhiji in the early 'twenties) could solve the problem. Lalaji did not find such preaching to be supported by his reading of history and by his assessment of the realities of the contemporary Indian scene. Today it is commonly recognised that the 'blank cheque' approach, while it alienated a certain amount of Hindu sympathy, was at the same time mistrusted by Musalmans as something insincere or at best evasive.

Lalaji did not set much store by the idealistic Gandhi approach of the early twenties. It lacked realism and in Lalaji's view could have little bearing on practical politics.

In his own way Lalaji remained consistent in his attitude towards the Hindu-Muslim issue; that is, remaining true always to certain fundamentals (with the sturdiness of the oak), yet always willing to make adjustment in details (with the suppleness of the willow). The phase in his thinking with which we are here concerned more particularly started during his stay in the States when he made that emphatic declaration against communalism which we have already quoted. When later on he found it necessary to organise the Hindus on a communal platform he kept the warning he had sounded ever before his mind's eye. He would not permit the Hindu Mahasabha to be used in the dangerous way he had condemned; till the end he did not even permit the Hindu Mahasabha to put up candidates in elections and thus fall foul of the National Congress. The phase of thought that began with the declaration on Hindu-Muslim dissension made during Lalaji's American days continued till the very end, for in his last days most of his time and energy were being devoted to work for the (Motilal) Nehru draft of a settlement. The last presidential address that Lalaji wrote out—the one delivered at the Hindu Conference at Etawah less than three weeks before his end—was a passionate plea for a Hindu-Muslim settlement along the lines laid down in the Nehru report. The fact that here Motilalji and Lalaji were in perfect accord is conclusive proof that the mature thinking of both on this problem had led them to basically the same conclusions and that the one was as keen on unity as the other. But their methods of work were different. For instance, Lalaji's utterance was made from a Hindu Sabha platform, which Motilalji would not have made use of. And as a practical politician Motilalji must have seen how useful and necessary Lalaji's influence over the Mahasabha was in the furtherance of the Nehru scheme.

Even after liberation—and partition—Hindu-Muslim unity continues to baffle statesmanship. But, basically the Indian Constitution adopted the Nehru scheme proposals on Muslim representation as far as they could be in the redrawn map of India. That this has not solved the problem only means that at best such adjustment can provide only part of the solution, not the whole of it.

Lalaji made an earnest, detailed, realistic study of the Hindu-Muslim dissensions in a series of thirteen articles which he wrote in 1924 for the press. Every page of the brochure reprinting these articles shows his keen desire for unity, and, many of the suggestions made therein hold good even today—though of course the map of India as redrawn in 1947 has outmoded others.

To anyone interested in a proper assessment of Lalaji's "communalism" and nationalism we would suggest a careful reading of the brochure as also of Lalaji's speeches at all the Hindu conferences.* His yearning for unity and his earnestness in seeking it is inescapable, whatever the merits of the detailed suggestions put forward by him.

Lalaji wanted not merely a settlement, being well aware that this by itself could not effectively solve the problem. The real integrational work had to come through education. And Lalaji's contribution here is found tersely—very pregnantly touching ticklish problems like that of the re-writing of the history of Muslim rule—given in his book on National Education. There can be little doubt Dr. Zakir Husain was particularly struck by Lalaji's contribution here when he wrote his highly laudatory foreword to the centenary reprint of that book.

It was not only for enlisting Hindu support to the Nehru scheme that 'Motilalji had to lean heavily on Lalaji; for even securing the support of an outstanding Muslim leader like Jinnah, if the relevant data of those days were fully examined, Lalaji's contribution would be found to outweigh that of any other Congress leader. Lalaji strove for a united stand against the Simon Commission, and secured full support from Jinnah. In his last days he was again in touch with Jinnah to secure his support for the All Parties Conference to consider the Nehru scheme.

Lalaji had generally not much difficulty in working with M.A. Jinnah. They had often worked together in the pre-non-co-operation days and though Jinnah left the Congress when Gandhi came into power; they had once again to work with each other when Lalaji went to the Legislative Assembly—and they were often seen discussing things not on the Assembly agenda but the broader aspects of the Hindu-Muslim

* This series on the Hindu-Muslim problem has been included in V.C. Joshi's 2-volume edition of Lala Lajpat Rai's *Writings and Speeches* (New Delhi, Servants of the People Society, 1966). See Vol. II. pp. 170-222.

relationship. They did not always see eye to eye and sometimes differed sharply and publicly criticised each other with zest and vigour, but it was always possible to know where the differences lay and to what extent they could work together, the boycott of the Simon Commission being an instance in point. During the Assembly session Jinnah would frequently walk into Lalaji's room without an appointment and unannounced. Sometimes he would do so several times in the course of the same day. Lalaji visited him likewise and very often they both would rise from a talk and go together to Malaviyaji to continue the discussion. There were no formalities, and whether or not the talks resulted in agreement there never arose a question as to who should seek whom—the trivial things that in the 'thirties and 'forties often hindered pourparlers. Jinnah had no Muslim League Party in the Central Assembly and was the leader of a small group of Independents. The relations between the Swarajist leader and the leader of the Independents were not as smooth as one would have expected between two opposition leaders. Lalaji and Jinnah may not have found a satisfactory formula for a communal settlement, all the same in most assembly matters, they could wholeheartedly co-operate with each other.

XI

Writing of the 1926 elections Jawaharlal Nehru has said in his *Autobiography* : *

"I had met Lalaji in Geneva that summer and from our talks I had not gathered that he contemplated taking up an aggressive attitude against the Congress Party.... But in the course of the election campaign, he made certain vague charges, which showed how his mind had been working. He accused the Congress leaders of intriguing with people outside India. He further accused them of some such intrigue in establishing a Congress branch in Kabul....

"I remember that when I read in the Indian papers . . . about Lalaji's charges I was astounded. As Congress Secretary,

* Pp. 158-159.

I knew all about our organisation; I had myself been instrumental in getting the Kabul Committee affiliated (Deshbandhu Das had taken the initiative in the matter);... I do not know how Lalaji was misled in the matter. He may have relied on various rumours, and I think he must have been influenced by the talk he had recently had with Moulvi Obeid-ulla, although there was nothing in that talk which seemed extraordinary to me."

Obviously Jawaharlalji, being away in Europe, had not been in close touch with things; otherwise he would not have given the Kabul Congress Committee such absolute precedence over the other issues which loomed large in Lalaji's campaign whilst the Kabul Committee was hardly ever mentioned in his public utterance.

But the Kabul Congress Committee too had made its own contribution, not so much in the actual campaign as a facto in the background which influenced Lalaji's own attitude as it filled him with deeper and darker misgivings than even those inspired by the recurring riots in Malabar and at Multan and Kohat and elsewhere.

The misgivings engendered by Habib-ur-Rahman in Lahore jail acquired poignancy through what we may call the Episode Obeidullah, after Màulvi Obeidullah Sindhi to whom goes the credit of having set up that branch of the Indian National Congress. Episode Obeidullah merits special consideration because of its influence, real or supposed, on the 1926 general election, and more than that on Lalaji's thinking and outlook and his relations with the contemporary Congress leadership, and above all because of its import as revealed by subsequent events.

First of all the tangible facts. In August 1924 Obeidullah saw Lalaji in Istanbul, his visiting card describing him as a functionary of the Kabul Congress Committee, and the Maulvi gave Lalaji a printed scheme about the federated republics of the sub-continent issued on behalf of that committee. On his return to India Lalaji who had never before heard of such a committee or its scheme of federated republics had enquiries made from the A.-I.C.C. headquarters (then in Allahabad) and these confirmed affiliation having been granted to a committee in Kabul in 1922 when Deshbandhu Das was President of the Congress and Lalaji a prisoner.

The visiting card had presented an anomaly: for a branch of the Indian National Congress in Kabul could make no sense and besides, how could he as a member of the Congress Working Committee remain ignorant about such an innovation? Perhaps it had come into being unauthorised. The scheme issued over this new imprint Lalaji's penetrating eye could see through at once as a camouflage for cutting up India, so that an independent Muslim state might be carved out thereby : Kabul could be interested in such a scheme. Obeidullah was a dark horse, but what could he be up to? And, above all, what business had the Congress to let him use its prestige and authority the way he liked a glimpse of which had been afforded by the Kabul Committee's scheme? About the camouflage he had no doubt : what lay behind it might or might not be actually or even potentially dangerous. But careful scrutiny and vigilance were certainly called for.

Filled with misgivings Lalaji tried to share these with the topmost leaders. And the real tragedy (it must be stressed) lay in their reactions which ranged from a "so what"? nonchalance to pooh-poohing the question raised. Such an attitude on the part of his colleagues and comrades at the helm made things infinitely worse.

It has become possible now to view the whole thing in retrospect in a factual objective manner, instead of indulging in conjecture about what had been camouflaged. A boy born in a Sikh family in Sialkot embraced Islam, styled himself Obeidullah Sindhi, and as he grew up, decided to dedicate his life to the service of Islam, identifying himself entirely with a school of Indian divines who, ever since the decline of the Mughal empire, had through generations kept up a determined secret endeavour to bring into being a theocratic Muslim state. No sacrifice was too big for achieving this end.

The means included camouflage, alliances with foreign Muslim powers, in later phases—World War I onwards—aligning themselves with Indian nationalist or revolutionary forces working for India's liberation. In the twenties it was difficult to get the real facts about the teachings, methods and aims of this school. Today no one who recalls that episode for a cold objective scrutiny can help admiring Lalaji's penetrating foresight which could straightway after the Istanbul encounter visualise what had been go deftly camouflaged, and had put all the other leaders, including Das and the Nehrus, off their guard... Lalaji smelt "secession" when others failed to suspect anything.

But he was hesitant to mention "secession" in public lest such lack of discretion precipitate things and go to make of it a live issue when it was still possible by vigilance and seasonable action to nip the sinister thing in the bud. His forebodings—for the most part expressed only in private talks with a few with whom he thought sharing these necessary—then described as cock-and-bull stories—became stern realities within two decades of his death. The controversy was closed by History's verdict which proved the forebodings prophetic. What needs mention here is that the Episode Obeidullah was an important contributory factor in the 1926 elections for even though he avoided talking about Obeidullah and his scheme or openly mentioning "secession" he found impelled to deplore the leaders lack of vigilance and their attitude of nonchalance in matters which he regarded of fundamental importance. The electioneering evinced a good deal of acerbity and thus, at least for the time being, it went to create an unfortunate estrangement between Lalaji and some of the leaders.*

The effect of the episode on Lalaji's outlook on politics, particularly on what constitutes the theme of the present chapter, may be summed up thus :

* For a fuller discussion of this episode the reader is referred to *The Unheeded Prophet* by the present writer. (New Delhi : Lajpat Bhawan, 1972).

(a) The camouflaged plans of "secession" or for a theocratic Muslim State went to confirm further his apprehensions about communal representation; in particular, it made him all the more adamant against communal electorates the logical outcome of which he foresaw in a demand for "secession". Therefore, it was necessary not only to be vigilant with regard to the camouflaged Obeidullah plans, but also to stand firm against the extension of communal representation, and firmly oppose all settlement formulas based on the communal electorate.

(b) Plans like the Kabul Committee had to be avoided like poison by nationalist leaders. Lack of vigilance here would jeopardise Indian unity.

Paradoxically, the Obeidullah school, in the early forties, seemed to oppose the League-evolved scheme of partition. The difference lay in this—that the Ulema of this school did not relish negotiation with the British as a means, and in their (still veiled) final objective they were completely theocratic Lalaji's misgivings of "secession" applied to both, though after the Congress-Khilafat honeymoon had ended the Obeidullah school—because of its secretive way, and its raising an insuperable theocratic barrier against real abiding unity—was a graver peril.

We have called attention to the main episodes which, over and above the general pessimism arising out of the riots, made Lalaji particularly pessimistic in regard to unity—the frank Lahore jail discussion, Mohammad Ali's presidential address, the Episode Obeidullah. Despite such depressing influences Lalaji never slackened his own efforts for unity. Because of such difficulties the efforts had to be redoubled! Coming out of prison he got busy, jointly with Ansari, in evolving a "National Pact". After meeting Obeidullah he wrote a series of thirteen articles, published simultaneously in the most important dailies, and soon after released as a brochure. This was Lalaji's best considered, most earnest contribution on this subject. I am not aware if anyone else has ever taken such pains to present all the problems and difficulties in detail, and striving to meet these has offered for serious consideration suggestions in a spirit of fairness and of mutual accommodation.

It is remarkable that though at the time of writing these articles Lalaji's mind was assailed by the "secession" foreboding he said in these not one word about the Kabul scheme or its author, but somewhat enigmatically he concluded the series with these words :

"I have not said all that I wanted to say. I have deliberately kept back some important and unsavoury facts that recently came to my knowledge in the hope that there will be no need to give publicity to them."

5

Last Years of His Life

Lalaji was a strong man and a great nationalist. Sense of National humiliation involved in the assault on him hastened his end. He was truly a great son of the soil.

—Jawaharlal Nehru

I had the good fortune of living and working in close contact with Lala Lajpat Rai during the **last eight year's of his life.** I met him for the first time in early 1920 at his house in Lahore. The Royal Amnesty, which had been proclaimed on the eve of the Amritsar Session of the Indian National Congress in December 1919, had enabled Lalaji to return to his motherland after seven years of exile in the United States. The two years 1920 and 1921 were a period of hectic activity for the country as well as for Lalaji. The Non-cooperation Movement launched by Mahatma Gandhi in August 1920 caught the imagination of the whole country and shook the foundations of the British Raj in India. But Lalaji realised that India's battle for freedom would be a laborious and long-drawn-out affair. He felt that there was great need of having a body of young men who would dedicate their lives to the service of the country. Accordingly, in November 1921, Lalaji founded the Servants of the People Society. At his request, Mahatma Gandhi came to Lahore and performed the inauguration ceremony of the Society. I was one of the first of the batch of youngmen whom Lalaji considered suitable for being taken into the Society as life-members.

The constitution of the Society stipulated that we were

to devote our full time to work in the field of pub. .ivity. We were debarred from earning money. We took a vow to remain contented with whatever subsistence allowance the Society paid us. Lalaji donated his spacious bungalow to the Society, and this served as the headquarters of the Society and the residence of some of its members. After Lalaji's death, this bungalow was named Lajpat Rai Bhavan. It had the privilege of having lodged almost all prominent nationalist leaders whenever they came to Lahore. It served as the venue of important meetings and conferences right up to the Partition, when Lahore went to Pakistan.

Lalaji was to us our *guru,* father, mother, guide, philosopher and friend,—all rolled into one. When he took us into his hands, he took complete charge of us. With his masterful hand, he was constantly chiselling us into shape. It was our misfortune that he left us before we had become finished products. He left us much too soon for us. as indeed for the whole country.

Lala Lajpat Rai was born on 28th January, 1865, in the small village of Dhudhike in Jagraon Tehsil of Ludhiana District in the Punjab. He died a martyr's death on 17th November, 1928, at Lahore. His existence on this earth was thus confined to just about sixty-four years. But every minute of his life was spent in selfless service. He was an all-rounder. He was foremost in every useful activity of his time. His personality was towering. He was enormously dynamic. He always remained active. His spirit was exceedingly restless. He was here, there and everywhere. To himself he never gave any rest, and allowed none to others. He was a perfect embodiment of the formula propounded recently by Jawaharlal Nehru : *"Aram Haram Hai",* which means that it is a sin to sit idle. He was brave to the extent of being reckless. He never fled away from danger. In fact, he always went out of his way to invite danger and challenged it to do its worst to him. Lalaji's frankness was proverbial. He always spoke and wrote exactly as he felt. It would never occur to him that his frankness would embarrass his friends or give handle to his enemies which they could easily use against him. He was never "tactful" in the sense of worrying how to save his skin or how not to jeopardise his own position. Two things he could never tolerate. One was humbug; the other was treachery. He was ultra-responsive to the dictates of his own very sensitive conscience. By his word and deed he was also constantly appealing to the conscience of his fellowmen.

Lajpat Rai was born in a very poor Agarwal Bania family. He was not born with the proverbial golden or silver spoon in his mouth. His father, Lala Radhakrishna, was a village schoolmaster. Although he was poor as far as earthly possession was concerned, he was endowed with a deep love of learning and a lofty moral character. He had a good mastery over Arabic, Persian and Urdu. He lived to a ripe old age. Lalaji's mother was illiterate, but in every respect she was an ideal Hindu woman. Lalaji used to say that whatever good qualities he possessed he had inherited from his parents. Even when he was engrossed in political turmoil in later life, Lalaji never allowed his filial devotion to falter.

Lajpat Rai was a precocious child. Even as a schoolboy he was a voracious reader. He was always among the top students in school. What is more, he gave evidence of qualities of leadership even as a schoolboy. He became a forceful writer and speaker in Urdu. He passed the Matriculation Examination at the age of fifteen and came to Lahore for studying in the College in the year 1880. He was studying for Intermediate and for Law together. He passed Law and became a *mukhtar* (a sort of a junior lawyer).

For some time, he practised at the District Court of Hissar. Then he shifted to Lahore, the capital of the Punjab. Here he quickly rose to the top position in the profession. His income shot up. But he neither indulged in luxuries nor hoarded money. Both these things were foreign to his nature. He spent the minimum amount of money on himself. He was also meeting the requirements of maintaining his parents, his younger brothers and sisters and his own wife and children. He earned so much and spent so frugally that, after meeting all these expenses, quite a big amount would be saved at the end of the year. His practice in those years was to donate his entire saving of the year to the Arya Samaj, which was his first love at that time.

Normally, any man in his circumstances would have become engrossed in amassing wealth and enjoying life. But Lajpat Rai was made of sterner stuff. Just when riches and the pleasures of life started coming to him in their full plenitude, he turned his back on them and chose a life of dedicated service and imposed poverty on himself. For some years, he was dividing his time between public work and legal practice. Then he gave up his legal practice altogether and became a. wholetime public worker.

Like most Hindu public-spirited young men of his time in the Punjab, Lajpat Rai was attracted by the then virile movement of the Arya Samaj. Swami Dayanand Saraswati, the great founder of the Arya Samaj, was the Father of Indian Renaissance. At that time the whole country was under the spell of the British rulers on the one hand and of European culture on the other. Every one in India, not excluding unfortunately our top-most leaders of the time, was suffering from inferiority complex. Swami Dayanand stopped this rot. In fact, he turned the tide completely. He created a superiority complex among the people. Lajpat Rai became one of the top-most leaders of the Arya Samaj. He became a wizard in the art of collecting money for worthy causes. When Swami Dayanand died, Lalaji and his associates founded the Dayanand Anglo-Vedic College in his memory.

Lalaji was fast moving into the wider sphere of the "Freedom Movement" of the country. The spearhead of this Movement was the Indian National Congress. The Congress was already becoming a force to reckon with. Lalaji's association with the Congress started when he was only twenty-three years of age. By the beginning of the twentieth century he became one of the top-ranking leaders of the Congress. The Congress had by that time got divided into two sections, popularly known as the Extremists and the

Moderates, led respectively by Lokmanya Bal Gangadhar Tilak and Shri Gopal Krishna Gokhale. Lalaji was equally friendly with both of them and enjoyed the confidence of both. For some time he played the role of conciliator. But gradually, by the force of circumstances, and because of his own temperamental set up, he became identified with the Extremist section of the Congress. The trio of Lal, Bal, Pal became a by-word in Indian politics, as representing the spearhead of the Indian Revolutionary Movement.

An interesting incident occurred in the beginning of Lalaji's association with the Congress. In those days English was the only language that was used on the platform of the Congress. Lalaji was already a fluent orator in Urdu. But he had never had any occasion to make a speech in English. When he made his maiden speech in the Congress Session in English, it was such a dismal failure that an Anglo-Indian newspaper seized that opportunity to remark : "Then spoke Lala Lajpat Rai, that master of bad English".

Lalaji was cut to the quick. He made a firm resolve to become a "master of good English". He started reading books in English voraciously and also started writing and speaking in English. His efforts were soon crowned with glorious success. In the year 1906, he and the great scholar-orator Gokhale were sent by the Indian National Congress to England on a lecturing tour. What tremendous effect the learning and oratory of both of them produced! What applause they won from the countrymen of the English Editor who had ridiculed Lalaji in his paper just a few years earlier! This was how Lalaji turned an insult from an adversary into a valuable asset.

By the year 1907, anti-British feeling had become almost as red-hot as it was half a century earlier in 1857, the year of the First Indian War of Independence. India was seething with discontent. A spirit of defiance and rebellion was abroad. Bengal and the Punjab particularly were veritable volcanoes. Lalaji was the idol of his countrymen and particularly of the Punjabis. The Government became panicky and did what

Governments usually do in a similar situation. They arrested Lalaji and *Sardar Ajit Singh* (uncle of the great martyr Sardar Bhagat Singh) and speeded them away in a special train to an unknown destination. Later on, it became known that Lalaji had been lodged in the Mandalay Fort in Burma. But the remedy proved worse than the disease so far as the Government were concerned. Only the Punjab and Bengal were till then the "trouble spots". Now entire India became the trouble spot. The ire of the people all over India assumed frenzied proportions. No single act after 1857 had aroused public anger and precipitated demonstrations and movements against the Government more as this single act of Lalaji's deportation to Mandalay did. So many of our public men who were at that time of youthful age have vouchsafed that it was Lalaji's deportation that bad turned them into opponents of the Government. Lalaji's deportation marked a great epoch in Indian history. The age of making petitions to the Government had gone. The age of resistance had started.

Lalaji had foreseen these developments. At the 1905 Session of the Indian National Congress held in the holy city of Banaras under the presidentship of Shri G.K. Gokhale, he had made a clarion call to his compatriots for service and sacrifice : "'If you have adopted this manly and vigorous policy (of resistance), be prepared for the logical consequences. Don't hide your heads. Don't run away like cowards. Once having adopted that manly policy, stick to it till the last, come what may".

It was not only in India that Lalaji's deportation created a crisis for the Government. In England also it created a tremendous stir. The Secretary of State for India, John Morley, realised the dangerous consequences of keeping Lalaji in jail. He, therefore, ordered Lalaji's unconditional release after he had been in jail for six months. Lalaji returned home a National Hero. He undertook a whirlwind tour of the country. People everywhere vied with one another in giving him rousing receptions. The enthusiasm of the people and the anti-British feeling among them reached red-hot proportions. The

Government repented at having ventured to twist the tail of the Lion and having got woefully mauled. They saw to their dismay that the Lion of the Punjab had become the Lion of India.

Nation-building work largely claimed Lalaji's attention during the next five years. The D.A.V. College has already become one of the premier educational institutions of India. Lalaji now devoted his energies to building orphanages, schools and widows' homes. He also worked hard to ameliorate the lot of the untouchables. Lalaji knew that Swaraj without *Swadeshi* would be a mirage. He promoted the establishment of indigenous industries, banks and insurance Companies, etc. The Punjab National Bank and the Lakshmi Insurance Company were two of his major creations.

In 1913 he went to Japan and the United States of America on a lecture tour. He was there, when War broke out in 1914. He remained in U.S.A. till the end of the year 1919. While there, he conducted an intensive propaganda in favour of the freedom movement in India.

On his return to India, he again came up on the crest of the country's public life. A few months after his return to India, he was called to the highest position of honour in the country by being asked to preside over the special session of the Indian National Congress held in Calcutta in August 1920. The session was momentous, because it was there that Mahatma Gandhi unfolded his non-cooperation programme for the attainment of Swaraj.

The last eight years of Lala Lajpat Rai's life were hectic years in the history of India. For Lalaji they were years of intense activity, of ceaseless effort, of bitter controversies, of success in some ventures, of failure in others, of fulfilment of hopes and also of disillusionments and disappointments. While Lalaji's whole life was chequered, the last eight years were particularly so.

Lala Lajpat Rai's death was the crowning consummation of his life. He had lived a hero's life; he died a martyr's death.

On 30th October, 1928, there was a demonstration against the "Simon Commission", outside the Lahore Railway Station. In spite of indisposition, Lalaji walked a long distance when the mammoth protest procession was proceeding through the streets of Lahore. When it reached Lahore Railway Station, the number had swelled enormously. Many of us who were with Lalaji in the procession requested him to rest his weary limbs. But Lalaji somehow sensed that the British Officers were bent on mischief and foul-play. Therefore, he said that, even though his body was aching, he would not go away and leave us exposed to the wrath of the British officers. The crowd was perfectly peaceful. Lalaji's presence ensured that the crowd would remain perfectly non-violent. And so it did. But the British Officers had pre-planned to teach Lalaji a lesson and, if possible, to remove this thorn in their side. I was by the side of Lalaji. A British officer suddenly assaulted him without any provocation at all, from Lalaji or from the crowd. There is absolutely no doubt in my mind that this was part of a plan to do away with Lalaji. Some of us, including other leaders of the demonstration, like Dr. Satyapal, Dr. Gopichand Bhargava, Raizada Hansraj and Dr. Mohammed Alam, tried to shield Lalaji. But the British Officer concentrated his attack on Lalaji. It was evident that he was inflicting blows on Lalaji, not merely to cause him pain, but to kill him.

Although the doctors advised Lalaji not to stir out of bed, he insisted on addressing the mammoth meeting held that evening. He was anxious to dissuade the people from indulging in any act of violence, which might provide the British Government with a pretext to enact another Jallianwalla Bagh.

Every speech of Lalaji's was a big event. But his speech that day was the most masterly of all. Listening to it, one was reminded of Mark Antony's funeral oration in Shakespeare's immortal play, *Julius Caesar*. If Lalaji had wanted to exhort the people to resort to violence, the streets of Lahore would have flowed with the blood of Englishmen that night. Instead, he asked the people to remain non-violent and adhere to the teachings of Mahatma Gandhi. He prophesied, however, that

Nemesis would strike the British imperialists : "Every blow hurled at us today will prove a nail in the coffin of the British Empire", Within nineteen years the coffin was sealed.

Lala Lajpat Rai breathed his last on 17th November, 1928, just eighteen days after the brutal assault. The Lion of the Punjab had passed away. The whole of India was plunged in gloom. Writing under the caption "Long Live Lalaji", Mahatma Gandhi said, "Men like Lalaji cannot die so long as the sun shines in the Indian sky. ....".

> *I am too deeply distressed by the news of the death of LALA LAJPAT RAI to be able properly to express the sense of loss the country has sustained by the passing away of a patriot, statesman, educationalist and journalist of his calibre.*
>
> *It is a misfortune to the country that a publicist so widely honoured whose aim in life was to serve the country and the community of which he was an ornament in the best possible way should have died just at a time when the need of his wise and sober guidance was the greatest. LALA LAJPAT RAI loved his country intensely and worked for it incessantly and unselfishly.*
>
> *His pure patriotism, his robust independence, fearlessness, sincerity and earnestness, easily won for him the respect which he so widely enjoyed.*
>
> *It is difficult to exaggerate the value of his services. It was needed and present to voice sound national public opinion and to guide the country into the right path of national self-government. LALAJI's death has heavily added to the loss of many public men, which we have sustained during the last few years. While his passing away inflicts a heavy loss upon the country as a whole, it inflicts a special loss upon the Hindu community, the interest of which he had so much at heart and which he tried to protect without letting it stand in the way of the growth of sound nation spirit,*

which was the very foundation upon which a national system of free government can be built up.

Madanmohan Malaviya

Return From War Time Exile

"The spirit of service should become part of our character as a necessary ingredient in our discipline. Cultivate the habit of service for its own sake, free from all motive and all thought of reward. Service of prisoners, unmindful of the 'waste of time' that this entails, feeding, protecting and loving the children of the poor even though they be shabby or filthy, helping womankind irrespective of faith, community, colour or nationality, and in general, to serve others, sacrificing one's own interest—that should be our insignia."

—Lajpat Rai

Lalaji's 'return from his wartime exile' had coincided with the birth pangs of a stupendous mass struggle, and the hectic times could not be congenial for long-term plans. But it seems the brooding in exile had shaped out several plans which should unfold themselves as opportunity arose after the exile had come to an end.

The first of these to be announced and to materialise was for a daily paper of his own. Next came, after a short interval, the Tilak School of Politics which, metamorphosed into an order of life-members, the Servants of the People, became the foremost of Lalaji's institutional creations. This chapter, devoted to the institutions set up by Lalaji after his return from exile, may benefittingly start with the Servants of the People Society which even chronologically may claim precedence if its long period of gestation be taken into consideration.

To trace the origin of the Servants of the People Society in its founder's mind, we have to go back to 1905 when the Indian Association in the Punjab collected about Rs. 3,000 to meet a part of Lalaji's expenses for a trip to England as a delegate jointly of the Indian National Congress and of the

Indian Association. On his return Lalaji announced that he had throughout been spending his own money, and that out of the amount collected stipends would be given to selected young men expected to devote their time to political studies and postgraduate research. He had been influenced by what he saw at Poona during his halt there before setting sail for England from Bombay. Gokhale had just founded his Servants of India Society; impressed by what he saw and heard Lalaji began to think of starting something analogous in his own Punjab. The scheme of stipends for political education was intended as a small beginning towards that end.

Many things intervened to delay the realisation of the 1905 dream. As Lalaji wrote when the Society was already five years old, in what has ever since been a sort of permanent foreword for the Society's periodical reports :

"But my deportation of 1907 prevented any definite action being taken.... My misfortunes in 1907, 1910 and 1914, and my public engagements and disappointments throughout this period gave me no rest and no time to expand my idea and give it a practical shape."

In the prefatory piece from which we have just quoted, after paying a tribute to the pioneering genius of Maharashtra for creations like the Deccan Education Society, and acknowledging his debt to Gokhale who founded the Servants of India Society, Lalaji speaks of certain American institutions that made a notable contribution in the definitive shaping of his idea. He "learnt and unlearnt much" during his American years, and at some of the American institutions he was both "a lecturer and a student off and on". He felt particularly attracted to the Rand School of Sociology, New York, which imparted instruction in Social Sciences to people denied by their circumstances the benefits of regular university education in these subjects, and to people who could not afford large fees. This school (he observed) "is run more or less on the lines of self-help. Lecturers are paid small honoraria from the fees collected.. ." Acknowledging a personal debt Lalaji says :

"I owe a great deal of education in Politics and Sociology to my stay at New York, and one of the ideas that I borrowed from there was the need of institutions of that kind in my own country."

The Rand School, as Lalaji points out, "is a centre of Socialism". From this centre Lalaji drew inspiration in formulating his plans for a School of Politics in his own country which he announced not long after his landing.

In less than six months after his welcoming Lajpat Rai from the presidential chair at a huge Bombay meeting Tilak departed on August 1, 1920 from this world mourned by the people of India who loved and adored him as the "Lokamanya" and for whom he had sacrificed all and undergone unique suffering. Soon after the sad happening Lalaji announced that he was starting an institution to be called the "Tilak School of Politics". To a considerable extent the memories of the Rand School influenced his initial plans for this School, but as we shall see the impact of subsequent events made him change those plans.

The Tilak School seemed to have made a very promising start—a decent home of its own, a fine library, and the collections in response to Lalaji's appeal and his effort adding up before long to a six-figure corpus. With such a start under Lalaji's fostering care the School could be expected to make rapid progress. But even in the quarter that intervened between the first announcement concerning the School and its actual start in December 1920, events were moving fast that seemed destined to have their impact on this nascent institution—as on a good many others very well established.

These events with such an impact were of course connected with the non-co-operation movement. The Congress session at Nagpur at the close of 1920 found Lalaji fully committed to calling upon college students to non-cooperate and many of them naturally demanded alternative arrangements for their study. In the Punjab a Board had to be set up for education on national lines and a Mahavidyalaya or

National College was set up under this Board. Though the Tilak School had not been conceived on identical lines, a good deal of overlapping and duplication was inevitable. As a result, when the Mahavidyalaya came into being Lalaji transferred the small lecturing staff that he had engaged for the Tilak School to that institution—one of them as its Principal. The School was thus bereft of its primary role :

At the same time the new situation presented an opportunity for something more ambitious. Some of the non-cooperating young men might be available for dedicated service for a long period. and so the dream of a devoted missionary band of whole-timers for social and political work—with the Poona Society as prototype—constituting a life order might now come true. The Tilak School teaching was taken over by the Mahavidyalaya—the assets (Home, Library, corpus) became available for founding a life order. It may be mentioned, however, that though the life order was named the Servants of the People Society, for many years the name adopted for the earlier phase—the Tilak School—continued in use. Particularly, Lalaji himself often used the two names as equivalents.

It had been Lalaji's practice always to give himself before he called on others to do so. Before inviting public subscriptions he announced that he was giving away his house at 2, Court Street to a trust for setting up the Tilak School of Politics. The announcement made a little reservation—Lalaji wanted a cottage built for his family in a part of the compound with a modest sum-out of the Trust funds. Perhaps this was only his way of breaking the news to his own family and of wearing down any possible opposition that he might have to face from them. After he had brought round the family one never heard a word about the reservation or the stipulation for the trustees—the southern portion of the compound remained with the family, but the Trust funds were not touched.

The Trust consisted of Duni Chand (Barrister), Bhai Parmanand, Ram Prasad and Jaswant Rai, with Lalaji as Chairman.

The idea of converting the Tilak School into an order of life-members like Gokhale's Servants of India took definitive shape at a political conference at Rawalpindi in the spring of 1921. Achint Ram, P.L. Sondhi and the present writer were the first three members.

The brief and simple rules—just one printed sheet—did speak of an undertaking to work for 20 years, but Lalaji did not set much store by signed undertakings or pledges, manifold vows or elaborate do's and don'ts. Word plighted before Fire was, however, a different affair. Even when dogmatic religion had sloughed off, something elemental in him gave profound solemnity to such a ritual.

About three weeks after the inauguration Lalaji went to jail.

Fully aware that the young initiates had missed their regular "training" under his own direction, from the jail came a letter to the "young men of the Tilak School of Politics (or the Society) in which Lalaji expressed in detail his wishes as to what sort of life he wanted them to lead and what sort of training he expected them to undergo. This letter, written in Urdu and subscribed "Your Friend, the Prisoner", became for the young initiates a basic document, giving them valuable guidance about a curriculum for study, as also about the Chief's idea of the other training that they would need to be adequately equipped for their mission in life; and it said golden words about the spirit in which they must go about their work and which must underlie all their doings, and without which their training and equipment and even their work would be mere husk with the really valuable kernel gone. The quotation preceding the narrative in this chapter is from this basic document.

A methodical systematic training in those hectic times was simply out of the question, but the hectic times were in themselves quite valuable schooling—intimate touch with the people, the countryside experience of mass propaganda, working with fellow-workers in a spirit of comradeship, experience as organisers, prison terms. Training through classes and courses of study could be valuable—the "hectic" training was simply invaluable. For anyone really eager for the requisite intellectual equipment, the opportunity offered by the Dwarkadas Library—as the library started with Lalaji's gift was named— and curricular guidance received through Lalaji's letter could be enough at least for the basic requirements. It was clear also that the training that Lalaji envisaged for his whole-time missionary workers, though fully recognising the need for proper intellectual equipment, was to be very different from that available through academic bodies. It was to come as much from living reality as from books, so even those who had to work, in what many would consider the intellectual sector, had to have adequate field experience. Nearly all the young men that Lalaji enlisted in his life order had done mass propaganda in the non-co-operation movement, and in the next phase when Lalaji launched his anti-untouchability drive almost the full strength worked for some time in this field under the Achhut Uddhar Committee.

Though our Founder had fully acknowledged the debt to Gokhale's pioneer institution, the two Societies were generally supposed to be very different from each other. The Poona Society had by the time ours came into being completely identified itself with the politics of the Liberal party, whilst the Lahore Society had been founded by non-cooperators. A more basic distinction was that our Founder did not want the changing political exigencies or programmes to be a permanent article of faith; the Servants of India had "British connection" written down intc its institution, as something with the sanctity of the Athanasian creed. Though an order of life-members was working in a missionary spirit Lajpat Rai's creation had very little of the Jesuitical ways—neither the vows, nor the cast-iron discipline nor the ban on dissent.

Strange as it may seem to many, our Founder himself was not a member of the New Order—a noteworthy difference in the set-up of the two Societies. Our succinct Constitution had to make a special provision to define his position as that of life-long Founder-Director. Gokhale as the founding member was the first to be sworn in, and then Gokhale administered the seven-fold vow to his colleagues of the founding batch Lalaji took no vows and administered none. His was already a life of perfect dedication—had been so for many years, a formal (re-) dedication would be a meaningless superfluity. And, though he had withdrawn from normal earning activity, he had never been a burden on public money. A deviation from that pattern would no doubt have meant a mental strain. Not being a member he never drew any allowance from the Society's funds. What may seem as anomaly to some, for us had a natural look.

His moral authority as *paterfamilias* was there, and the constitution recognised this by making him life-long Director. His guidance as Director and his fatherly affection were ever available, but he did not like to lay down the law for the members, not much even when they still underwent training. Unhampered discussion and a free exchange of views often resulted in accord; but where this did not happen, dissent was fully recognised. Did this work in such a Society? The answer is that though casualties did occur, now and then a member seeking release before completing his 20-year term, this never happened because of political differences. Political contingencies were a changing pattern, and programmes must be periodically reviewed. No durability could be found in these, so a pattern had to be evolved in which only the durable essentials had to remain intact, and for the rest harmony was to be aimed at rather than uniformity. Accord was generally desirable but where this could not be achieved, harmony based on a catholic tolerance of others' views was to be looked for.

As I look back and reflect I cannot help noting that our training and our career of service owed far more to the impact of the Founder's personality than to all the other factors I have mentioned. The perennial source of inspiration was his own perfect dedication to the cause of freedom and of the Indian people and, for harmonious working, his own broad-minded catholicity and respect for convictions earnestly held even if these happened to be different from his own. His affectionate hug for Achint Ram as he came home after casting his vote for the Swarajist candidate pitted against Lalaji in the 1926 election—the story of which is told in the narrative for that period—was a thing of rare beauty and abiding worth, a beacon that would shine undimmed for many years and withstand many a squall—and became the noblest part of our tradition, of the legacy that the Founder left us.

After his return from prison, the Society was seen functioning through a number of centres or branches in the Punjab and the U.P., and in most of Lalaji's work one or more of Society's members were associated with him—in particular, to begin with, in the anti-untouchability work. But they were assisting him besides in the Congress work, and later on in journalistic work and under his direction started other departments of activity like the trades-union centre at Kanpur The *Bandemataram* was being looked after by P.L. Sondhi, and Chhabil Das ran the National College as Principal.

When the Society was well out of its infancy and the Founder felt satisfied about its stability and about its having to its credit enough useful work to entitle it to the public support in March 1927 for the first time publicly celebrated its "anniversary". The Society needed an auditorium and the library and offices were finding the old yellow bungalow very inadequate. A new double-storey block was planned at the same time. The funds needed for this had, some time prior to the first public celebration, led the members to discover the Founder's birthday, and his completing sixty years had brought a few substantial cash gifts which constituted a good start for the Lajpat Rai Hall—so the new block was named—the foundation-stone of which was laid by Malaviyaji on the occasion of the 1928 anniversary.

The Founder-Director had already taken one member in Kathiawar, Balvantray G. Mehta, and in Orissa he had started a branch of the Society under Gopabandhu Das, who was also chosen Vice-President of the Society. The *Samaj*, its printing press, and some of the Gopabandhu's lieutenants (Lingaraj

Misra, Radhanath Rath) were parts of this branch. Gopabandhu Babu on the return journey after the 1928 anniversary fell ill and shortly after died. Orissa of course mourned for a beloved leader. Lalaji and the Society deeply felt the loss. In Gopabandhu Babu's place, Lalaji (and the members) selected the present writer for the vice-presidentship. The U.P. membership had considerably increased—including four Kashi Vidyapith Shastris—Algurai, Hariharnath, Lal Bahadur (under Draining in Lalaji's days) and Raja Ram—besides Baldev, the seniormost (Harnam Singh having resigned) and Mohanlal Gautam.

After the '47 partition the Society set up its headquarters in New Delhi, and in course of time it has expanded a great deal, adding to the number of its branches and the area of its activity. It has been particularly lucky in its succession of Presidents—Purushottam Das Tandon, Balvantray Mehta, Lal Bahadur, the present incumbent being Biswanath Das. Of these, Balvantray, and Lal Bahadur had been taken into the Society by Lalaji himself. Tandonji had on Lalaji's persuasion moved from Allahabad to Lahore (as Secretary of the Punjab National Bank) where he kept in close contact with Lalaji and the Society. Lalaji no doubt desired Tandonji to join his life order one day, but he hesitated thinking that it might not be fair to ask for his sacrifice till the family had found bread-winners in its younger members. The sacrifice had to be made after Lalaji's death, in deference to the wish that some of us knew had been in our Chief's mind.

A notable creation of Lalaji's last years was the Tuberculosis Hospital named after his mother. More correctly, the hospital had a posthumous birth: Lalaji had merely created the Trust and given it a corpus of more than Rs. two lakhs. Tuberculosis which had taken away Dalpat Rai, the most promising of his brothers, in the prime of life, and then the most promising of his sons, Pyare Krishna, when he was barely twenty, naturally claimed his special attention.

Lalaji sent his tentative plan for the Gulabdevi Trust to a few friends, including Gandhiji, for comments. Gandhiji observed that the idea was noble, but that the execution called for improvement; so the original plan was amended in the light of Gandhiji's observations.

At the time of the '47 partition of India the Gulabdevi Hospital was a well-established institution doing highly useful work. The hospital and equipment could not of course cross the new boundary line, and presumably the old hospital near the Lahore airport "continues to serve the people in Pakistan.

The Gulabdevi Trust was not the last of what may be called Lalaji's philanthropic ventures. For his last gift, in his last months, was for the creation of a centre of physical culture for women. This was a minor project which could go into action without an elaborate project stage. But Lalaji was not spared to see it through.

For the conceiving of the project we have to bear in mind the grave misgivings that (in his closing years) filled his inmost mind. The project and the misgivings both had their genesis in the intractable posture that the Hindu-Muslim problem had assumed. He had begun to visualise a demand for "secession" with large-scale violence, particularly the mob and *goonda* varieties, and he wanted our womenfolk to be prepared for such eventualities and to get some training that might be of some use in such situations. He had somewhat earlier, when this phase in his thinking had started, given a *Katari* (a small dagger) as a present to one who had been very close to him, explaining to her the underlying purport of such an unusual gift along the lines we have here indicated. He was being inspired no doubt by the way indicated by Guru Gobind Singh, who had made the *Kirpan* part of his followers' apparel. India's, integrity and freedom demanded that Hindu women should follow that model, cease to be helpless weaklings and take to a hard, militant way on the Rajput or Khalsa lines.

One aspect of this chain of philanthropy must not be missed. Philanthropy as commonly understood and practised it was not 'Renunciation' one hesitates to call it—out of deference to Lalaji's own allergy to some of the connotations or undertones of that word. But whatever label one might give it, this chain had started when he announced his resolve, in the prime of life, to accord public work a clear priority over professional work and, further, to neutralise the pull of the money incentive he resolved to give away all his earnings after meeting the household expenses.

It was in accordance with the resolve we have recalled above that he had virtually denuded himself of all his worldly assets —all that in the form of investment or savings had still been left over from his earlier career plus all that out of "by-product" earning in the twenties remained after meeting his frugal household.

To Cecil Rhodes, a regular and outstanding "philanthropist" is ascribed the saying that philanthropy is good but philanthropy plus 5 p.c. is better. One of Lalaji's institutions of this period, the Lakshmi Insurance, may be said to conform to the Rhodes dictum. From a personal angle, this venture was conceived as solution to the problem of retaining K. Santanam who had thrown away a promising career at the bar in the non-co-operation movement, and who was considered by Lalaji amongst his top lieutenants. If he was not to go back to the bar he might have to leave Lahore and go back south for starting a new career. A life office with Santanain as Managing Director was the solution that Lalaji conceived—and, of course, a good life office must have been a part of Lalaji's Swadeshi programme. Lalaji was the chairman of the new venture—and this made for astoundingly rapid success. A special feature during Lalaji's days was that controlling interest possibilities were totally ruled out, as (because of the Chairman's insistence) no application for more than 100 shares (of Rs. 100 each) was entertained by the Board, not even Santanam being permitted to go beyond this limit.

Lalaji's newspapers were a vitally important part of his work. A" daily paper of his own he must have decided on before he got back from his exile. For as soon as he had settled down he registered a joint-stock venture called the Punjab Akhbarat & Press Co. Ltd., which launched the Urdu daily

Bandemataram. Lalaji was Chairman of the company and Editor of the daily. None of the shareholders had a controlling, interest, but Harkishan Lal had a handsome holding and served on the Board of Directors till his becoming a Punjab Minister when the Montagu-Chelmsford Reforms took effect.

The *Bandemataram* was a powerful organ from the very start. Its career forms an important chapter in the annals of Urdu journalism, and it made a creditable contribution in the fight for liberation. Lalaji had not just lent his name. Though he had no editorial desk at the office in Gowalmandi, occasionally he called there for a brief while; but the next in command, Ram Prasad, his trusted lieutenant from the Arya Samaj days, would be sure to call in the forenoon at 2, Court Street—provided Lalaji was in town for the editorial conference at which the two could review the previous day's performance and plan the issue to come out in the afternoon—morning papers started in Lahore some time later, and the *Bandemataram* was among the first to effect this change.

In no time the *Bandemataram* became the foremost Urdu daily, wielding influence on public opinion in the Punjab as no other paper did. It made an all round contribution in raising the standards of the Urdu press—by the fare presented, its variety, its comments and contributions at once thoughtful and forceful, by its bold and high professional ethics, by its superior production and decidedly more liberal payment to workers.

The *Bandemataram* had gained circulation, popularity and power, by becoming the fearless, vigorous evangel of the great mass movement launched by the Congress under the Mahatma's leadership. The weekly in English, *The People,* was born when the non-co-operation high tide had ebbed away. The role of *The People* offering a varied weekly fare with a stress on educative value was decidedly different. In particular it acquired a high reputation for its cold objective scrutiny and stock-taking and for its independent, fearless, realistic analysis and examination of political programmes and, policies and slogans and shibboleths, no matter how high the authority from which these emanated. It was not afraid of being charged with heresy, nor, in the name of "discipline", being made to forego the right (or neglect the duty) of dissent—a task which required much more of moral courage than might be needed for vigorous attacks on alien rule.

As a prisoner Lalaji had made a resolve to do what he could for prison reform—in the interest not merely of jail-going leaders, but for the sake of the "common felon". This promise was to be made good through his papers. The *Bandemataram* exposures of prison doings led to a defamation case— which led to further exposures, and then to the appointment of a Committee and to legislation on its recommendations Lord Oliver (Secretary of State for India) paid a notable compliment to *The People* and the *Bandemataram* for this.

It seemed to be the privilege of Mrs. Sarojini Naidu to act as an angel radiating peace and goodwill whenever in Indian politics, at the top, tempers were frayed. During her term as Congress President, in 1926, enormous calls were made on her magic talent for soothing the troubled waters. Her success achieved by extraordinary exertions at Kanpur and Sabarmati did not last long, and on the eve of the autumn session of the Legislative Assembly she seemed to have her heaviest task on hand. Watching "Delhi sessions from the distinguished visitors' gallery, she had often found an excellent pastime but the Simla sessions, usually brief and unimportant, had not much attraction for her. The problems of 1926, however, were peculiar and the call of duty urgent as she was the head of the Indian National Congress.

Lalaji returned from abroad in mid-August and within a few days the Assembly was to begin its autumn session.

When he was leaving India at the end of April, the Sabarmati pact had just been entered into; though perhaps before his boat had left the Indian waters, misgivings about it had already started. From Calcutta at the same time news was pouring in of communal rioting and bloodshed.

On his return Lalaji found his Sabarmati pact already buried seven fathom deep. The pact had (in Motilalji's words) proved still-born, for almost from the outset each party put its own interpretation on it. The Swarajist-Responsivist feud therefore continued. The stink of communal orgy had made the atmosphere thick and foul.

When Lalaji returned from Europe he talked to a few friends here and there of his having heard of certain schemes fostered by certain "revolutionaries" of slicing up India and of a "Congress committee" having been formed at Kabul to further them.

We have dwelt at some length on this Kabul committee affair elsewhere. What is relevant here is that though Lalaji thought it inadvisable to start a public controversy over this matter, he found that though no one was able to explain what for such an anomalous thing had been set up, there was nothing but mischief of grave import such a thing could be. Their refusal to take him seriously was to Lalaji even a graver symptom than the original anomaly. This created a hiatus between him and them. This was an important factor though in the background in the sequel.

Put more briefly, Lalaji did not approve of the nonchalance which it was the fashion with certain leaders to affect regarding "communal" questions. He had never much approved of a parliamentary programme to consist largely of abstention from the Assembly. He had now further begun to realise that by their abstention the Assemblymen injured or at least neglected the interests of the constituencies they represented, and as the abstainers mostly were the representatives sent up by the Hindu constituencies, it was exactly the Hindu interests that suffered most by such tactics. Some of those who were keenest on this policy for the last session of the Assembly looked upon the walk-out as a striking gesture, as in fact an investment that should yield a handsome dividend on the not so distant polling day. Lalaji on the other hand thought the voter might as well tell his representative that having neglected his post he had lost his confidence. In the Simla session, two important official measures were coming up, one embodied the Government's decisions on the recommendations of the Royal Commission on Currency and Finance and therefore of the utmost importance to India's industry and commerce, and the other proposed an amendment of the Criminal Procedure Code that would affect civil liberties. It was possible the Government were in a hurry about these measures just because they thought the Swarajist walk-out gave them an excellent opportunity to rush to the statute-book whatever best suited their own wishes.

Thus full of doubt about the wisdom of the walk-out policy and brooding sadly over having again been torn asunder from his Maharashtra friends by the non-ratification of the Sabarmati pact, Lalaji arrived in Simla.

He took counsel with Malaviyaji, who shared much of his own doubt and misgiving and who, at any rate, had never accepted the Swarajist discipline or tactics. He tried at the same time to discuss things with Motilalji and other Swarajist friends. As these talks tended more and more towards a split. Sarojini Naidu, anxious to preserve the unity, got busy using all her womanly tact, and with infinite patience, trying to explain the position of each to the other, and carried whatever messages, formulas, queries and replies were entrusted to her, even at odd hours, up and down between Firgrove (where Lalaji stayed) and Shantikuteer (where Malaviyaji was) and Hotel Cecil (where Motilalji had his G.H.Q.). But the soothing unction compounded of tact and wit and charm and patience failed to produce the healing effect. The Swarajists lifted the ban for a day to attend the Assembly for the Currency Bill debate, with the result that the Government not feeling sure of the majority put off the proposed currency legislation to the first session of the new assembly. After that the party executive decided to ignore the rest of the session. This did not suit Lalaji. On the 24th the party had an important meeting. Overnight Sarojini Naidu and A. Rangaswami Iyengar had given Lalaji a message from Motilalji requesting him to be present at the meeting and saying that Motilalji would like to see him at his room at Cecil before the meeting. As he thought the pourparlers were at an end, he did not call on Panditji before the meeting, but in response to the special message he attended the meeting at which his resignation from the Swaraj Party, a longish typescript, was read out.

Sarojini Naidu even then kept up her efforts in the hope that the differences might be composed and the resignation withdrawn. Instead, three or four days later the resignation was passed on to the press and became the opening shot in the most memorable political bout of the year and of many a year perhaps.

The long opening paragraph of the letter of resignation was devoted mostly to a criticism of the walk-out tactics, and Lalaji complained that the March resolution of the A.-I.C.C. had been unfair to him.

"At Kanpur I insisted on my amendment relating to the budget debate being accepted as a necessary condition of my supporting the resolution. The party accepted this, though reluctantly. But two months later the amendment accepted at Kanpur was again negatived by a lesser authority than the Congress. I voted against this change and questioned the jurisdiction of the All-India Congress Committee to do so. But I was overruled. Still in the interest of discipline, I walked out along with the rest of the party." Bur he maintained that because of this later tampering with the resolution his own obligation to abide by it was at an end.

"Slowly and gradually," the letter read, "I have come to share the belief of many other Hindus that the Swaraj Party, as at present constituted, is distinctly harmful to the Hindus not so much in the matter of their differences with the Muslims ... as in matters between the Government and the Hindus" inasmuch as the walk-out meant neglect of the normal duties towards the constituencies. The Hindu constituencies which returned us are thus deprived of the services of their representatives .... I consider this to be a breach of faith with the constituencies and I cannot any longer be a party to such a breach of faith."

And lastly he suggested that the peculiar need of the political situation was not that a vigorous party policy be pursued, but that all progressive public men and groups should get together.

Some papers called the letter a formidable indictment of the Swaraj Party. It is true the Swarajist tactics were subjected to rather severe criticism in it. But on the whole while forcefully setting forth the stand he took, Lalaji was trying to avoid importing acrimony into the discussion.

Motilalji came out with a reply to the "indictment". This reply did not much seek to justify the walk-out tactics, which had been the main ground of resignation and were certainly the main theme of the letter under reply; but it let go no opportunity for sarcasm and ridicule. On merits, Motilalji's principal contention seemed to be that Lalaji was as much bound to the Swaraj Party as if he had been actually elected on the Swarajist ticket—an academic futility when the last session of the outgoing legislature had but a couple of days left, and a general election was already in the offing. We have already given the facts relevant to this issue raised by Motilalji in his two letters and need not repeat them here. From these facts let the reader form his own conclusions and frame his own replies to Motilalji's queries and contentions (as formulated in the second of his two letters).

But the choice bits in Pandit Motilal's letter were not its facts nor any arguments adduced in defence of Swarajist tactics but its sarcastic flings. He opened characteristically by congratulating Lalaji on "the well-deserved compliment paid to you by such a friend of Indian rights and aspirations as the *Pioneer*". Discussing the objection to the walk-out tactics, Motilalji underlined, again and again, to Lalaji's having been a party to the decisions (as at Kanpur), or having acquiesced in them—or even when differing (as at the Delhi A.-I.C.C. meeting) not straightaway taking things to a rupture. "Slowly and gradually" came here very handy to Motilalji to exercise his sarcasm on—perhaps it relieved him of the obligation to meet the argument. He went one still better in picking on another phrase which he found rather inviting—in Lalaji's pronouncing the Swarajist tactics a breach of faith with the constituencies and his declaring that he could not *"any longer"* be a party to this.

Motilalji disowned responsibility for non-ratification of the Sabarmati pact for "if the agreement was as I take it to be, who was in the wrong in not confirming it?" and not without an undertone of sarcasm added, "I am glad to note that on the question of accepting offices your views remain unchanged, and trust you will adhere to them at least for some time to come." If in veiled sarcasm he wanted to suggest a prophecy, this never came true.

The Working Committee resolution enabling one community to block legislation, Motilalji too did not endorse. He said it had been passed "in my absence under a misapprehension and is being Reconsidered". The resolution of his own Provincial Committee recommending that the elections be fought by the Swaraj Party, as had been done before the Kanpur resolution, instead of by the Congress direct, Panditji dismissed on a technical plea taking shelter in an allegation—denied by the chairman of the meeting among others—that "it was the result of permitting, a number of non-members to attend the meeting, and the Working Committee of the Congress had refused to took at the resolution." He did not wish to take any notice of the growing feeling among Congressmen that the Congress imprimatur be not embroiled in election squabbles. Another choice fling came in dealing with the point in the letter of resignation—pleading for a united front instead of party antagonism.

There were other taunts too scattered in the body of the letter which accused Lalaji of 'moderatism'—taunts in which some saw a boomerang readiness to rush back to the glass-house from which they had issued forth. Motilalji's letter concluded—like Lalaji's—on a note of cordiality, though even here he could not resist once again and at the wrong place rubbing in the "slowly and gradually" that he had picked out from Lalaji's letter as a target for ridicule—"I do not expect you to change your mind in a hurry; but am hopeful that 'slowly and gradually' you will find the faith that is in you, and proclaim it to the world in no uncertain terms."

Blow and counter-blow followed in quick succession. The day Lalaji's letter was published, Motilalji wrote out his and sent it on to the press. (Sarojini Naidu, hoping against hope, still continued her efforts; but Motilalji fittingly changed his emissary and sent his reply to Lalaji through Lala Girdharilal of Amritsar.) Motilalji's letter was delivered to Lalaji on the 30th night (of August) and on September 2 Lalaji sent his second letter, for he had found Motilalji's reply "full of insinuations and innuendoes, half-truths and misstatements which I cannot let go unnoticed and unanswered".

Motilalji did not care to say whether he regarded the proposed amendment to the Criminal Procedure Code, which Lalaji had said was going to be a serious infringement of the citizen's liberty (and in particular of the liberty of the press), as not sufficiently important to warrant Swarajist attendance in the Assembly. He chose rather to take advantage of Malaviyaji's having supported the measure, and the jibe thrown at Malaviyaji was what Lalaji resented most of all in his reply. Referring to Malaviyaji as "your present comrade in arms" and recalling his speech in support of that bill Motilalji asked, "I put it to you to say what place a Swarajist can have in company like this."

The criticism that the walk-out was a vigorous demonstration had lost its value because of the exceptions—the "walk-ins" and that it had otherwise proved a failure; for, the expectation that the Swarajists would leave of the parliamentary pastime so that they might devote themselves to plying the charkha, propagating khadi and to promoting the other items of the constructive programme had not much been fulfilled. Here too Motilalji neither denied the allegation nor yet owned its truth, but told Lalaji that the "walk-ins" had been sanctioned to oblige him and that if the "constructive" work had not been taken up, Lalaji as a member of the party was as much responsible as anyone else, even though apart from other things Panditji knew well enough he had spent the recess in Europe.

Lalaji's second letter once again sought to prove that he had been returned to the Assembly an independent candidate and that he had given no pledge to his voters, nor any assurances to the Swaraj Party that he would join or remain in that party. And about the walk-in clause and the use made thereof—Motilalji's seeking to pass on the responsibility for these to Lalaji—"All walk-ins took place in my absence from India and I did not participate in any decision relating to them."

These walk-ins, had included many sanctioned by the special committee and some even without the formality of a sanction and yet connived at and silently accepted.

Again he referred to the shabby sequel to the Sabarmati pact.

The fling about the *Pioneer* congratulations and that about "moderatism" evoked a ready reply :

"The sting in your congratulation on the *Pioneer's* comment is only an electioneering tactic. It does not come with good grace from a gentleman who had been the recipient of many praises from that and other Anglo-Indian journals for his levelheaded moderate politics in the Assembly. You have followed a course which was a judicious combination of moderation and extremism, a very proper thing to do as was evidenced by your speech relating to the desirability of Indian appeals being decided by the Privy Council in London rather than by an Indian Supreme Court in India and also by your support in the first stages of the Contempt of Courts Bill. Both these actions I presume had the approval of the *Pioneer* and the Government."

But above all, Lalaji resented Motilalji's dig at Malaviyaji.

In the concluding paragraph, he once again made an appeal for avoidance of acrimony—"Let us fight a clean fight, if fight we must."

The epistolary bout concluded with a further reply from Motilalji. "My last unwilling contribution to the unbecoming controversy started by the publication of your letter of resignation." No fresh points were raised in this nor any fresh contribution made on the issues already under discussion. Panditji again referred to Lalaji's election to the Assembly and crystallised his allegations on this subject into "four central facts". "I shall take your denial of the four central facts...as conclusive and throw myself on your mercy."

He went on to explain that Lalaji was entirely wrong in making out that "I do not share with you the sentiments of respect and esteem which you have for Pandit Madan Mohan Malaviya," and sought to sum up the controversy about the resignation as a series of shifting and inconsistent attitudes, all equally untenable, to which the sender of the resignation had been forced to take resort.

There ended the fight with paper missiles, with two shots from each side. Interviewed by the *Tribune* (September 5), Lalaji repeated that in going to the Assembly he had accepted Raizada Hans Raj's unconditional offer, that the other Punjab members too had offered to make room for him, and none had laid down any conditions. He contended that the walk-out policy was harmful to the country, specially to the Hindus. He disclosed further that he was not likely to have resigned from the Swaraj Party if the party had decided to participate in the debates on the Criminal Law Amendment Bill, and on the communal resolution, and that the pourparlers which continued even after his handing in the resignation came to a sudden end with no chances of resumption in the immediate future, because of the insult to Malaviyaji in Pandit Motilal's letter.

The letter of resignation had sought to raise certain political issues—the Sabarmati pact, and the March resolution of the A.-I.C.C, the walk-out policy and its effects, and whether the Congress organisation should participate in the election fight or whether Congressmen might, as they had done in the past, fight through a separate organisation for parliamentary work. But these issues were given comparatively little attention, and whether or not any assurances or commitments accompanied Lalaji's entry into the legislature became the central topic of controversy. There Lalaji was able to take care of himself us the facts were strongly on his side, his trenchant criticism of the Swarajist tactics too was bound to make some impression, but though many who studied the correspondence not for political enlightenment but merely as a contribution to the literature of controversy, to see which of the participants wielded more deftly the weapons of ridicule and sarcasm thought that the honours lay with the illustrious lawyer of Allahabad.

The two rounds of hard hitting, of thrust and parry by two experienced duel-fighters, gave a foretaste of the big fight that was to ensue in the general elections two months later.

The letters were but preliminary to the real tournament of the general election, for which the teams were already being selected by the two parties. Officially now the selection of Congress candidates rested with the Working Committee of the Indian National Congress, and Lalaji still continued as a member of that body. The Working Committee started selecting its team and making its plans early in September. Lalaji deliberately kept away from that and subsequent meetings. He got busy instead forming another party of those Congressmen who wanted to have a parliamentary programme and who at the same time were dissatisfied with the Swarajist tactics—those who in general shared his own outlook and that of Malaviyaji and the Maharashtra group.

A whirlwind campaign was launched by Motilalji and his lieutenants on the one side and by Malaviyaji and Lalaji and their friends on the other. The latter decided to call themselves the Independent Congress Party, following unconsciously perhaps the British I.L.P. pattern. They not only refused to appeal to the voters in the name of the Hindu Mahasabha; they claimed they were as good Congressmen as those in the Swaraj Party, though they did not believe in the Swarajist formula about obstruction. They made it clear besides that they did not approve of the Congress as such participating in the elections.

The question was often asked whether the real clash was that of principles and policies or of personalities. The differences in principles and policies we have already explained, and these differences were by no means unreal or trivial; but it is possible the clash of personalities lent them an exaggerated sharpness and precipitated matters. When originally the Swaraj Party was formed, Lalaji was still in prison (though he was helpful even from there); when he came out not being eligible for the legislature, he did not deem it necessary to join the party. Das and Nehru were the founders of the party and they did well in demarcating their respective areas—Das was President of the party, and in the Bengal Legislature its leader; Nehru, Secretary of the party, its leader in the Central Assembly. After the death of Das, Nehru was both President of the party and its leader in the Assembly when a seat was found for Lalaji. In spite of the differences in their outlooks, Lalaji and Motilalji had collaborated with each other very well as long is Lalaji did not formally come to be one of Motilalji's flock. From this point of view his entry into the legislature was a mistake, for an adjustment with the leader of the party now became more necessary and more difficult. Occasions often arose when either he felt that the discipline was too irksome or that the leader was overbearing, or when the leader felt that Lalaji was too big for the handling that he had devised for his flock. Lalaji as second fiddler to Motilalji was to many an inept situation, though a split was not the only solution for ending it, for Lalaji could easily remain out of the Assembly, and then he could have continued to help Motilalji while maintaining his freedom to criticise him.

The campaign proved an enormous tax on Lalaji's energies. His was the main responsibility for the party nominations from the different provinces and for deciding the main questions affecting the plan of campaign. He had, of course, to visit many constituencies in his own province as well as outside, to help the candidates of his party and to explain to the voters what the new party stood for. He was besides being fiercely opposed personally. When Motilalji came down to Lahore to beard the lion in his own den, many Congressmen desired that Lalaji and Malaviyaji should not be opposed, as their personal standing demanded that they should be in the legislature even if in certain matters they differed from the parliamentary leadership of the Congress, and also because it would unnecessarily embitter things and leave behind a bad legacy. Their point of view was placed by a few spokesmen before Pandit Motilal. It was urged before Panditji that the setting up of candidates against patriots of such eminence would.be disliked by the voters and generally go against the Congress Party. But Motilalji had been assured of thumping victories by some of his lieutenants in the Punjab and because of (thanks to) their enormously miscalculated assurances he rode the high horse. Quoting Lloyd George, he told his interviewers he preferred the cobbler of his party to the leader of the rival one.

But though he rode the high horse, he rode for a fall. When the results of the polling came he had to own not a defeat but a rout. He could still continue as leader of the opposition in the Legislative Assembly, but that was merely because Malaviyaji and Lalaji gave him fight only in northern India and not on the peninsula. Motilalji would now be no longer leader of the opposition but for the Madras M.L.A.'s at his back. In his own province the voters punished him very severely indeed.

In the Punjab the Swaraj Party was almost obliterated out of the local council, but for a solitary seat regarding which out of personal regard for the candidate Lalaji was persuaded to keep away from the constituency. At a late stage of the polling when Lalaji's own polling was over, he was persuaded to leave alone Bodh Raj (of Multan) and thus Bodh Raj was permitted to be elected with a very narrow majority. Not one Swarajist was sent by the Punjab to the Central Assembly. Lalaji took the unusual step of offering himself from two constituencies, and the double personal fight notwithstanding he kept busy running about to help his party candidates not only in the Punjab but even in other provinces.

In his two constituencies he was being opposed by Ruizada Hans Raj and D. Chaman Lall. Raizada Hans Raj was most unwilling for the fight and tried to dissuade his leader from putting up a candidate against Lalaji, but his advice was ignored and he was ordered to contest the seat. He loyally abided by the orders and entered the lists and for a while put forth his best, but it did not take him long to realise that he stood not the ghost of a chance and so he virtually withdrew from the contest a good while before the actual polling.

The Lahore Congressmen's deputation that had waited on Pandit Motilal only to be subdued and dismissed with Lloyd George's terse stinging words had included some from the Servants of the People Society, who had given full assurances that they had no interest in the new party being launched by Malaviyaji and Lalaji and no intention of diverting their loyalty as Congressmen in the altered context and that Lalaji had never asked any of them to join his party. (The present writer was one of the deputationsts..)

Though hurt deeply by the rebuff of that interview, Achint Ram, a founder-member of the Society, went to the booth to cast his vote for Chaman Lall. When he came home after this, Lalaji straightaway hugged him affectionately and patted him for having acted up to his convictions. Achint Ram may have himself been unhappy over his conduct because of the mischievous use to which some of the Punjab Swarajist leaders (who no doubt had egged him on) put it in the next day's paper.

But Lalaji made no complaint. A sequel to Lalaji's own double victory in the poll is noteworthy. D. Chaman Lall has tened to 2, Court Street to make sure for himself of the seat that Lalaji must needs vacate. "If not in the Assembly, I am just nobody and nowhere," said he. What he had been doing during his campaign against Lalaji was simply a closed chapter. Lalaji readily conceded that he had done creditably in the

Assembly and therefore readily made room for him retaining for himself the Raizada's (Jullundur) seat. Raizada Hans Raj too came down to Lahore; they met with the same cordiality as ever before, and things were so managed that he got into the Punjab Legislature. Had Lalaji adopted the Lloyd George canon, neither Chaman Lall could get back into the Assembly nor Hans Raj become an M.L.C.

Elections are a queer phenomenon and the values governing the conduct of contestants often seem paradoxical. Thus Lalaji's nomination was objected to on behalf of the Congress Party on the ground that he had been debarred by the Chief Court for having written a book or books which being considered seditious were banned by the Government. He was, therefore, disqualified from being elected to the Assembly—so urged the Congress rival at the scrutiny of nomination papers! But Lalaji had forearmed himself against this possibility and by a representation to the High Court had had the absurd order of 1917 set aside.

Though bitterly opposed and harassed by the Swaraj Party and declared by Motilalji to be of less account to him than any Swarajist cobbler, Lalaji for his part, when he heard that some of the U.P. lieutenants of Malaviyaji were keenly pressing the desirability of setting up a candidate against Motilalji, strongly opposed the proposal and wrote to Malaviyaji :

Oct. 14, 1926

My dear Pandit Malaviya,

I have read a statement in the Press to the effect that the members of the Independent Congress Party in the U.P. are pressing you to contest the same seat as Pandit Motilal is expected to stand for in the coming elections of the Legislative Assembly. I hope the statement has no foundation in fact. In any case, I would beg of you not to follow the advice of your friends in this matter, as in my judgment the country needs both of you in the Legislative Assembly.

As for myself, I think I can take care of myself. I do not believe in the doctrine of retaliation.

Yours sincerely,

Lajpat Rai

In the wider context of the fight for liberation Lalaji did not attach an exaggerated importance to party labels. Here as also in regard to the notions of discipline within a political party—were very different from those upheld and proclaimed by the Swarajist chief.

Lalaji fought vigorously but tried his best to keep the tight clean and honourable, even when he knew mud was being thrown at him. The one regrettable episode on his side—but in which he had no hand—was the publication, in the *Bandemataram* (along with some other papers) of a slanderous story against Motilalji. Lalaji was away from Lahore when this happened, but as soon as he came to know of it, he expressed his strongest disapproval; and after the elections he made the guilty paper apologise to Motilalji unconditionally and to make amends to the Swarajist chief's satisfaction.

Jawaharlal happened to be in Switzerland by the side of Kamala Nehru in her illness. Just when he had finished the campaign tour and even before all the results had come, Pandit Motilal wrote to him a very despondent letter. The routhad so depressed him that he was seriously thinking of resigning from the Assembly and retiring from public life! Though "still acclaimed as the leader of the strongest party", he could not forget that not only in the Punjab he had been beaten hollow, but in his own U.P., what had happened was "nothing short of a disaster"*.

Not being accepted by the electorate one could understand, but the most amazing confession was—"I had hardly any workers worth the name to help me in my own

* A bunch of Old Letters, p. 49.

Province."* This surely could not be put down to the credit of "Birla's money" or the "lies" of the "Malaviya-Lala gang"! But whatever the reasons the upshot was—"I am thoroughly disgusted and am now seriously thinking of retiring from public life."** He wanted to keep quiet about this till the Congress met at Gauhati in 3-4 weeks from the date of the letter. He was thinking of sending in his resignation from the Assembly after the Congress session, but it seems the favourable session trends changed his plans.

In the Central Legislative Assembly

In the Assembly eventually Pandit Motilal of course continued as the leader of the opposition. In the south no fight had been offered by Malaviyaji and Lalaji; they sought the verdict particularly of the North India Hindu voters, and this went convincingly in their favour. Central India and the Western presidency were not neglected, but the southern presidency was left out of the campaign. The result of the poll was overwhelmingly in their favour (in the region of the campaign), but the campaign put a heavy strain on Lalaji's health. In the Sind tour he nearly broke down. The Independent Congress party contained in its ranks enough both of talent and of genuine patriotism, and it got sound leadership from Lalaji and Malaviyaji. "I am the leader of the party, and Malaviyaji is my leader," Lalaji used to say. The two leaders got on quite well. Their new party kept up the fight—for freedom—splendidly. In all fights against the bureaucracy the Swarajists and the Independent Congressmen stood shoulder to shoulder.

Soon after the elections the Congress was meeting at Gauhati (in Assam) under the presidentship of S. Srinivasa Iyengar. Lalaji's colleagues were for making a determined effort to get a fair hearing and, if possible, a favourable verdict from the Congress. Malaviyaji strongly urged Lalaji's participation in the Gauhati deliberations. So also did M.R.

* *Ibid.*, p. 49.

** *Ibid.*, p. 50.

Jayakar. Lalaji perhaps made no particular effort to canvass support and to collect forces at Gauhati, but he himself agreed to attend the Congress session. The news of a grim tragedy overtook him *en route*—that of the martyrdom of Swami Shraddhananda at the hands of a fanatical Muslim assassin. Gauhati was bound to be enveloped in gloom, and against the background of such a tragic happening all political controversies of the moment would seem pale and puerile. No one could predict what might be coming in the wake at Delhi or elsewhere in northern India. On his way, at Calcutta, Lalaji's very first impulse was to rush back to Delhi and the Punjab. Mahatma Gandhi agreed with him. Instead of proceeding to Gauhati Lalaj'i made a dash for Delhi. (Kelkar and Jayakar having been kept back by illness, the field was left clear to the Swarajists.) His last Congress it seemed was to be a U.P, one—the 40th session at Kanpur—as even his first had been, the 4th at Allahabad.

The Assembly session started soon after at Delhi and his work as party leader was very strenuous. He had been able to get no test since his return from Europe in mid-August the previous year, and throughout the session he had been feeling the strain. When the Assembly session was over, he made up his mind he must give himself some rest and again arranged three to four months' trip to Europe like the previous year. Wrote he in *The People* :

"I am not going to Europe on a mission of any kind. The trip has no object except that of rest and recuperation. From repeated experience of Indian resorts of health (the hills and the seasides) I have found that the climate and the environments do not give me the rest I need. The climate of the hills does not suit me. My stomach gets deranged. Moreover the call for speeches and meetings, etc., is so incessant and insistent that one finds it impossible to resist it without giving grave offence to friends and constituents. Life on Indian hills is no less expensive than in Europe. I can live in Europe fairly cheaply because I do not go in for pleasure or luxurious living. I believe that 3½ months' trip (because that is all I will get) to

Europe will re-set me for serious work in India and I therefore hope that my friends and countrymen will forgive me for this absence from India for a short time. On my return I shall again be at their disposal for such service as I am fit to render."

On May 4,1927, he set sail by the P&O boat S.S., *Rawalpindi.*

This time he eschewed political work in the interest of his health, during his stay abroad. On his return in mid-August he wrote :

"I will be absolutely frank with them. I saw nothing in particular, and did nothing but take rest and get treated by doctors. From the very first I had determined on this trip being an absolutely non-political one. In November last I had had a nervous collapse and I did not recover completely therefrom even up till the end of March. In April again I had a bad attack of liver during my tour in Sind. So I kept to my decision. On board the ship while going outward I did no work and for the first ten days felt very well indeed—much improved and much refreshed. In the Mediterranean, unfortunately, I had a chill and contracted a cold from which I suffered more or less for five weeks. I was in London only for four weeks and a few days. During this period I did no work, saw no one in particular except a few friends of the Labour Party. I did not ask the Secretary of State for India for an interview and did not even go to the India Office. I met the Under Secretary for India at a dinner at the House of Commons, where I said or heard nothing political. The talk was mostly about poetry, literature or the prayer-book."

When he returned however he seemed to have in hand a job that might take a good deal of his time during the next few months. This was shaping out of a book that had just been published as he was returning from Europe and that he like many of his fellow passengers carried with him on the steamer. This, was none other than the calumny perpetrated by Katherine Mayo—*Mother India.* On his return early in his stay at Simla—for he had to go there for the Assembly session—he seemed to have made up his mind to publish a reply to the slanderous book. In fact when he returned from Simla to Lahore he already seemed to have finished a substantial part of his manuscript. But work progressed rather slow in Lahore. He could not find much leisure. Besides he wanted me to edit his hastily done manuscript and to give it proper shape, and I too was in the fetters of other routine. So he decided that we might both go to Calcutta and shut ourselves up till the task was finished. To Calcutta we went and more than a month's hard work gave us *Unhappy India*—so Lalaji chose to call his last book—in the final shape fit for the publisher. The book actually did not come out till about the end of spring 1928.

His assembly work took up an exceptionally large amount of time as he served on two committees—one on age of consent and the other regarding roads, and both involved a good deal of touring about. The work on the Road Committee had enabled him amongst other places to visit Adyar and to meet Mrs. Annie Besant after many years. When the committee's work was finished on April 4, he went to Sabarmati on April 6 to meet Mahatma Gandhi who was then planning a trip to Europe. The trip had to be abandoned largely because of the Simon Commission situation. Lalaji discussed with the Mahatma a campaign for the boycott of spinning franchise for the Congress which he had in the past opposed. The plain fact is that he wanted a vigorous boycott campaign worked up and he did want to safeguard against the mill-owners exploiting it at the cost of national good, and also he felt that with the output of the mills alone India could not meet all her requirements in cloth. In Mr. Gregg's book the chief thing that impressed him was the way the colossal waste through 'unemployment' in India was being caused and how this could to an appreciable extent be remedied by home-spinning and weaving.

By June the no-rent campaign in the Bardoli taluk had been launched. When he happened to be in Poona, he wrote to Vallabhbhai Patel if he could be of any use at Bardoli, but the Sardar wrote back :

"The rains have set in and villages have become unapproachable. Japti (Zabti) operations have ceased and the people are all busy with their agricultural operations. It would be impossible for me to take you to the various camps or to any of the important villages. In fact you can only come to the Bardoli Ashram where it would be possible for you to meet me and some of my co-workers working in this Ashram." So he decided not to go there.

The election fight had already become a mere 'bygone'. Lalaji and Pandit Motilal were working together in a friendly spirit in the Assembly. But the way Lalaji endorsed the Nehru report and magnanimity with which he put himself at the disposal of Pandit Motilal for all work required for a complete success of this venture opened the way to their working together even with greater trust in each other than they had done in 1921 or 1924.

At the end of August the Nehru report was considered by an all-party meeting at Lucknow, and after slight alterations adopted. Lalaji, along with Dr. Ansari, Mrs. Besant, Malaviyaji, Mr. Jinnah and C. Vijayraganavachariar, was added on to the committee. Lalaji threw himself heart and soul into the campaign. The true picture of the co-operation that now subsisted between Lalaji and Pandit Motilal could be formed by some of the letters that passed between them during this period.

6

The Simon Commission and the Sunset

"When you advise an attack, do not say, 'Go' but 'Come'." Mrs. Annie Besant very fittingly recalled this saying of Charles Bradlaugh's in a tribute she paid to Lalaji.

The Simon Commission landed for the second time in the dark hours of October 11, 1928 and, according to their schedule, would be expected in Lahore on the 30th. On the twenty-seventh and twenty-eighth Lalaji presided at Etawah over the deliberations of the Agra Provincial Hindu Conference. He had gone there to mobilize Hindu opinion in favour of the Nehru report proposals, the Nehru scheme and the Simon boycott being his two preoccupations at the moment. From Etawah he hastened to Lahore to be in time for the Simon Commission's arrival in his own city, so that in the boycott demonstrations he should be able to say "come" instead of ordering from afar "go".

"Come," he said on the thirtieth morning as he marched along at the head of a huge "Go back, Simon" procession—a vast concourse whose enthusiasm found vent in their lusty shouts of "Go back"—and yet the despondency of their hearts was well symbolized by the gloomy little flags that most of them carried and waved. The black flags betokened that they did not want John Simon and his colleagues, and they waved these constantly to reinforce their demand of "Go back, Simon". The demonstration was amongst the most orderly and the best controlled that Lahore had witnessed. Lalaji's presence at the head engendered great enthusiasm, but it was the best guarantee that there could be that the demonstrators would be a disciplined peaceful body of men. He could lead crowds like Browning's Pied Piper, but he ever led like a veteran responsible general.

The authorities had made their preparations in advance. Overnight they erected a barbed-wire barrier at the western approaches to the railway station, and it was arranged that the Simon Commission would be led out of an exit at the eastern extremity. The procession stopped near the barricade. They knew their full-throated chorus would be loud enough for Sir John Simon and his companions to hear as they got into the motorcars waiting for them outside the railway station. Their greetings would reach the ears they were meant for even though the black flags be too far away to darken the horizon for the unwelcome intruders.

There the procession had to stop and wait for the signal which would indicate the arrival of the Simon team. There they halted whiling away the time. Ataullah Shah Bokhari. that great charmer of crowds who could continue to sway an audience even when the night was running into the short hours, was present and Lalaji found him very handy in keeping the crowd busy. It was a long wait and it was not early morning either. The day was getting hotter and Lalaji stood beneath an umbrella, in supreme satisfaction that the crowd was so perfectly well-behaved in spite of the great barbed-wire irritant that was provoking them all the time.

Law-and-order, however, was in a different mood. It had its policemen ready with Regulation lathis. Not only with the demonstrators, but even towards the pressmen its behaviour showed that it was 'standing no nonsense.' The Senior Superintendent of Police questioned the genuineness of the permit armed with which the *Tribune* representative had worked his way on to the railway platform. He had him insulted—and later on lost a law-suit to him paying him substantial damages!

It would be useless to inquire how exactly the police felt-provoked into ordering an assault on the demonstrators. They just seem to have made up their minds in advance. If a 'reason' you must have, the time-worn Aesop fable of the lamb and the wolf would give you all that is relevant.

The peaceful crowd was charged, in particular the leader who kept them restrained and orderly in the face of all provocation. On him the lathis rained. The chief assaulter was Mr. Scott, the Senior Superintendent of Police himself. Another was an assistant of his, one Mr. Saunders. The leader beneath the umbrella was the special target that day for John Bull's 'splendid brutality'—a short-statured elderly man with a walking stick in his hand who commanded an unarmed crowd and kept them restrained and peaceful, even when the blows rained on him, hard and true.

A rather frail puny thing he looked, but his spirit was dauntless. He could receive the blows like a man. He did not flee. He did not flinch. He did not budge. He did not permit his people to hit back. His lieutenants tried to surround him and to share the blows aimed at him. He still received the lion's share so that one of his doctors—Gopi Chand Bhargava, who gauged the force of the blows not as a mere eye-witness but more intimately and more exactly as one of those who took on themselves some of the blows meant for the Chief-wondered how it was that he stood up to it at all without collapsing on the spot.

Manfully he took the blows and shouted with a lion's roar at his assailant, asking for his name. More lathi blows were the only reply. Again he shouted and challenged the assaulter's manhood demanding his name once again. The challenge was lest on the unmanly, inhuman thing with the lathi. The brute automaton just delivered more blows. He did not get the name—not at least from the unmanly thing itself. But his roar was effective in keeping the crowd firmly rooted where they stood—furious but perfectly under control.

When the assault had halted and the occasion for the demonstration was over, badly mauled, and wounded mortally in mind, but still undaunted in appearance, he marched at the head of the procession on the way back.

In the evening the citizens of Lahore assembled in a

mammoth public meeting outside the Bhati Gate. The injured lion roared again. Lajpat Rai narrated what had happened, congratulated his own people on their splendid behaviour in the face of grave provocation and gave his memorable reply to the morning's brutality. One sentence that he uttered was being repeated next day by the whole town, and soon after it was echoing all through India. To this day the echo is heard as the voice of prophecy well fulfilled. "Every blow that they hurled at us drove one more nail into the coffin of the Empire." And he said also that if he died and if the young men whom he had kept under check decided on a contrary course of action his spirit would only bless whatever they thought fit to do. What eloquence in gilded chambers or learned assemblies with all the aid that rhetoric might give it could ever have matched the pealing thunder of the lion that had that moment been injured! Such rhetoric and oratory at their best would, in comparison, seem a pale absurd affair.

His audience was worked up into a high pitch of expectancy—a 1,00,000 Irishmen awaiting that O'Connell 'would give the word', or soldiers *qui vive* for the General's command to start the march on the enemy's citadel. But he did not give the word and he did not order a march. He ordered a firm cold resolve, a grim determination to continue their struggle and for its continuance to be ever prepared to suffer and sacrifice.

Next day an official version of the happenings was put out. This was followed by a departmental inquiry which completely exonerated the police. Some two weeks later another inquiry was announced. Mr. D.J. Boyd, I.C.S.,-Commissioner of the Rawalpindi Division, was deputed to conduct it and to submit a report. Lalaji and other leading publicmen declined to appear before Mr. Boyd. Lalaji had alternative suggestions to make :

"I have read the Government communique regarding the attack made by the police on me and others on the 30th October. It is as usual an extremely one-sided document full of lies. I will make no comment on it just now and await Mr.

Boyd's report. The official version is changing from day to day and we will wait and see what further changes are made therein by the time Mr. Boyd's report is out. We do not accept this inquiry and I have no intention of appearing before Mr. Boyd to give any relevant evidence. I will advise all my friends to do likewise, I frankly confess that I expected nothing better from the Punjab Government. We do not want a departmental inquiry and we do not want an inquiry by a single I.C.S. officer. If any inquiry is to be made it must be an open inquiry by a commission consisting of two non-officials and one judicial officer. The police officials must be subjected to cross-examination if the falsity of their statement is to be exposed, I cannot do better than repeat the challenge already given by me."

In the legislature, when it was too late to be of any interest to Lalaji, a resolution demanding an inquiry was thrown out by the Government vote.

His own eye-witness account he had given publicly at the meeting that very evening. His doctors had examined him soon after the assault and found two longitudinal contusions on the left side of the chest. They had him photographed 29 hours after the assault and the photographs showing the contusions appeared in the press. He did not content himself with vague allegations, but in a signed item in the next issue of his weekly, under the caption "How the Guardians of Law Behave" named some of the guilty officials and threw out a bold challenge :

"Evidence is accumulating of a complete demoralisation of the ruling powers in India. I never saw such a conclusive proof of this demoralisation as witnessed on Tuesday in connection with demonstrations directed against the Simon Commission...."

Narrating the happenings he described how the procession had stopped near the barbed wire barricade that had been erected leaving a gap of about 5 feet or more towards the wall of the Railway Industrial School, having "absolutely no intention of crossing the barrier. The statement made in the official version that I or anybody else attempted to cross the barrier is a contemptible lie, invented to justify the unprovoked and cowardly attack launched by one Mr. Scott, Superintendent of Police, Lahore, and other police officers on me and others who were standing near the gap, towards our own side. The way in which this man Scott and one or two other European officers behaved showed to me completely their demoralisation. There was no provocation and yet these men lost their temper because they thought that it was too much of an impertinence on our part even to have come there and then the way in which they belaboured us in spite of the fact that we were all unarmed—I had a small walking stick in my hand, others had not even that—to my mind showed that the British officers now ruling in India have lost their grip of character which had obtained for them the rule of India.

There was no decency, not even a show of courtesy. . . . I shouted several times for the names of the officers who had assaulted me. The Punjab M.L.C.s standing by my side sent slips to the Magistrate and to the Deputy Commissioner asking for the name of the man who had assaulted me but no reply was given. I shouted to my assailant that if he was a man he should give me his name but there was no reply. It was several minutes after the occurrence that the idea struck them of collecting some evidence to show that the crowd had thrown some stones at them. This charge against the non-violent crowd is absolutely false, and whoever be the man who has dictated or written the so-called official version published by the *Tribune,* I have no hesitation in saying that he is a damned liar, and I challenge him to prosecute me for this statement. The statement contains several lies and the whole trend of it shows that things have been deliberately concocted to make a show of justification."

After describing earlier events since the early non-co-operation days that had earned for the Punjab officials "a name for lack of knowledge of law, lack of statesmanship, and of a great inclination towards high-handedness" Lalaji went on with his narrative :

"The Senior Superintendent of Police is said to have questioned the genuineness of the Government permit which the representative of the *Tribune* showed to him when seeking admission to the railway platform, and on this side of the railway station where the demonstrators were gathered, the same police official showed gross incompetence in handling the situation. May I ask His Excellency the Governor if he is going to rule this province with the help of this class of men? If so, the politicians in this province will not have much to do, as these guardians of the peace will pave the way for a bloody struggle... and the Government will be helping us substantially if they depend on officers of this class to stem the tide of the coming revolution."

In a press paragraph acknowledging the numerous messages of sympathy that poured in, he said :

"I am deeply touched by the numerous messages of congratulations and sympathy that I have received from my countrymen all over India in relation to the recent incident of police attack on me. I cannot sufficiently thank the senders of these messages for their affectionate kindness and goodwill. I think the attack of the police has been on the whole a help to the national cause than otherwise. My first and foremost thanks are due to those who took on themselves the blows that were aimed at me, amongst them being Dr. Satyapal, Dr. Gopi Chand, Raizada Hans Raj, Dr. Alam and others. I accept Sardar Sardul Singh Caveesher's statement that the blows were really aimed at me and but for these gentlemen taking the blows on themselves injuries would have been much more serious and perhaps fatal."

Yet he went on with his usual work every day. The A.-I.C.C. was meeting at Delhi on November 3 and 4, and he attended that meeting and addressed it and took an important part in its deliberations. But he found that the strain was too much for him; he had to leave the meetings and run back to Lahore. In fact he left a public meeting, for which he had been announced, to Annie Besant. Back in Lahore he wrote in his paper *(The People,* November 8) :

"My speech at the All-India Congress Committee has not been properly reported. I was a little bit excited and nervous. The injuries caused me at Lahore by the police attack are not serious in any way, but I think their after-effects have resulted in a great shock to my system, which is affecting my health. All the time at Delhi I felt very much pulled down and on Monday owing to fever I had to absent myself from a public meeting where I was advertised to speak. I left the Nehru Committee on account of a kind of influenza from which I am still suffering."

In his A.-I.C.C. speech he had joined issue with Jawaharlal Nehru. In his *Autobiography,* Nehru has referred to this :

"A short time after the Simon Commission beating, Lala Lajpat Rai attended a meeting of the All-India Congress Committee in Delhi. He bore marks of injuries, and was still suffering from the after-effects.... The question of Independence came up for discussion in some form or other .... I remember speaking at some length .... The speech had no importance and I would have forgotten it but for the fact that Lalaji replied to it ... and criticised some parts of it ....

On returning to Lahore, Lalaji reverted to the subject of my speech at the A.-I.C.C, meeting, and began a series of articles on various issues connected with it in his weekly journal, *The People.* Only the first article appeared; before the second could come out in the next week's issue, he was dead. That first unfinished article of his, perhaps his last writing for publication, has had a melancholy interest for me."

He had, as a matter of fact, paid high tribute to Jawaharlal and Subhas Bose as "of the younger men the only two whose sincerity, high character and scholarship I value". But he was not much in agreement with the "Complete Independence" talk for one thing because it seemed at the moment a bit academic, and, what is more important for another because certain people, in his opinion, were exploiting it, just to torpedo the Nehru draft, out of their dislike on other grounds of that draft or of Motilal Nehru.

"Those who are not with us are against us," Lalaji had said in the challenge he threw down in *The People* for November 1—taking the slogan from what had been said by his opponents some two decades earlier. This he amplified in another article which remained unpublished, the last bit of writing by him and one written in the same vein as part of his speech on October 30, in which he had said his spirit would permit the younger men to act as they themselves deemed best—and bless their doings!

"Every blow...drove a nail into the coffin of the Empire." It injured the assaulter, not him. How did the Great Teacher himself say in his last and immortal discourse?

"Nothing will injure me, not Meletus nor yet Anytus—they cannot, for a bad man is not permitted to injure a better than himself. I do not deny that Anytus may, perhaps, kill him, or drive him into exile, or deprive him of civil rights; and he may imagine, and others may imagine that he is inflicting a great injury upon him; but there I do not agree. For the evil of doing as he is doing—the evil of unjustly taking away the life of another—is greater far. And now; Athenians (the 'great and mighty and wise' Britishers) I am not going to argue for my own sake, as you may think, but for yours,... For if you kill me you will not easily find a successor to me...."

And yet he went on with his work—in particular, with doing his very best for the Nehru report. He kept busy seeing Hindu leaders, converting them to his own ways of thought, meeting their objections, sending them back to their towns to canvass support there for the Nehru settlement, making arrangements for press publicity and platform propaganda for it. He kept himself busy and denied himself the rest that his doctor told him he needed. The injuries still intruded themselves on his attention by an occasional pain and sometimes a slight temperature, but otherwise he did not talk much of them. Within his bosom no doubt he carried a heavy load all the tune and keen humiliation kept gnawing at his inmost heart. His doctor noticed that he looked rather exhausted and paler than he used to; but his pleading for rest had no effect.

Diwali seldom failed to touch in him the chords of natural mirth. He took a boyish delight in the candles and the sweets. So he asked some of his younger friends to break bread with him on November 12, the Diwali evening. A vivid picture of this evening was drawn by one* of the company later on :

'But, Sir, I am not free this evening.' He was asking me to a meal that evening. I was leaving Lahore the next day for a fortnight, and had innumerable little things, trifling and otherwise, to attend to. My protest and anxiety were both in vain. He had put a hand on my shoulder, in the manner of old old days, when I had been a mere boy, and said : 'Yes, I know. But you are coming to us this evening. I may be going away very soon, and not return for a long time.'

"There we sat in a room, squatting on the ground. It was a little chilly. He leaned against the wall. The room was full of laughter—his overflowing the room with its merry boyish peals. It was a rich meal and we ate heartily—but none cared for what they ate. We always listened to him, and wondered how he ever so wise in counsel could be so gay in banter. At times the voices were subdued, and a little sadness fell over us all, as his voice failed him. We knew he was still suffering. There was a throb of pain. He had never complained—no, not even in the days when he lay in bed cheerfully laughing at the blows that had sent him home a dying man. He was lion-hearted, as we knew, as the world always said.

"We had shifted to another room : his bed-room. He lay in bed resting; he had exhausted his strength. He always let us take too much out of him. He never grudged us the smiles we valued, the laugh we shared with him. But this evening more than ever before he had been happy. He had talked of the work that lay before him. We had come to the parting of the ways in the affairs of the country, he said. We must choose the right path. We must depend on our past experience alone. We had nothing else to go by Sagacious and practical, he built on sure foundations. He left little to chance; he knew the odds against us, and was for preparing us to meet them. His own

* Madan Mohan Singh.

suffering was but the beginning, but the foretaste of what was coming. He saw it as clearly as if he had been in the thickest of our battles.

"Yes, we were all a little subdued now. I was sitting next to him, the nearest, at the foot of his bed. Perhaps that was why I was the saddest. He was not sad: only a little grave, a little looking into the distance, foreseeing and retelling. It was not his usual mood; he always kept his dreams to himself. He talked only of what was—not of what would be. But tonight it was different. That's why it all comes back to me, as if it were yesterday.

"Yes, I sat nearest to him and listened as he lay on his bed. He had suffered, but never complained. How could we know, we who suffered less and complained more? Only a little tired, at the end of the day's work, we thought. He took all out of himself for our sake. So they left him one by one, all the seven or eight of them. I could not make up my mind to go. I looked up at him, and would have gone, but he understood and said--'Wait yet a while. You come to me so seldom. They are always here; they work with me.'

"There was no reproach in the voice or the words—only a wish unfulfilled, a desire unrealised. Yes, I had tied myself hopelessly in a mess of things. I had been useless to him, or to his great work. But he had always understood me, and never talked of it except at my wishing. And had we not so often planned and thought how I could get out of my angle of a life into a freer, simpler and nobler being? But his voice never sounded to me as it sounds today—a wish unfulfilled.

"Yes, I had disappointed him. For the end came sooner than I expected. He had indeed gone on a journey to a distant land and I was never to see him again."

Thus things went on at 2, Court Street.

November 16 afternoon : As was his wont he was talking to friends and visitors. In particular he had had a business chat, punctuated with hearty laughs with talented journalist G.S Raghavan when he more or less told him that he would be appointing him to organise press publicity for the Nehru report. Earlier, his doctor, N.R. Dharmavir, had called and had spent about an hour with him. Lalaji told him that he was refusing an invitation to preside at an important meeting as he did not feel equal to it and asked him to take him in the evening for a drive. But before the doctor called again to pick him up he had decided on a stroll instead and marched out leaving word for him to follow. Not having been able to find him, the doctor called again after dinner.

The family are having a game of bridge, probably because Lalaji is not feeling equal to serious work. Lalaji plays too and then gets the doctor to examine him. The doctor notices that his exhaustion has developed into aching all over together with some neural pain on the right side of the chest, and near the spine. No disturbance is noticeable in the heart or the pulse. The beats are normal, so is the temperature, though the respiration is slightly above the normal. The tongue is somewhat furred; but there is neither headache nor thirst and the pain is very mild, though Lalaji fears he might be developing dengue fever which he has never had. The doctor notices that the exhaustion which used to disappear with rest or massage or a stroll or drive in fresh air, has since October 30 become rather persistent. The thought makes him anxious of course. But he sees no cause for alarm, just gives Lalaji an aspirin and at eleven bids him good night.

November 17 : In the grey hours Lalaji's man comes running from his rooms to the old bungalow where live the Servants of the People. Not all of them are yet out of bed. Presently, everybody rushes to Lalaji's room. Wife and son and daughter and the rest of the family already stand there stock-still. Doctors have been rung up and are anxiously awaited though obviously all seems up. The perfect serenity that reigns seems to whisper that the 'fitful fever' is over.

The "doctors arrive and declare it to be so.

After the doctor had left the previous night, he had retired. But he had seldom been favoured with quick sleep and that night Bharati, his grandson, continued to massage him till about half past one. At 6-30 Bharati heard him complain that the pain was increasing, and immediately went to Amrit's room to wake him up. Before 6-45 when the two stood by his bed the end had already come.

Who could explain the exact cause and dabble with the mystery of death? But Dharamvir and Gopi Chand and the other medical friends who had been in touch with him had no doubt that the physical and psychological injuries, result of the savage assault on him on the fateful thirtieth of October, had contributed their sinister share.

It is a matter of moments before the news spreads through the town. Lahore, old and new, (the walled city and the Civil Lines) pours out to have the last glimpse, to do the last honours to its most distinguished citizen. Not a soul amongst them but links November 17 immediately with October 30. Not one but is sullenly thinking of that day's savagery outside the railway station, visibly hitting the Chief, but invisibly and far more grievously causing a lesion in a people's psyche. In sullenness they think of this: in pride they all recall the lion's last roar that evening—"Every blow . . . drove a nail into the coffin of the Empire."

By the afternoon a sea of humanity in solemn mourning is seen marching to the Ravi, and on its bank solemnly hands back the Son of Fire to his Primal Parent.

A city in mourning stood round a pile of burning wood the flames of which rose sky high and fell reflected on the quiet waters of the Ravi. As we stood and watched, motionless and still, a mass of humanity, the sunset. Man, nature, and flames all bathed in one colour—quiet and resplendent, rich and glorious.

Yes, it was a glorious sunset.

A Montt Later

No homily is it that in the bosom lies hid
From the scaffold it can be revealed,
But not preached from the pulpit.

—GHALIB.

December 17 : Towards dusk revolver shots are heard near the District Police Office. Grim reports spread with the wings of lightning. In the dark hours the people recall the memorable meeting on October 30, the memorable sentence : "Every blow ... drove a nail into the coffin of the Empire." Had that been a prediction from one becoming vaguely aware of his own approaching end? 'And now, you who have condemned me, I would fain prophesy to you; for I am about to die, and in the hour of death men are gifted with prophetic power. And I prophesy to you who have sentenced me to death, that immediately after my departure, punishment for heavier than you have inflicted on me will sure await you . . . For I say that there will be more accusers of you than there are now, accusers whom hitherto I have restrained; and as they are younger they will be more inconsiderate with you, and you will be more offended at them .... that is the prophecy which I utter before my departure . . ."

The prophecy, commentators assure us, was fulfilled soon after the exit of Socrates. His accusers were universally despised and shamed—one was torn to pieces and the other fled for shelter, and in addition a raging plague desolated Athens. Of the assaulters of Lajpat Rai, the principal one, Scott, was sent away from his Lahore job to take shelter in a secure haven. One of his younger men was shot at by lads (who perhaps really wanted Scott rather than Saunders), and died on the spot. But these events and the "plague in Athens" that raged for several years are beyond the scope of our narrative. Jawaharlal Nehru has very aptly said :

"Bhagat Singh ... did not become popular because of his act of terrorism, but because he seemed to vindicate ... the honour of Lala Lajpat Rai, and through him of the nation. He becomes a symbol; the act was forgotten, the symbol remained, and within a few months each town and village of the Punjab, and to a lesser extent in the rest of Northern India, resounded with his name. Innumerable songs grew up about him and the popularity that the man achieved was something amazing."

Let these events be the historian's domain. In 1907 Lajpat Rai's deportation had been a deciding factor for the younger elements' resort to violence. In 1928 the assault on him, the national humiliation that this implied, and his death acted once again in the same fashion. They decided the younger party which was already getting restive. The 1907 sequel was inimitably told by Lalaji himself in his *Young India : An Interpretation and a History,* the author referring to himself (like the Greek historian Thucydides) in the third person, and narrating events connected with his own person, with rare detachment. The 1928 sequel may miss that masterly handling. But whoever the historian of those events and whatever his style of narrating them, through his pages will echo the prophecy and its fulfilment.

"For I say that there will be more accusers of you than there are now, accusers whom hitherto I have restrained; and as they are younger they will be more inconsiderate with you, and you will be more offended at them .... That is the prophecy which I utter before my departure."

In 1907 the Punjab authorities had made of Lajpat Rai and Ajit Singh a sort of 'binary system'—deporting the two under the same Regulation, keeping both in detention in the same Fort, though the two were not permitted to meet even when the same train carried them back to Lahore for release. It was this same Ajit Singh's nephew, Bhagat Singh, whose name in 1928 became indissolubly linked with Lajpat Rai's and who became the *beau ideal* of the younger party—as one who sought martyrdom by avenging within a month the assault that had deeply humiliated a whole people and conferred martyrdom on its victim.

Young Bhagat Singh had inherited a rich family legacy—his father, Kishan Singh, had started life as a social worker under Lajpat Rai's direction and been in extremist political movements since the "Bharat Mata" days in the century's first decade. A far more potent influence had been his uncle Ajit Singh—the legend of his exploits, for the lad had had no personal contact with this uncle long in exile; and yet as he grew up locating him and establishing contact with him had become a passion with young Bhagat. Reinforcement came in his years at the National College, Lahore, with Bhai Parmanand as its potent inspirational influence, and an atmosphere surcharged with India's yearning for liberation. Here he heard and read about the Kuka Revolt, and the doings of certain young revolutionaries like Kartar Singh Saraba who had sacrificed themselves for the cause.

Endued with rare courage and determination and with many qualities that marked him out for leadership, and saturated with the influences we have mentioned, Bhagat Singh seemed destined for the martyr's role. The present writer had ample opportunities of watching him for several years and as he tries to recall his image, the total impress of his personality, he finds it effectively given in Ghalib's Persian utterance cited (perhaps through a rendering not quite adequate) at the top of this Epilogue.

The assault on the people's leader and the extreme national humiliation involved therein acted as the stimulus for the in most secret to come out and announce itself from the scaffold : the decisive goad that precipitated and clinched matters came from the challenging statement of Basanti Devi (Deshbandhu C.R. Das's widow) who as a "woman of India" demanded from India's youth a befitting reply to the affront to the nation.

The youth of India could ill afford to decline such a challenge. Through Bhagat Singh the reply must come. Again and again he pored over Basanti Devi's statement and seemed haunted by the challenge. He pondered deep till he saw the light—and he made his resolve.

Despite the utmost official arrangements for secrecy and suppression the scaffold revealed and broadcast the message. *Inquilab Zindabad* may have remained a mere slogan : from the scaffold, Bhagat Singh endued it with unique potency. The scaffold's broadcast straightway caught fire.

7

The Memorials

Altogether I submitted two memorials protesting against my deportation and imprisonment and praying for my release. The first was handed over to the Superintendent of Jail on the 29th June. A few days before this, I came to know that a question had been put in the Parliament enquiring from the Secretary of State for India if I had protested against my deportation and if so what was the substance of my protest.[1] The conversation led me to think that my friends in the British Parliament probably wanted to know what I had to say against the Government's high-handed action in deporting me without trial. Till then, I had not made up my mind on the question of petitioning for my release, although I had already applied for a copy of the Government of India's order relating to my arrest and also of the grounds on which it was based. In reply thereto, the Superintendent of Jail supplied me with a copy of the Warrant of Committal bearing date 7th May, 1907, in pursuance of which I was arrested and deported in order to prevent "commotion within the dominions of His Majesty the King Emperor of India."[2] The copy of the Warrant supplied is reprinted below :

"Home Department, India.

To the Superintendent of Jail, Mandalay.

Whereas the Governor-General in Council, for good and sufficient reasons, has seen fit to determine that Lajpat Rai, son of Radha Kishan, shall be placed under personal restraint at Mandalay, you are hereby required and commanded in pursuance of that determination to receive the person above-named in your custody and to deal with him in conformity to the orders of Governor-General in Council and the provisions of Regulation III of 1818.

By order of the Governor-General in Council.

(Sd) H.H. Risley,

Secretary to the Government of India,

Home Department.

Dated the 7th May, 1907.

I had, besides, asked permission of the authorities to let me have newspapers to read and while away my time with. This was refused by the Local authorities. I could not possibly think of any reason why they should have deprived me of this, considering that I could not communicate with the outside world and attributing this refusal to the narrow-mindedness of the Local Officers, I wrote a letter to the Superintendent of Jail asking him to ascertain if such were the wishes of the Government of India. He forwarded my query to the proper authorities and on the 22nd June officially informed me that the matter had been determined upon by the highest authority and that no newspaper could be allowed to me.[3] The want of newspapers was felt by me as the greatest deprivation, for I naturally wanted to know what was happening in my country.

A few days before, I had received a copy of Regulation III of 1818 from home in compliance with a request made by me to that effect. I read the Regulation very carefully and could find nothing therein which justified the refusal to allow newspapers. I considered this to be a great hardship and consequently decided to memoralise the Government of India on the subject as well as to enter a written protest against my arrest and deportation. Having arrived at this conclusion, I wrote down the draft of the Memorial the same day. Before making a fair copy of it, I read it to the Superintendent of Jail and asked him if he had any objections to it. He advised me to strike out the portion about my ill health, as well as the request contained at the end of the Memorial but I did not agree to it. I regret I do not possess a true copy of this Memorial. On the 20th July the Superintendent of Jail asked me for a copy, which was required by the Government of Burma, and I had to reproduce it from memory. I do it again for the information of my countrymen, so that they may know what I wrote to the Government. To the best of my memory the memorial printed below is a substantially faithful reproduction of the original, except that a word here or a word there might be different.[4]

To

H.E. the Viceroy & Governor-General of India.

SIMLA

May it Please Your Excellency,

That your petitioner is a State Prisoner confined in Fort Dufferin, at Mandalay, Burma; that he was arrested at Lahore and deported therefrom on the 9th of May, 1907 in pursuance of a warrant issued under the authority of Your Excellency in Council, in accordance with the provisions of Regulation III of 1818 and bearing the date of 7th May, 1907;

That neither at the time of his arrest, nor subsequently, was your petitioner informed of the charge or charges against him on the basis of which action was taken against him under the said Regulation;

That your petitioner is not conscious of having done, or having attempted to do, any thing which could make the Regulation applicable to his case;

That your petitioner respectfully but emphatically denies that at the time of his arrest, or immediately before or after it, there was any reasonable apprehension of any "commotion" taking place in any part of the dominions of His Majesty, the King Emperor of India;

That your petitioner very, respectfully but very emphatically denies ever having done or attempted to do any thing which was likely to cause "commotion" in the Indian dominions of His Majesty the King Emperor or which could otherwise justify the application of Regulation III of 1818 to him;

That your petitioner believes that he has been the victim of false information given against him by his enemies and of the biased reports of misinformed officials based upon misunderstandings and misapprehensions on their part;

That your petitioner respectfully prays that he may be informed of the grounds on which action against him has been taken under Regulation III of 1818, so that he may be in a position to reply to or explain the same, at least, for the consideration of Your Excellency in Council;

That your petitioner has always been a peaceful worker, devoting most of his time in furthering the cause of education amongst his countrymen, organizing and distributing charity for the relief of orphans, widows and other famine stricken people in time of famine and in organizing relief to the sufferers from the great earthquake in the Kangra Valley in the year 1905;

That he worked as a Municipal/Commissioner for a period of three years and has been practising as a lawyer for about twenty-five years;

That never in his public life extending over a period of twenty-five years has he ever been suspected or known to do anything which was likely to cause "commotion" in the dominions of His Majesty the King Emperor or to do any other act which would justify the application of Regulation III of 1818 to him;

That your petitioner is a constant sufferer from enlargement of the liver and diseases of the stomach; that he suffers from sleeplessness also; that in case of doubt, the facts may be ascertained by reference to his medical attendants at Lahore; that his prolonged confinement in a strange land and a strange climate and under conditions of restraint without sufficient opportunities of exercise is likely to tell heavily on his health;

That he prays that if his immediate release cannot be ordered he may be informed of the grounds on which action has been taken against him and his petition may be forwarded to His Majesty the King Emperor of India. The petitioner further prays that in the meantime, pending consideration of his petition, he may be permitted :

(a) to read Indian and English newspapers, as being deprived of the right of reading them, he feels extremely lonely;

(b) to send for a servant of his own home to attend upon him;

That the petitioner shall further deem it a favour if he can be informed of the probable duration of the period of his confinement; for which your petitioner shall, as in duty bound, feel grateful and pray etc.

Your Excellency's Humble

Petitioner,

Lajpat Rai of Lahore

Fort Dufferin, Mandalay,

Dated 29th June 1907.

From the copy of the Regulation received for me, the Superintendent of Jail came to know that the law required him to submit a report about me to the Government of India on the 1st of July. He asked me if I wanted him to recommend me for any privileges. I told him that I would like to be permitted to take drives out of Fort; to have the police-vigilance reduced a little and also to be allowed to see my friends. He said he would see what he could do for me. The Regulation lays down that "every officer in whose custody a State Prisoner may be placed was to submit a report to the Governor General in Council, through the Secretary to Government in the Political Department, on the conduct, the health and the comfort of such State Prisoner." Consequently the Superintendent of Jail submitted my memorial and his report thereupon to the Government of India direct. On the 6th August he read to me the orders of Government of India, on my petition, which were altogether unfavourable.[5] I asked for a copy of Government of India's orders and was supplied with a slip-containing the following Memorandum of the Government's decision which is here reproduced *verbatim :*

"Government of India decided that you cannot go for drives beyond Fort Dufferin",

"Nor reduce police vigilance (terms of request vague.)"

"Regarding desire to be informed of charges against your Government of India direct that no more particulars can be given beyond the reasons already given. (The only reason given was that I was deported in order "to avoid commotion within the dominions of His Majesty, the King Emperor of India".)' You must submit your memorial to the King through the local Government.

"Can't have your own servants nor newspapers, (already refused.)

"Nor any information regarding duration of confinement."

"No strong objection to your seeing your relatives but meetings and individuals to be restricted and only with permission of the Punjab Government."

Of course, I was quite prepared for such a reply. The only point on which I had hope, was the request as to newspapers. For drives I did not care much. But I was greatly amused at the directions given to me about the despatch of my petition to His Majesty the King and at the decision of the Government of India, refusing to forward it to His Majesty as it had not been received through the proper channel. I thought it was extremely ludicrous to say to a prisoner, who had been refused all access to legal or other advice, that a petition handed over by him to the Superintendent of Jail, the only person to whom he could do so, had not been sent through the proper channel. To me it appeared that the Government considered the matter too ugly to send it to the King at that stage and hence this pretence to cause a delay. It was certainly absurd on the face of it to be told to send my petition through the local Government as it was the business of the Superintendent of Jail to find out the proper channel for such petition and if on account of his ignorance of the rules, he did not do it, it was preposterous to hold the prisoner responsible for it.

I was so much disgusted with this reply that I resolved to send no more Memorials. I have never had any faith in petitioning. I knew well that His Majesty being a constitutional monarch was not likely to interfere in the Government of India's action which had received the seal of approval from a statesman of Mr. John Morley's political principles. My only reason for asking my petition to be laid before the King was just to let him know the heartlessness of his Government in India, in refusing newspapers to a political prisoner of my position and education. This evasive red-tape reply convinced me that the Government of India did not want my case to go before His Majesty at that early stage. They were yet trying to fish out some evidence against me. The accused in the riot cases at Lahore and Rawalpindi were being pressed and in some cases, tortured to implicate me in these disturbances and the Government of India evidently hoped to get something substantial against me. Indulging in these thoughts, I decided to drop the idea of sending a fresh petition to the King, *through the proper channel,* though the Superintendent of Jail reminded me of it several times. I replied that there was no hurry and that I would take my time. Knowing a bit of history as I did, I despaired of getting any justice or fairplay from despots and resolved to settle down in the life of bondage to which I had been doomed by the latter's verdict. I thought that it was sufficient that I had entered a written protest and a denial to the general charge against me.

In September, however, I happened to read in an English magazine, which had been passed on to me by the Superintendent that one of the charges against me was that of having attempted to tamper with the loyalty of the Native Army. I considered it to be a gross libel on my intelligence and good sense and thought that I was in duty bound to enter a protest against it. Consequently I drafted another memorial this time to the Secretary of State for India. The ran as follows:

To

The Right Honourable

The Secretary of State for India,

London.

May it Please Your Excellency,

"That your petitioner is a State Prisoner confined in the Fort at Mandalay, Burma;

"That he was arrested at Lahore and deported to this place in pursuance to a warrant of committal under the authority of His Excellency the Governor-General of India in Council, under Regulation III of 1818;

"That neither at the time of his arrest nor afterwards, has your petitioner been informed of the charge or charges on the basis of which action has been taken against him under the aforesaid Regulation;

"That your petitioner has already in his petition addressed to the Viceroy and Governor-General of India submitted that he had done nothing which could justify the application of the aforesaid Regulation to him;

"That he had never done nor attempted to do anything which caused or was likely to cause commotion in the dominions of His Majesty the King-Emperor of India : That in fact there was no reasonable apprehension of any such "commotion" taking place at the time of petitioner's arrest;

"That your petitioner has been a victim of false information given by his enemies or of the biased reports of misinformed or prejudiced Government officials; and that if informed of the grounds of his deportation, he would be able to explain the same to the satisfaction of Your Excellency;

"That your petitioner being kept in entire ignorance of the allegations against him is not in a position to make a more definite statement or to point out proofs of his innocence;

"That newspapers having been steadily disallowed to him, your petitioner is not even in a position to explain away or refute the "supposed grounds" of the Government of India's decision against him; that he, however, takes the liberty of respectfully repeating that the action of the Government of India in applying Regulation III of 1818 to him was quite unjustified and uncalled for; that there was no occasion for it, and that the Regulation was never meant for times of settled administration and for persons of your petitioner's humble position in life;

"That your petitioner further begs to submit that he took no part in the Lahore or Rawalpindi Riots; that he did not directly or indirectly encourage any person to bring about the same; that he did not make any seditious speeches; that he was always within the bounds of Law and the Constitution in expressing his disapproval of certain measures of the Government which were at the time of and immediately before his arrest exercising the public mind ; that he never advocated any violent or illegal methods of redress; nor did he associate himself with any people who, to his knowledge, advocated such measures; that the suspicion, if entertained against him, of having tampered with the loyalty of the Native soldiers of His Majesty's Army, is entirely devoid of any foundation, your petitioner having had no opportunities whatsoever of mixing or communicating with the same;

"That the petitioner respectfully begs to add that in depriving him of his personal liberty without ever informing him of the grounds thereof; in condemning him unheard and undefended; in acting on information given behind his back, and in refusing him access to legal advice, the Government of India have on this occasion failed to act in accordance with those principles of justice and fairplay which are generally believed to be characteristic of British Administration;

"That the petitioner has reason to think that the Regulation which has been enforced against him is an unconstitutional act of the late East India Company, beyond the powers granted to them by their Charter; that being opposed to the letter and spirit of the British Constitution and British Laws it is *ultra vires*; That it has never been approved of or sanctioned by the British Parliament. That the provisions of the said Regulation giving permanent powers for all times to the executive Government to deprive British Subjects of personal liberty without a proper trial by a Court of Justice are opposed to all notions of natural justice and Government by Law;

"That the petitioner very respectfully begs to point out that the "personal restraint" mentioned by the Regulation could not have contemplated more than what was absolutely necessary for the object stated in the preamble; that the Regulation ostensibly aimed at prevention and not at the punishment of a man who had no trial;

"That looked at in this light the decision of the Government of India in disallowing newspapers and refusing to let the petitioner have a private servant of his own or a cook of his nationality are hardly just and necessary; nor can there be any justification for not allowing him to see any of his friends at all and in laying down that only such relatives can be permitted to see him as have received the previous sanction of the Government of the Punjab to that effect and that only in the presence and immediate hearing of an official;

"That the said restrictions are opposed to the practice observed in Great Britain for the treatment of political prisoners or persons confined under special acts of Parliament without a trial;

"That your petitioner is a married man having a wife and several children (including a young widowed daughter and her baby) to protect, educate and support;

"That in any case there can be no justification for his confinement continuing after the supposed apprehension of "Commotion" has ceased to exist;

"That your petitioner very earnestly hopes for that justice and fairplay for which the British Nation and their Government are renowned and that they will order the petitioner's release with permission to return to his home and resume his ordinary vocation in life;

"That, lastly, in case His Majesty's Government find it impossible to order the *unconditional* release of the petitioner and his restoration to his family, they may graciously be pleased to permit him to leave India for such time as they may in that behalf choose to fix, with liberty to reside in Great Britain or any other country on the continents of Europe or America, for which act of justice, the petitioner shall as in duty bound pray, etc.

Your Excellency's humble servant,

Lajpat Rai of Lahore.

Mandalay

Fort Dufferin,

22 September, 1907.

Of course I never received any reply to this Memorial, unless the order of my contemplated release at Lahore, communicated to me by the Commissioner of Mandalay on the 11th of November, be considered as a reply to the said Memorial.[6] The argument that Regulation III of 1818 was an unconstitutional act of the late East India Company was suggested to me by the perusal of a short history of the East India Company known as "Ledger and Sword" which I was reading in those days.

I may state here, once for all, that no undertaking of any kind was required of me nor was any given by me about my future, behaviour, nor were any conditions imposed on my release. In fact, no other communication passed between me and the Government of India either in writing or by word of mouth but what has been stated above, with the sole exception of the warning that was given to me by the Commissioner of

Mandalay on the 11th of November when communicating the orders of the Government as to my intended release at Lahore.

I was supposed not to know that Sardar Ajit Singh was also at Mandalay, although as a matter of fact I came to know of it the very day he reached there.[7] It was also known to me, that he was being searched for. The very next day after Sardar Ajit Singh's arrival the Superintendent excluded the Eastern side of the Fort from the range of my walks and I at once understood the reason thereof. Shortly after this, a Sergeant asked me, if I knew where Ajit Singh was. I said I was not supposed to know it and that he knew it better than I did. He smiled and then told me that Ajit. Singh was also confined in the same Fort in a house located near the Eastern Gate. A few days after, I saw Sardar Ajit Singh from a distance walking with a European Sergeant by his side. After this I heard the police talking freely of Sardar Ajit Singh and of the events that occasionally happened at his house when they were on guard there, though the higher officers still pretended to believe that I had no knowledge of Sardar Ajit Singh's presence at Mandalay.

Release and Return Home

On the 11th November, 1907 the Commissioner of Mandalay Division accompanied by the Superintendent of Police and the Deputy Superintendent of Police came at 10.15 a.m. to the bungalow in which I resided. The Commissioner took me apart and said that I was going to be released, but would be conveyed home under escort to Lahore and set free there. In the meantime I should not attempt any communication by telegram or otherwise with my friends or others. To this, the Commissioner added a warning on behalf of the Viceroy that in case I was again found doing any thing seditious, I would be arrested and immediately deported.[8] The only reply that I gave him was that I understood it.

The Commissioner told me that a train was ready for me and the time fixed for its departure was 10-45 a.m. and that I should lose no time in packing up my things. Having said so, the Commissioner left the bungalow and with the assistance of the police I packed up my luggage in less than half an hour. The Superintendent of Police accompanied me to the railway station where, on a siding, a special train was ready to start and some European officers were standing.

The Superintendent of Police then gave me a cordial shake of hands and I got into the train which whistled off immediately. A First Class compartment was reserved for me and the Deputy Superintendent of Police who was escorting me. In the yard I noticed a Sergeant, who I knew was on duty that day with Sardar Ajit Singh. I concluded that Ajit Singh also was in the same train and enquired of the Deputy Superintendent of Police if it was so. He did not give a straight reply, saying that he might be following me in another train. I learnt, however, before the sun went down that Sardar Ajit Singh was in a Second Class compartment in the same train with a European Inspector of Police and a European Sergeant as his escort. Besides the officers, twelve native constables formed the escort. The Deputy Superintendent of Police made all arrangements for our food and was generally courteous.

At 5-10 a.m., on the 12th November the train reached Poozoundaung, suburban station of Rangoon, where I was taken down and put in a hackney carriage with all the windows closed. Thus we drove to the same jetty where I had landed six months before on my way to Mandalay. When all the luggage had been removed to a steam launch, the Commissioner of Police, rather haughtily and without the least consideration for my comfort, ordered me to go down the hold where rigging, etc., of the steam launch were stored. This was a terribly suffocating hold, with hardly standing accommodation for two of us, *i.e.,* myself and a European Sergeant. Sardar Ajit Singh was given a place on the deck of the launch. It took them 15 minutes to reach alongside *S. S. Guide* during which time I was freely perspiring. After everything had been removed and Sardar Ajit Singh taken on board, I was asked to leave the hold and follow. On board the steamer I and Sardar Ajit Singh were asked to stand at two different corners pending cabin accommodation being arranged. Shortly after, a cabin was placed at my disposal and two others were occupied by the European Inspector and the European Sergeant. Sardar Ajit Singh was assigned a place on the deck. The *Guide* left Rangoon at 7-10 a.m. on the 12th. For the first two days the sea was rather rough, but on the third it was pleasant. The officers of the ship were generally courteous, one of them, Mr. Cooper, Additional Chief, being particularly kind. On the 15th at about 3 p.m. the *Guide* came in sight of a pilot brig, *The Fraser,* and an order from the captain of the ship was communicated to me to stick to my cabin, as the steamer was to be anchored alongside the pilot brig. Sardar Ajit Singh was told off into the hold the same time.

Some communication passed between the two Captains (of the *S.S. Guide* and *The Fraser)* which took about half an hour. After that the anchor was raised, and then at about 7 p.m. the Steamship *Guide* entered the mouth of the Hooghly and anchored opposite the Saugor Light House for the night. Early next morning at 5-30 the anchor was raised. At about 8-30 a.m. the steamer passed Diamond Harbour, and at 10-00 a.m. she again anchored at Raipur, some twenty-five or thirty miles from Calcutta. There the party stopped till 4-20 p.m. when the anchor was raised and the steamer was once more moving towards Calcutta. We landed near Budge Budge about sunset. Once again I was on Indian soil. A special train was in readiness on a siding of the Bengal Nagpur Railway. Inspector Mathews of the Bengal Police joined us while landing. A First Class carriage was allowed to me and my guards, the two European Inspectors, and a second class carriage was given to Sardar Ajit Singh. Mr. Clark, the Traffic Manager of the Bengal Nagpur Railway, was also in the train and so was the Assistant Traffic Manager. Mr. Clark provided dinner to me in his (Mr. Clark's) own saloon and was very courteous and kind. At noon on the next day, the 16th November, the train reached Bilaspur (C.P.) on the Bengal Nagpur Railway, from where it took a branch line to Katni. All this day we had to live on tinned food, though Mr. Clark did everything he could to give us plenty and make us comfortable. Early next morning we found ourselves at Bina on the G.I.P. Railway, from where we travelled *via* Jhansi to Delhi. The arrangements for food, etc. were excellent. From Delhi we travelled on the Southern Punjab Railway to Lahore *via* Bhatinda. The train was running under a false name and particular care was taken to keep the platforms clear of Indians so long as the train stopped.

During the whole of this journey, which took seven days, Sardar Ajit Singh and myself were kept quite separate, and on the railway journey the shutters of the windows were kept generally closed and at times attempts were made for secrecy which were simply ludicrous and excited laughter. Otherwise the behaviour of the officers in charge was all that could be desired. No newspapers, were allowed except the *Times Weekly,* dated the 13th November, and a copy of *Fry's Magazine.* The train reached Mian Mir West (Lahore Cantonment) railway station at 5-30 a.m. on the 18th instant, immediately after which myself and Sardar Ajit Singh were taken to a saloon where Major C.H. Bensley, the Superintendent of Lahore Central Jail, read us first the warrant of transfer from Mandalay Jail to Lahore Jail and then the writ of release. This over, a landau was placed at my disposal and a tum-tum for luggage. Every assistance was given in the removal of the luggage. Mr. Rundle, the Superintendent of Police, Lahore District, drove in front of me in his tandem and left after I had entered the compound of my bungalow.

Thus after an absence of six months and nine days I returned home.

References

1. Before Lajpat Rai had reached Mandalay questions were asked in the British Parliament on 13 May about his arrest and deportation without trial. Prominent among those members of Parliament who frequently asked questions in the Commons on this subject were V.H. Rutherford, O'Grady, William Redmond, Frederic Mackarness, and Henery Cotton. John Morley, the Secretary of State for India,

made a full statement on the question on 6 June, but it was a repetition of the views of the Punjab Government. It was on 18 June that Mackarness asked if Lajpat Rai had made any protest against his arrest and Morley had replied that he had no information.

2. This was done under instructions of the Government of India and the authorities did not consider it necessary to convey to Lajpat Rai any details regarding the reasons for his detention.

3. The request for supply of newspapers was considered by the Government of India but was refused.

4. Lajpat Rai's memory served him well. The memorial reproduced here is substantially the same as the original in the official records of the Government of India.

5. The Government of India turned down the requests made by Lajpat Rai in his memorial of 29 June, 1907 without reference to the Secretary of State for India. The memorial had been forwarded direct to the Governor-General in Council by Captain H.H.G. Knap, Superintendent of Jail, Mandalay.

6. This memorial had no connection with Lajpat Rai's release; in fact it was not forwarded to the Secretary of State until 5 December 1907, long after he had been released.

Morley had initially approved the action of the Government of India in deporting Lajpat Rai and Ajit Singh but immediately after their deportation, Morley found that there was no tangible evidence against Lajpat Rai which would justify the action. Morley persistently demanded the release of the two deportees in his private correspondence with the Governor-General and finally Minto too changed his earlier opinion and was convinced of the injustice done to Lajpat Rai. In his communication of 5 November Minto wrote to Morley : 'Lajpat Rai is undoubtedly a man of high character and very much respected by his fellow countrymen, and if when I was asked to arrest him, I had known what I do now, I should have required much more evidence before agreeing. Ajit Singh is of much lower standing in every way and I shall regret associating them in their release".

7. Ajit Singh arrived at Mandalay on 16 June 1907.
8. Lajpat Rai was released unconditionally and this warning by the Commissioner was un-called for.

Index

K

L